The Folkloral Voice

by
Ian William Sewall

Routledge
Taylor & Francis Group
LONDON AND NEW YORK

First published 1998 by Qual Institute Press

Published 2016 by Routledge
2 Park Square, Milton Park, Abingdon, Oxon OX14 4RN
711 Third Avenue, New York, NY 10017, USA

Routledge is an imprint of the Taylor & Francis Group, an informa business

Copyright © 1998 Qual Institute Press

All rights reserved. No part of this book may be reprinted or reproduced or utilised in any form or by any electronic, mechanical, or other means, now known or hereafter invented, including photocopying and recording, or in any information storage or retrieval system, without permission in writing from the publishers.

Notice:
Product or corporate names may be trademarks or registered trademarks, and are used only for identification and explanation without intent to infringe.

Canadian Cataloging-in-Publication Data
Sewall, Ian William, 1949–
    The folkloral voice
    Includes bibliographical references and indexes.
    ISBN 0-9683044-1-9
    1. Storytelling. 2. Folklore. I. Title.
    LB1042.S48 1998   808.5'43   C98-900193-8

From "Neither out far nor in deep": THE POETRY OF ROBERT FROST, edited by Edward Connery Lathem, Copyright 1936 by Robert Frost, © 1964 by Lesley Frost Ballantine, © 1969 by Henry Holt and Company, Inc. Reprinted by permission of Henry Holt and Company, Inc.

From "It was a dark and stormy night": DANCING AT THE EDGE OF THE WORLD: THOUGHTS ON WORDS, WOMEN, PLACES, by Ursula K. Le Guin, Copyright 1989 Ursula K. Le Guin. Reprinted by permission of Grove/Atlantic.

POEM from HARD WORDS AND OTHER POEMS by URSULA K. LE GUIN. Copyright © 1981 by Ursula K. Le Guin. Reprinted by permission of HarperCollins Publishers, Inc.

Oden, Thomas, PARABLES OF KIERKEGAARD. Copyright © 1978 by Princeton University Press. Reprinted by permission of Princeton University Press.

Graphic Design: Murray Pearson
Deer Hide Paintings: Ian William Sewall

ISBN 13:978-1-59874-285-5 (pbk)

Deer Hide Painting:
The Storyteller

The best storyteller is one who lets you live if the weather is bad and you are hungry. (William Smith-Smith, cited in Anderson, Aubrey, & McDiarmid, 1979)

Contents

Acknowledgements — vii
Preface — viii

1 To places that are remote — 1

2 Orality — 27

3 Metaphor — 115

4 Laughter — 177

5 The intergenerational conversation — 223

6 And if the fiddle string hadn't broke — 267

Bibliography — 291
Index — 305

Kitchen Table of Contents

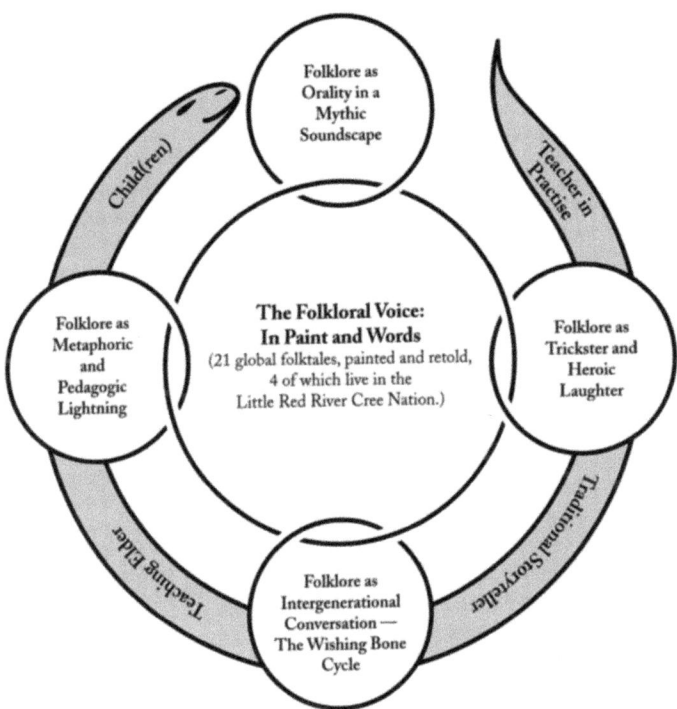

In the Far West, where Brigham Young ended up and I started from, they tell stories about hoop snakes. When a hoop snake wants to get somewhere—whether because the hoop snake is after something, or because something is after the hoop snake—it takes its tail (which may or may not have rattles on it) into its mouth, thus forming itself into a hoop, and rolls. Jehovah enjoined snakes to crawl on their belly in the dust, but Jehovah was an Easterner. Rolling along, bowling along, is a lot quicker and more satisfying than crawling. But, for the hoop snakes with rattles, there is a drawback. They are venomous snakes, and when they bite their own tail they die, in awful agony, of snakebite. All progress has these hitches. I don't know what the moral is. It may be in the end safest to lie perfectly still without even crawling. Indeed it's certain that we shall all do so in the end, which has nothing else after it. But then no tracks are left in the dust, no lines drawn; the dark and stormy nights are all one with the sweet bright days, this moment of June—and you might as well never have lived at all. And the moral of that is, you have to form a circle to escape from the circle. Draw in a little closer around the campfire. If we could truly form a circle, joining the beginning and the end, we would, as another Greek remarked, not die. But never fear. We can't manage it no matter how we try. But still, very few things come nearer the real Hoop Trick than a good story. (Le Guin, 1980/1981)

DEDICATION

To

BETTY (BEAR WOMAN) SEWALL

Whose belly laugh
causes the sun to rise
on Dunvegan Hill

Acknowledgements

To all those storytellers and their pure gestures of friendship that I might listen and then tell of it: Sparrow, Rattler, Dafna, Sabochees, Pesimwastches, Mosum, Je-Nee, Tololwa, Nitotem and Saskastenohk.

And to those who graciously made it possible:

The Ralph Steinhauer Award of Distinction,
The Social Sciences and Humanities Research Council Doctoral Fellowship
and
The Walter H. Johns Graduate Fellowship.

And a particular gratitude to Jean Clandinin, Merle Martin, Sherilyn Grywul, Janis Blakey, Daiyo Sawada, Gordon McIntosh, Myer Horowitz, Nophanet Dhamborvorn, and Bear Woman Sewall for their sushi, saskatoons, and smiles.

Preface

They say that if you kennel a cow dog under the summer trees, trees full of birds and birds on a wire, that the dog will chase the birds in his mind. He will just lay there busy on the inside, chasing and herding in his head. There is a danger to this, they also say. Given enough birds on a wire and enough rotations of the earth, there is a chance that the cow dog will overheat his mind, just plain burn out from all that mental herding.

And that little story darn near explains me and this story business.

I have loved them all, the little stories, the ones some call metaphor, the stories that should have ended and did not, the stories that ended before the telling, I have loved them all. I have chased them in my mind like an old collie dog chases the birds on a wire. And at times this old mind has overheated, not from the telling, mind you, but from the silence afterwards.

The Folkloral Voice is about this love, this hearing and telling. It is also about friendship come flesh. The breath in my narrative travels belongs to Jean Clandinin. She has a way of looking at you and seeing the real story. She has an eye and ear for possibility. If *The Folkloral Voice* brings an important moment to anyone, it is because of her.

The other storytellers have brought me to the flame. They have told of the sweet spot we call life. They have poked with narrative fingers at the embryonic silence. They have told. And now, I come to the moment of a poem. It is my prayer for each of you who approaches:

Sunrise on Narrative Hill

just as the day begins with a rising
so my book of stories
must begin too
must begin with the concert of the Great Spirit and I and you.
I by the window and spectator to the theatre of a new day
and the Spirit......well......She does what spirits always do
that is...leads me to the mystery
leads me to the holy land just beyond syllables.
She leads me to a dance of the undanceable
to the place where silence owns the wee puffs of sound.
She leads me to you

my good friends
you have something of the sunrise about you
if not the mystery
and I do cry for our morning watercolor of sunup
I do cry for our part
that we should only now be where we go.

I like to think prayers like this
cause such a rising
and

THEY SAY that if you kennel a cow dog under the summer trees, trees full of birds and birds on a wire, that the dog will chase the birds in his mind. He will just lay there busy on the inside, chasing and herding in his head. There is a danger to this, they also say. Given enough birds on a wire and enough rotations of the earth, there is a chance that the cow dog will overheat his mind, just plain burn out from all that mental herding.

And that little story darn near explains me and this business of story.

Ian Sewall

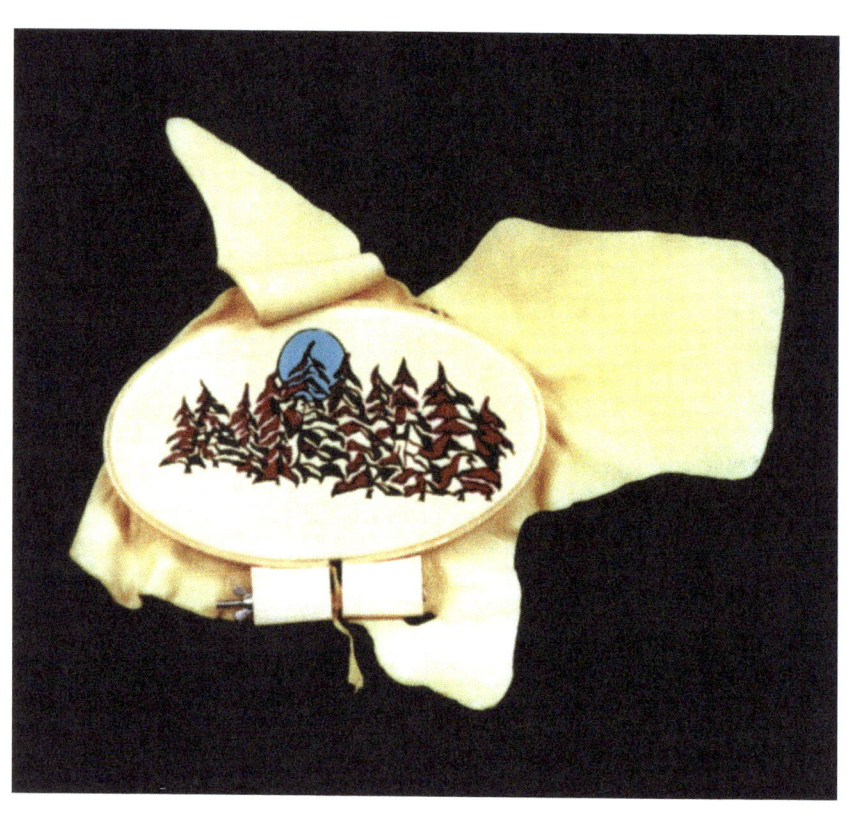

Deer Hide Painting:
Was and Was Not

Chapter 1
To Places That Are Remote

IN THE BEGINNING WAS AND WAS NOT

For in the beginning was and was not sound
And within sound was found and found not
The laughter of word
And the word became and became not a story...

We story-teachers must have joined hands, in our turn then
In that first folkloral moment of telling...then...
In that moccasin round to the hide
And chokecherry stick rhythm of a heart,
Telling round softly, and back upon ourselves,
Foot rhyming and join'ed hands to Sol.
We each and each not Trickstering along, telling
The lakeshore of our childhood and sound...
We story-teachers must have joined hands, in our turn.

We story-teachers must have tea circled, in the beginning
And circled not our drummers of silence
And nodded respectfully to the Ancestors, telling
To the song-back-upon-itself,
In the red evening dust that rose

From our narrative steps...along...
Our days each coyote yips to the moon of laughter.

We story-teachers, mamawe, and together we're bound
By child loves under these eyebrows of spruce
By the tea dance sound of our telling
And we came and came not along,

And would be dancing still and telling, telling
If the rawhide drum had not stretched
  In the beginning
    And someone else, maybe you
      Had taken their turn...and

If any man say that there are now no such animals to be seen (...as gryphons), I answer that that may be so, but simply because they are not seen does not mean they do not exist or that they have perished, for maybe they have moved to places that are more remote and softer because they are inaccessible to man. (*Arcana Microcosmi*...Andrew Ross refutes Dr. Browne's *Vulgar Errors*, Nigg, 1982).

I have lived much of my life, first, in search of gryphons, the beast half eagle and half lion, and then later in defense of them. For once upon a time, there both were and were not such composite and wordy creatures, both religious and mythic. They represent for me "geste," both the thing and the story of the thing, the beautifully blurred line between the deed and the articulation. What we cannot see, we intimate and tell of; we leave off our search for gryphons that we might paint and write of them. Our lives hang in the balance of the thing and its representation and in the transubstantiation of sound into space.

Perhaps the gryphon speaks also to our search for a metaphor, our search and propensity for the honeyed trail that connects this side, the living side, to the other side, the place where shadows evade ownership. And what better gryphon than a good story! By the talon and feather of metaphor they fly over the dualistic nature of thought and join things together. They, the good stories, are the *corpus collosums* of our lives.

Le Guin (1980/1981), as one wizard of the word-sea, as one who takes singular pleasure from her dance on the edge, gave us the metaphor of the hoop snake. First she described the eastern lands where Jehovah designed the snake for belly travel. In the western lands, however, one particular snake was able to join mouth to tail, beginning to end, form a hoop and roll and roll and roll. There was a catch: some hoop snakes were poisonous, and therefore, the art of hoop travel came at great expense, a quick death. We bipeds face just such a dilemma. Do we lie on our bellies in the forever sun, or do we attempt the hoop, the perfect circle, mindful but unmindful of the cost? Le Guin (1980/1981) eloquently reminds us that there just may be no gryphon flight, no perfect circle. But we can come close, close my friends, with a darn good story.

My research, and this telling, is an attempt at gryphon flight. It is a campfire act in celebration of the storyteller's primal art. It is a celebration of storytelling as the ancestral template of good teaching. And as John Cage threw open the doors of his concert hall to incorporate street sounds, so I have gone to several storytellers, in the act of their daily lives and at their kitchen tables (Schafer, 1969). I wished to know the storyteller as teacher, the one who by her/his artistry of the oral, the metaphoric, the laughing, and the intergenerational gives almost full circle to the kitchen table telling of the classroom. It is the classroom storyteller who creates a misty world of inner appearance from the throaty resonance of everyday sound. It is the classroom storyteller who connects the stories to children and stimulates all the suggestive medicine therein. Perhaps it is in the very nature of the classroom soundscape that the story-teacher finds and finds not his/her own personal telling moment, his/her soul, within a privately constructed silence.

To understand teaching and myself, to understand that relationship, I have gone to those who live and tell of gryphons, the storytellers. I have travelled in the red evening dust, and if the rawhide drum had not stretched, I would be listening still, in my turn.

The Hearthstone of Orality

> The sound of speech and pausing for a friend to contribute sound is one of the earliest needs. (Scott-Maxwell, 1968, p. 148)

The power and the glory of the spoken and storied word is beautifully illustrated in an aged tale of Hasidic Judaism:

> It seems that the founding Rabbi, Ba'al Shem Tov, visited a particular small village and once there, learned of a sick child. Being close to the child, the Rabbi knew that he must do something. And that something consisted of taking a candle late at night, following a path through a nearby forest to a particular tree that was as high as the stars, wording a particular chant and prayer...and you know what? It was enough, for by the time the Rabbi returned to the village, the child was

better. Years later, it happened that a disciple of the Rabbi visited the same small village and again there was a sick child. In an attempt to help the youngster, the disciple took the candle and path late at night to that particular tree as high as the stars, but once there...forgot the prayer, and so whispered the name of his master over and over again and you know what? It was enough, for when he returned to the small village the child was better again. Years and years passed, generations passed, and it so happened that a Rabbi, a descendent in the tradition, visited the same village only to find a sick child there. He remembered hearing something of an earlier elder's experience and so late at night walked out into the trees, walked out with neither chant nor prayer nor direction. He recounted the story instead and you know what? It was enough, for when he returned to the village, the child had grown suddenly well. Years passed again and a time of great confusion settled upon the people. Great confusion. And one day a dearly loved child grew sick. The people remembered something about a story and the sick growing well and so they began to tell and share their stories...and you know what? It, too, was enough, for the child grew well. (Sinclair & Rosenbluth, 1986)

It was the purpose of this study to consider the impact, the rebound and medicine of oral language, particularly as it appeared in its storied and folkloral form. While at the kitchen table, our conversations create a kind of vibratory soundscape and our oral words fill the body of experience, fill by naming the primal places. By our stories and by their telling we become native to the land, situated. Culture and nature interplay and negotiate a place in our words. As Klein (1986) suggests, the world and the people in it become explained to itself through the oral. The storytellers find their way through the trees as high as the stars and bring smiles to the children. The human voice can perhaps "more powerfully than any other agency, put into our deeper consciousness those lasting patterns which belong to the deeper consciousness of the race" (Colum, 1927, p. 364). By our words we flesh the young, we sing and sometimes cry and ultimately inhabit an ancestral place.

When a northern elder speaks of his earlier travelling days from family home community to family home community and all along a northern river, he is describing by means of oral narrative a path taken. Each moose hunt, each dry meat cache, each summer gathering becomes part of the narrative line that linguistically binds and guides the people. And in the manner of an Anansi and his webbed stories, the people become inextricably bound together by the narrative ceremony of their days. They become caught in their own story webs. The cycle and journey of the seasons from spring hunt to summer gathering to fall hunt to winter trapping become an oral path taken. Just as the aboriginal people of Australia are said to move about through the songlines of a dreaming time, so the rest of us find direction and place from our personal and public narrative lines. In telling of the day, we spin inward and secure some sense of self. By our speaking, we bring the thing into our reality. Each activity, every event and relationship, each ceremony and visit and healing of a sick child becomes not just the thing, but, in its telling, the story of the event. It is this storymaking that connects each to the other, connects the happenings, infuses the human engagement with the power and burn of language. And you know what? It is enough.

Folklorists have helped us appreciate the manner by which an oral culture achieves memorability. There is in voiced transmission perpetuated a "pristine aggregative, paratactic, oral style thinking" (Ong, 1982, p. 28). In the oral world, the telling is itself a joining act. It brings people together. The storyteller creates an audience, a campfire circle, a hoop, in a way that the writer can only imagine. Fewer words have to mean more for as the context shifts so the words, once uttered, continually slip away into the perfect sound of silence. When Odysseus faced Menelaus and that individual's elegant speech, he first mumbled about until his audience grew bored and weary, "then he recaptured them with a stream of words 'coming down like snowflakes in winter'" (Havelock & Herschell, 1978, p. 122). And in those syllabic snowflakes could be found the memorable. For the needs of the memory have an enormous influence on the nature of the syntax. Ong (1982) describes, with typographic eloquence, oral communication as additive, aggregative, redundant, traditionalist, agonistically toned, participatory, situational and homeostatic. We can infer that sensitivity to and the understanding of a typographic or electronic culture necessarily begins with a study of a primary oral culture, the kitchen table context in this instance. A western culture much given to the celebration of the face of type does well to remind itself of the face of the storyteller. And whereas the written enjoys a "stored away" ability, the oral lives in its own breath and touchability. Thus the technology that was created to tool our world not only transformed our speaking, but also the deep patterns of consciousness that underly it. Writing, with its wonderful sense of introspectivity, serves to separate the knower and the known, whereas orality struggles to join them back together again. Like this, the written has a way of standing alone and inviolate, separating the writer from his/her utterances, the created from the creator. And with time the written word becomes much less of a recording and much more of a thing. Thus, we live in the Canadian middle as gryphons, somewhere between the fixed pointedness of the written word and the gestural hand dance of oral verbalization. It is the oral word, however, that "first illuminates consciousness with articulate language, that first divides subject and predicate and then relates them to one another, and that ties human beings to one another in society" (Ong, 1982, p. 179). It is the oral word that joins together the silences; it is the pausing between friends:

> *We would be dancing still and telling, telling*
> *If the rawhide drum had not stretched*
>   *In the beginning*
>   *And someone else, maybe you,*
>   *Had taken their turn...*

THE RATTLESNAKE OF METAPHOR

> If I had not bene a peece of a Logician before I came to him, I think he would have persuaded me to have wished my selfe a horse. (Sidney, 1950, p. 5)

We live in our metaphors, I believe, and in our names. And it is students who fill up the name "teacher" with a body. Agnes was such as lived beyond the classroom world of *in parentis*. She began for me as a grade 6 student, and as those first teaching days at Chipewyan Prairies unfolded, Agnes became one of the family. And as the years went by and we travelled about, we stayed in touch, as one does with children or parents who leave the nest. Then one fateful evening, miles and stories away, we received a call from Father. Agnes had been in a car accident and in escaping from a twisted wrecked vehicle, she had stepped into an electrified pond beside the gravel road. She instantly lost the bottom half of her left leg. I asked myself then and I ask myself now if anything, anything at all in the metaphoric life of our classroom had helped Agnes when she woke up to one foot. I asked myself the big questions: like what could I say to this youngster now and why Agnes anyway. When we finally met months later on a doorstep at Chipewyan Prairies, I tried with "Hey, you look great Kid!" while Agnes replied with, and of all the things she might have said, "Do you have a copy of my journal Mr. Sewall?" Her yellow pencil, made from the wood of a tree as high as the stars they say, bled that night.

It is students who fill up the name "teacher" with a body. You see, Agnes did lose a leg. That is true. She did, however, gain a story, was chosen by story, as was "teacher." Stafford (1986) describes memory as a bit of quilt work whereby "from the whole cloth of time, frayed scraps of sensation are pulled apart and pieced together in a pattern that has a name" (p. 15). As storytellers and educators, we may not be able to prevent the burn of lightning;

we can, however, assist our youngsters in storying the pain and the joy of survival. We can help our little elders-in-waiting pull the "scraps of sensation" together into a pattern that names and sustains. We can intimate through our orality and laughter a metaphoric world awaiting. Again, like Stafford (1986) suggests, "a story does not rescue life at the end, heroically, but all along the road, continually" (p. 29). Agnes, through the metaphor of language, would find a way to live deeply and truthfully and metaphorically. She would find a way to live in a world that did not always explain itself, in a represented world where fire lived inside of trees as high as the stars.

Nietzsche (1968) suggests that the act of knowing is simply the manipulation of one's favorite metaphors. By this study and through my storytellers' conversational disclosures, I have attempted to appreciate and understand the metaphoric power of language and specifically the manner by which folklore bridges life and art or, as Skiff suggests, how our species makes public representations of private experiences (Sacks, 1978, p. 106). I am mindful here of Agnes' journal and how in crafting her story, in the blood of her yellow pencil, Agnes was able to explore the relationship of self to story, to experience the interiority of metaphor. Through conversation and the interplay of sound and silence, we seek out a metaphoric life and attempt to capture implicitly what language fails to do explicitly. Socrates was driven to the dialogical mount, Plato considered his way to the philosophical cave and foundation myth, Black Elk to Harney Peak, Joseph Campbell to the invisible life of the mythic, Roger Jones to the metaphor of physics, Ursula Le Guin by hoop travel to the Earth-Sea, and my storytellers in a particular way to the kitchen table weave of folklore. As story-teachers, we recognize an ethnocentricity about our lives and continuously struggle for metaphoric postures of fidelity. We wish to tell with a competence of our represented lives. We wish to move with word and gesture from the known to the unknown and back again. And it may be that in the person of the storyteller we best embody our pedagogic acts. When Agnes became storyteller and hero of her own journey, she was able to affirm something of the human spirit and of the holy land. It was the spirit that could walk on one leg. It could move the listener from confusion to compassion to insight. Agnes as storyteller became teacher, and in the act of storying, she put flesh upon the ghost of our perception. Agnes was able to find a way past the paradox of pain, past the roasting fire. Like all my storytellers, Agnes was able to transubstantiate sensation and experience into the metaphor of story, the kind that saved life:

I think we'll be born again,
an implosion perhaps

when we look up into our story-stars
and where once only wordy-thoughtlines appeared
now will forever be the ruffled grouse of metaphor
and the continuance of our grins.

LAUGHTER: THE SHAPESHIFTER

He yelled just before he died Cass. He sat up in bed and yelled "Where in hell are my green socks!" Then he died. That was all. (MacLachlan, 1982, p. 107)

It was September 1, 1973. We had flown in by Cessna 185 and arrived at Chipewyan Prairies only hours before. Now, green as the summer grass, I, teacher, stood before my Grade 6-7-8-9 class. And there sat Mary Ann, elder student. We carefully but casually glanced at one another, and I faced an immediate truth: as Mary Ann went, so went the class, so went the year, and so went I. It was going to be as simple as that. Mary Ann and I politely chatted after registration and early dismissal, as I recall.

The horse-drawn school caboose arrived promptly the following morning, and the northern dance of the multigraded and multidisciplined began. We were in earnest. And just prior to first break, I nonchalantly circled over to Mary Ann's desk and quietly urged her to finish up the mathematics review before recess. "I'm tired," she tersely replied. "Well, tired or not, I'd like everyone to finish up before recess. I want to go on to something new after our break," I countered diplomatically and professionally. "Then you do it!" Mary Ann muttered. Well, as you might imagine, Mary Ann and I were exchanging insults before many seconds had passed, and I was rapidly "losing it." "If you think I was hired and flown in here to take your abuse young lady," I bellered, white knuckling my yardstick and shaking it in Mary Ann's direction. Mary Ann then suddenly burst from the mobile classroom, a stream of bilingual and northern invectives in her path. I, teacher, pursued, out of the classroom, with ruler and language blistering aloft. I pursued. And as our rage unfolded, you could have heard a beading needle drop. It was that quiet, and the students were that stunned by our abandon. Less than a minute later, and I swear this is true, the other classroom door burst open. We returned. But this time, however, it was I, teacher, running into and then through the classroom, all the while being pursued by a yardstick-swinging Mary Ann. Again, as we raced from the room, the student shock and student silence was almost palpable. Mary Ann and I reappeared a few moments later, as I recall, hand in hand, together carrying the yardstick that had been crafted from a tree as high as the stars. Silence, then the ruffled grouse of laughter rocked the old trailer. We had them! "Now my new and young friends, let's talk about what you thought you saw," I giggled, a wink to my colleague Mary Ann.

For the next 400 teaching days, friend Mary Ann and I exchanged many a glance, and they always held the tricksterish twinkle of those on the inside. We had begun our Chipewyan Prairies' pursuit of truth with laughter. Our laughing back, our daily pauses, enabled a looking ahead. Laughter suggested to students and teacher alike that reality was perhaps the most interesting of all worlds to live in. It was so often laughter that glued the story of our instructional and personal lives together.

Lincoln (1983) writes that "to back into the old tales, reversing and suspending historical time is to re-enter that protective burrow of tradition looking out on the future, as Kwakwu [i.e., the porcupine] does" (p. 28). Thus, when Wesakychak, the Cree Trickster, travels north, we learn of the south country by his passing. We learn to live by the humor of his movements. By her laughter, Mary Ann was able to live with the serious and the unfunny and finally accept a part in the triangulation of story, storyteller and listener. Smith-Smith, when he talked of learning, cautioned that some things "won't be easy to hear…inside the story, but it's there. Too easy to find you might think, it was too easy to do" (Norman, 1982, p. 172). I believe it is laughter that brings us to the story, reversing and re-entering as does the porcupine its burrow, and that it is laughter that keeps us in the story, even when it is not easy to hear.

Through the laughter of this study, the laughter of the conversational and the contrary, I came to a better understanding of this most folkloral of all sounds. Laughter so often revealed the way to the inside of story and things. The storytellers and I ceremonialized our friendships with a laughing and by its resonance found the metaphoric bridge that led to our own tricksterish elders. Our puffs of storyteller-listener laughter became corner posts that held the fence of our experiences up, joining together the negative spaces of conversation.

Norman (1982) points out that "the Swampy Cree say stories live in the world, may choose to inhabit people, who then have the option of telling them back out into the world again. This all can form a symbiotic relationship: if people nourish a story properly, it tells things about life. The same with dreams. And names" (p. 200). And what better nourishment than the kind of laughter that moves one's belly into the throat. Surely my storytellers and their narrative weavings existed as evidence that such "creation is born in exuberance" (Baughman, 1979, p. 26). Just as laughter nourishes the stories, so the stories nourish those who wield yardsticks as high as the stars.

THE INTERGENERATIONAL CONVERSATION

When [Grandmother] told me those old stories, something strange and good and powerful was going on. I was a child, and that old woman was asking me to come directly into the presence of her mind and spirit; she was taking hold of my imagination, giving me to share in the great fortune of her wonder and delight. She was asking me to go with her to the confrontation of something that was sacred and eternal. It was a timeless, timeless thing; nothing of her old age or of my childhood came between us...you see, her words were medicine; they were magic and invisible. They came from nothing into sound and meaning. (Momaday, 1966, p. 88)

My own grandparents, particularly Grandpa Willie Fraser, held me like that: I was the red pheasant in the snare of his words. He brought me into his presence with the stories that each like "a little marble prism...burst open the words as bones which come rattling out like dice" (Garfield, 1985, Preface). His telling and my listening were a timeless thing. Neither his great broody body nor my sunburnt little boy person got in the way. The stories were free to rattle out like dice, and we wished ourselves nowhere else.

My Grandpa Willie had sent leather love postcards to Edna, his betrothed, as he plumbed his way from Canadian Pacific Railway hotel to hotel, his tin and rivet suitcase the home of pliers and handgun and Edna's replies. Two years later and with Gaelic stake in hand, Edna and Willie relocated from Van Kleeck Hill, Ontario, to Medicine Hat, Alberta. Their wedding gifts had been duly packed, shipped by rail and then unpacked in their new prairie brick home. And at some point, in the unpacking, the newly married couple discovered a 200 pound saddle shaped rock. We suspect that Willie's friends were having a last laugh about their own rocky pastures. What could be more appropriate than taking a rock to the holy land? Throughout my childhood and our family's pilgrimages to the Fraser's elm treed home where the trees grew as high as the stars, my little boy times were filled with chicken weather vanes, coconut-covered marshmallows, and long rides on this Ontario rock. And while I rode rock saddle, Grandpa Willie talked and talked and talked, stories rattling out from his bones like dice, stories of trotting horses and tomato plants and one legged chickens that lay silver eggs. We talked, and I rode rock saddle in the timeless presence of story. And now, years and generations later, the rock has moved to my mother's home. Several times each year, I bend and caress its saddle on my way to the kitchen table and parent tales. The voice of my northern education tells me that the rock saddle is alive. Mighty in silence and stone, the saddle still gives gallop to the spirits of the little ones.

There was an intergenerational conversation in and around the words of all my storytellers. At times, it rattled out like dice, and in other moments, it lived in the silence of the saddle rock. It was the orality that connected child to elder and to the child in the elder. It was the oracy that connected beginnings and endings into almost perfect narrative hoops. As Le Guin (1979) says, "I believe that an adult is not a dead child, but a child that has survived" (p. 39). And whereas we adults of middle age and middle earth busy ourselves with one another and our computer searches for a distant truth, the very young and the very old inhabit a metaphoric landscape less encumbered by details and information. It is a folkloral place where saddle rocks gallop into the night and little eyes grow large at the story of a scar and survival. Campbell (1989) describes with joy reaching the age and the day that held no future. It meant the elder freedom to live in the immediacy of the momentary, as do the very young. The intergenerational conversation of my storytellers taught that as well, that the sacred mountain is here now. As Campbell (1989) professes, "The central mountain is everywhere. Is everywhere. It is not going to be everywhere. It's here now. That's the real message of myth" (p. 137). Perhaps that is also the real message of the intergenerational, that the tellers of the central mountain are here now, and they are both very young and very old. It is their intergenerational footprints that we discover on the unknown island of our middle-aged experience.

I have also been taught that the child and the child in the elder best live in this metaphoric land where the ancestral voice can still be heard over the oscillation of a motor and where the ancestral face of the storyteller is not yet blinded by the glare of the electric light. When the centenarian Stella was asked how she had managed to get so old, she gaily replied, "I picked my ancestors carefully" (Heynen, 1990, p. 117). And so by the archetypal laughter of the Heyoka, the elder and the child brought us to the elm treed places, where trees as high as the stars tickled the firmaments of our imagination. In this intergenerational dialogue of the kitchen table, we celebrated our uncertainty with the "unswerving focus that persists in a quiet kind of gusto, in a nonaggressive determination or in a soft fortitude" (Heynen, 1990, p. xiii):

> In old age wandering as a trail of beauty,
> lively, may I walk.
> In old age wandering on a trail of beauty,
> living again, may I walk.
>   It is finished in beauty.
>   It is finished in beauty. (*Navajo Night Chant* in Momaday, 1966)

ON MATTERS OF FOLKLORE

> And I meant to get there....Even if it meant climbing a mountain of words. For now I had begun to believe, despite all the talk of science around me, that there was a magic in spoken words. (Ellison, 1947, p. 288)

There is a Central African story told and told and told of a honey gatherer and his three sons:

> The boys were named for the nature of their abilities: Hear-It-However-Faint-The-Sound, Follow-It-However-Great-The-Distance, and Put-It-Together-However-Small-The-Pieces (or Hear, Follow, and Piece for the hurried). One memorable day, the old man left his small village and travelled throughout the forest in pursuit of honey. Finally, the honey gatherer came to a promising tree, one as high as a hill, and then climbed it. Unfortunately, a rotten branch broke and the old man tumbled to the ground...where he broke into ten pieces. Back in the village the son Hear, fortunately, heard the fall and called upon his brothers. Follow easily tracked the old man to the tree whereupon Piece promptly put his father together again. Together and honey in hand, the family returned home.
>
> The following day, the old man went out again while the boys remained at home and each bragged of their importance to the rescue of their father. At some distance from the village, the honey gatherer found a promising tree as high as a cloud, climbed it, but again stepped out on to a rotten branch and fell to the ground. This time, the old man broke into 100 pieces. Again the sons heard, followed and then pieced together their father, but very grudgingly for each son believed he was the indispensable part of the rescue team.
>
> On the third day, as you might imagine, the old man discovered a honey tree as high as the stars, but in climbing it, fell and broke into 1000 pieces. All three sons could guess of their father's dilemma, but each waited for an acknowledgement of his importance from the others. And as a result, the honey gatherer lays in pieces yet...or not, if you prefer. (Burton, 1962, pp. 39–41)

Grimm (1944) describes the old stories, folklore, as

> fragments of belief dating back to the most ancient times in which spiritual things are expressed in a figurative manner. The mythic ele-

ment resembles small pieces of a shattered jewel which are lying strewn on the ground all overgrown with grass and flowers, and can only be discovered by the most far-seeing eye. Their significance has long been lost, but it is still felt and imparts value to the story. (p. xiv)

So, like the honey gatherer, folklore lays scattered about, disclosing its mythic riches only to the willing and the discerning. And similarly enough, in this study, I found folkloral gems scattered throughout my storytellers' art. This folklore, by virtue of its third person nature, also carried within itself a consonance or spirit of piecing back together. Be the stories sweet and from Anansi or be the stories not so sweet and of a northern girl's lost leg, it was folklore that provided much of the body of our kitchen table conversations. Hardy (1978) and others argue that folklore is not so much an isolated act of oral entertainment as a "primary act of mind," a piecing together of experience. Thus, it was folklore that provided a way to call upon narrative and bring story to bear on this experience. For my storytellers, the old stories seemed to provide a way by which a private conversation could undergo a public disclosure. The folkloral allowed the storytellers to deal with humanity, but from a gentle distance. The situation could be named; the journey could be described. Personal meaning lay hidden like gems in the public text of folklore, and a necessary matter-of-fact spirit was brought to the situation. And understanding for both the storyteller and the listener probably came more from engagement in the folkloral than from a thick description of it.

For the purposes of this extended research conversation, I took the term "folkloral" to mean not only those stories most often found at the kitchen table or in the bedtime narrative, those old stories transmitted by word of mouth from one generation to the next, but also the very act of telling, be it religious, realistic, repetitional, humorous, or magical in delivery and guise (Pellowski, 1977, p. 359). In calling upon and searching out a "folkloral voice," this inquiry sought to celebrate the very synaptic fuse that drives the human and cerebral flower: voice. Our fate, as Le Guin (1989) says, is "that which is spoken" (p. 269). Thus, kitchen table conversation was the context, the voice folkloral. As Campbell comments, "If ever there was an art on which the whole community of mankind has worked—seasoned with the philosophy of the codger on the wharf and singing with the music of the spheres—it is this of the ageless tale" (Grimm, 1944, Appendix). And the ageless act of tale telling is essentially affirmative. Sometimes subtle, always suggestive, the voices of my storytellers affirmed life; life was indeed worthy of the folkloral telling. Life was worthy of the ritual of story. Thus, by both the story and its telling, my tablemates animated and pieced together things, honey gatherers to wooden legs to scholarly print. Their folklore, as the psychology of their past and the dreams of their future, squeezed into the songline and stories of their present. Hardy (1978) asks, "How often do we as students of politics, self or literature, make the move from realism back to fantasy again, and translate the despair and pain as stoicism, the madness as aesthetic eloquence, the disorder as a new order? It is hard to stop telling stories" (p. 12).

The folkloral impulse is both echo and vision. As Achebe suggests, "Two heads, four eyes. You can see around the problem if you have four eyes. If you first have two eyes, one head, you can't see around the corner" (Baker & Draper, 1992, p. 23). It is the old stories and the old practice of their telling that give us the other eyes. It is that folkloral impulse that enables the species to look around corners and hear the echoes. This is reaffirmed by Havelock and Herschell (1978), who write that "the very task which literate communication sets itself—the creation and the conservation of knowledge, technological and cultural—was first confronted and solved in the uncounted millennia of oral experience when man knew no knowledge other than that which was contained in the sounds of his language as they were pronounced" (p. 20). And with the telling, with the polishing, those sounds and pronouncements became, and are today, the strewn about folkloral gems of oracy:

I have good friends
Who leave tobacco on the river
As gifting to the spirits below the surface
And for their folkloral journey ahead.

And why not our words too…
Let's gently place them on the surface
That by their watery release
Might become great stories.

And journeys ahead.

ON MATTERS OF STORYTELLING

So each storyteller everywhere, as he fills his lungs to tell his story also fills his heart with the ceremony of life. (Y Maestas & Anaya, 1980, p. 8)

There is a South Korean tale told of a young man who had an insatiable appetite for stories. As a youngster, he was indulged by friends, family and servants and told stories daily. He insisted on it. Instead of passing them on, however, instead of retelling these tales, the young man chose to put the spirits of the stories into a leather bag and hang them on the wall. The story spirits grew increasingly congested and frustrated and by the time of the lad's wedding day were plotting revenge. Thus they decided that on the young man's wedding route, they would poison the creek of its drinking water and, further on, poison the patch of strawberries by the side of the road. If that failed, they would place a hot poker in the rice bag near the bride's door. Upon dismounting, the young man would be fatally impaled. And if by some act of fortune that failed, then a venomous snake would be secreted under the wedding bed. Fortunately, for the lad, an old and trusted servant hid behind a tree that was as high as the stars and overheard the plotting of the story spirits. Not only that, the servant managed to accompany his master that fateful day and rescue him from each act of revenge. In doing so, his good deeds were misinterpreted for a time as only a meddling presence. By the end of the Korean tale, however, the servant's loyalty and courage were revealed and a much chastened young groom agreed to release the story spirits. And from that experience onward, the young man faithfully retold those stories told to him, as the spirits of the stories so wished. (Zong, 1952, pp. 154–157)

In a similar fashion, it was the purpose of this study not only to identify or recognize the folkloral voice in others, but to actively engage in the celebration of storytelling. To that end and like the Korean bridegroom, I had come into the acquaintance of a wide host of story spirits. It was my pleasure and my purpose to pass them along. Thus, the telling of some 20 cross-cultural tales helped to situate the kitchen table conversations into a folkloral environment. I wished to know the story river not simply by watching it flow by, but by travelling with it.

Pellowski (1977) steers the student of story to the first written description of an action that resembled storytelling. It appears in the Egyptian Westcar Papyrus, around 2000 BC, and consists of a dialogue between Cheops and his sons. The father asked if there was one in the company who could tell of the deeds of magicians. The son, Khafra, replied with the tale of a forefather. Thus, Cheops demonstrated that "readiness to have something done to us." Our human way, however, requires that we live in both the Cheops and the Khafra side of the tale. We are told, like the bridegroom, that we might tell of it. Our storytelling engagement is an ancestral act and one that connects all deeds and all magicians.

An overview of storytelling necessarily intimates the bardic, the religious, the folk, the theatrical, the institutional, the playground and the therapeutic (Pellowski, 1977). Throughout the story of storytelling, we hear the echoes of it all. We hear of a time when oracy meant something quite different than the verbalization of a written text. My storytellers suggested also that this time of primary orality is yet upon us. And although the storyteller's voice is increasingly taped and technologized, it is here still, however it is scripted. The storytelling impulse yet drives each human day from first sun up to sun down. For all our attempts at the systemization of story, the happenchance of kitchen table conversation still whispers, shouts and thrives. For my storytellers, their oral way lived somewhere between the fast forward of a performed text and the province of a trained expertise. Their stories eluded, in a way, both science and art, for they were here first. They lived by telling about it and probably told it best at the kitchen table and in the metaphoric and storyteller embrace of their own clans. Their storytelling involved a truth, which, as Gadamer (1986) might suggest, predates post-Enlightenment definition. They were both the creator and the creation of the story spirits and revealed something of the ancestral campfire in all their words. By bringing us to the hearth, they reminded us of our need for holy places.

In Sabochees' Woodland Cree story of *Masquematuay*, a spiritual bag of meat comes to the hunting people during a time of starvation, and through the belief of a small child, the family group is saved. Now as important as that particular dried meat was to the particular people of that particular camp, the story of their rescue went on to spiritually sustain so many others. Thus, it is the storyteller in each of us that opens the moosehide bag, the grouse's pouch, and releases the tale, be it the "masquematuay" of the Cree, the story bag of the Korean, or the Nyame box of Anansi's people. All of the stories released by the storyteller are the "roomy repositories of an oral culture's lore" (Ong, 1982, p. 139). And whereas generalization and acts of intellectualization may fall short, these specific stories always move us on. It is this interplay of the stories of long ago, what the Tlingit called the "tlagu," and the stories that really happened and are happening yet, the "ch'kalnik," that occupied this study (Bierhorst, 1985). How is it that story speaks to this interplay of reality and its representation? How is it that story speaks to this interplay of the professional and the private? As Pevere (1992) observes, "If the medium truly is the message, then myth, to a certain extent, must be the media itself" (p. 13). And it is the storyteller who first and best began that mythologizing of human experience, letting loose the spirits to the inside:

You can hear of the people
In their pipe times of deep snow...
You can tell of the people
In their pipe times of deep snow...
Give thanks
Give thanks.

Story Meets the Teller: Methodology and Terminology of the Kitchen Table

In the ring, and even in the depths of their voluntary ignominy, wrestlers remain gods because they are for a few moments, the key which opens Nature, the pure gesture which separates Good from Evil, and unveils the form of a Justice which is at last intelligible. (Barthes, 1972, p. 25)

Storytellers, too, are gods for a few telling moments. By their words, they become the welding arc that fuses reality to its representations, the wrestler of shadows to form. Preoccupied as I was with my own research wrestling match, and that was the manner by which the folkloral voice informed the crosscultural educator, my first methodological concern was in determining "the ring," the where of the matter, Amy Tan's (1989) mah jong table. I felt it vital that the research ceremony be situated as close to the telling heart as possible. To that end, I chose several kitchen tables as my ring. It was there that I expected my storytellers to be most engaged "in living, telling, retelling, and reliving stories" (Connelly & Clandinin, 1990, p. 4). It was at the kitchen table that I expected the narrative gesture to be most pure and forthcoming.

In almost 20 years as a learning educator and about the same length of time as a teaching student, I am hard pressed to describe even one of the desks I have occupied. My best description would be guesswork and highly creative in the retelling. The kitchen table I grew up at, however, that is another matter. It was made from the mature oak of a tree as high as a star, Grama used to say. Its scars were as much from the telling and the finger tracing as from the original injury. It was where in those green-as-the-grass years I left from each morning and returned to each evening. It was there at the kitchen table that my parents kindly listened to a young wordsmith's stuttering poetry. It was there that I most told and told not of the secret places where I lived. It was there that the narrative tartan of my family was cross-barred and wove.

And years later as a northern curriculum weaver, I had the single good fortune of working with a group of parents in the ceremony and celebration of story and culture. For these 4 years, I travelled from and to the kitchen tables of artists, storytellers, and translators, friends all. I became forever changed. It convinced me then, in the depth of the journey, that it is at the kitchen table where acts of intimacy are most common and where the public and the private are most telling. It was there that I found good will or, as Barthes (1972) describes it, a meeting that represented "a space of speech divested of aggressiveness." It was at the kitchen table that we drank mint tea and laughed at our children, and it was there that the elder Jimmie cried when he whispered of the future of his grandchildren. It was at the kitchen table that my storytellers suspended the roles and rigors of speech and slipped into their natural narrative selves.

The intent of my study was to enter into an expansionist kitchen table conversation with several individuals, several fellow wrestlers, all from very diverse kinds of backgrounds. Conversation came to mean both experienced or visualized talk and the more removed or formalized tales. Perhaps the single commonality was that each individual had a way with words, each appeared deeply involved with the narrative songlines that bind us together, and each engaged in their way in the triumph of good over the proved and privileged (Wrightson, 1991, p. 165). At this table, as high as the stars, were commonly seated Sparrow, Rattler, Dafna, Mosum, Sabochees and Pesimwastches. Less often, but no less worthy, the table felt the added presence of Je-Nee, Tololwa, Nitotem, and Sakastenohk.

The willowy and black-ponytailed Sparrow was my youngest, my "littlest storyteller." These words will not fully capture her person; for in its animation and smiles and speech, it continually hopped from narrative branch to narrative branch. Like all my storytellers, Sparrow was much more than the sum of her silences and sounds, more than relationship, Grade fiver, athletic, competitive, rural and northern Albertan, daughter and granddaughter, heir to a French and Ukrainian ancestry. Sparrow liked nothing better than a good scare and a good story. They allowed her a celebration and a life of theatre. Pure joy for Sparrow often meant Canadian pizza and talk and an "awesome" movie. Pure joy was the night before Christmas, snuggling into the blanket of colored lights and brother and sisters and anticipation. To Sparrow, each day began with a question and ended with a reluctant sleep. Life meant engagement, and her delightful word tumblings and stories stood as testimony to that pursuit. Throughout the study, Sparrow continually reminded this grey-whiskered writer of the holy land called childhood.

Oh that Rattler, his stories slowly uncoiled, and then during a sip of hazelnut cowboy coffee, they struck the unsuspecting. As I listened and laughed and listened again to Rattler, I felt the warming presence and talent of a teacher elder (now retired), an archeologist, artist, folklorist, historian, snowshoer and road runner, homesteader, father, grandfather and friend and more. Rattler could both do it and then tell of it. I felt related to him as his incredible stories had a way of connecting everybody to everything. If I had listened long enough, I am sure that their narrative pluralities would have all merged into the one narrative river and tale, a creation story perhaps. Rattler was living testimony that the best stories were found closest to home. And as he told of one-room prairie schools and willow airplanes and bootleggers along the Red Deer, I laughed both quietly and uproariously. He sat, elder athlete that he was, near the edge of his chair, stirring his coffee and his tales as he occasionally glanced over the top of his glasses to where I should be sitting. Always he made me laugh until my middle-aged ribs were sore, and I would return home to pick the cactus insights from the flesh of his tales. Rattler held me in the stare and laughter of his words. Listening became no ordinary island.

Dafna brought another kind of presence to the dining room table, that of Israeli educator and mother, scholar and wife, international traveller and philosopher. Her life was filled with great and small passions: the passion of an Israeli loyalist, the passions around a Hebrew sense of ceremony, passions of family and talk and good literature, good music, good friendships, good chocolate. And when Dafna told the stories of what she called ordinary, she did so with the alternating abandon of laughter and tears. Life consisted of both principles and freedoms. It was a story that so connected the memorability and principles of a Hebrew past to what would be memorable in the freedoms of an Israeli future. By her laughter and strength of person, Dafna was able to situate her family into the context and ceremony of a people. And although her unique and eloquent character charmed the listener, one was also brought into the presence of culture, history, and nationhood. As Wrightson (1991) writes, "The life of story is in our many hands, and without authority, it will die" (p. 170). Similarly, as much as Dafna called upon the grand narrative or meta-narrative of her countrymen, she brought authority to it. Our conversations came at a narrative time of pause for Dafna, a scholarly time during which she was engaged in looking back for the future.

Sabochees, Pesimwastches, and Mosum collectively brought a fourth presence to the kitchen table of this inquiry. All three were grandfathers and modest custodians of the Cree way.

Sabochees, trapper, tall, mustached, pony-tailed and lean, was himself the son of a well-respected storyteller. He had, at a relatively young age, been given the respect and acknowledgement of the elder. When he story told, he did so with an intensity that held me like a mule deer in frozen camouflage. Normally and naturally he spoke Cree, a High Cree his friends said, and each story took on a beautiful oral cadence in its delivery. Language meant almost everything to the hunter Sabochees: culture, survival of the spirit. And as he lovingly enunciated and gestured his impassioned oral way, the little ones climbed off and on his knee, off and on his knee, children and grandchildren, watching his hands as they empathetically signed each notion. Sabochees was a traditionalist and built his house upon the old ways.

Our friend Pesimwastches languished in great bouts of story and laughter. His holy land was a northern place where good friends shared mint tea and salted moosemeat and long stories around the tamarack campfire. And as much as the kindly Pesimwastches honored the spirits and the ceremonies of the ancestral, he also firmly situated himself in the western world of all terrain vehicles,

Platonic fashioned classrooms and economic development initiatives. In that sense, the storyteller Pesimwastches was the old spirit in modernistic guise. Like Rattler, he lived to laugh. It was his gift, the comic. When people saw the bear-like figure of Pesimwastches approach, they readied themselves for a good laugh and the antics of the trickster. It was quite enough if the world was happy, quite enough for the young grandfather Pesimwastches.

Of the three northerners, it was Mosum who was most elderly and perhaps statesmanlike. Although he was invariably kind, even unassuming, I felt that I was in the presence of the best my species had to offer. The great grandfather, Mosum, spoke with great stretches of silence and a kind of whispered authority. I mean he had presence whereby even the ordinary acts of tea drinking or smoking took on a significance and symbolism. I sensed, too, that Mosum had many friends and loved ones on "the other side," for there was the ancestral about his manner. I sat straight up when I listened to Mosum. I hoped that when I wrote of Grandfather I would be able to do so in a way that left him with what mattered; I hoped that my need for pattern and explanation would not interfere with my listening (Farella, 1993, p. ix). I hoped also that I would always understand our primary reality to be a place of trees and wind and water and earth.

My storytellers have alerted me to not only the unique stories and the unique lives they tell about, but also to the compositional weave that connects them. Thus, in an attempt at Le Guin's campfire act or Barthes' pure gesture, I have gone also to the kitchen table of others: the South Korean colleague Je-Nee, the Tanzanian storyteller Tololwa, the northerners Nitotem and Sakastenohk. These four have provided more ring, more crosscultural hoopedness and the additional authority of oracy to the inquiry. The combined tales, whether their origins be scholarly or folkloral, give voice to my education and authority to my pursuit of truth. All the storytellers and all our conversations have reminded me that we the already living are not alone. Only together are we the key that opens nature.

I have purposely chosen the term "conversation" over the more rigorous "interview." A conversation seems to admit to more listener presence and perhaps a more flexible agenda, with the expression "a visit" more appropriate in northern homes. Narrative inquiry allowed the process and the product to remain an indivisible one. Thus, the stories, the conversations, were their own end. They were the third person at each table. It was my challenge to seek and celebrate narrative understanding, not to delimit or frame it. As participant and observer, I filled my masquematuay with both personal anecdotes and acrylic deer hide gestures. These interpretive story paintings visualized a world where silence still waits for story. In giving away the hide paintings, I am able to share something of the heart yet retain something of the soul. As in storytelling, possession and person come from the giving away.

Bruner (1990) describes narrative by its properties or "sense of sequentiality," its "indifference to extralinguistic reality," its "ability to forge links between the exceptional and the ordinary" (pp. 43, 44, 47). I similarly imagined the ordinary and private kitchen table tales to provide a profound entanglement, a connection into the public and packaged parts of our educational lives. The conversation and the visit created its own reality and fragile relationship between the family of the moment and the family of humankind. Each of my visits carried with it that "enabling possibility." To be a good listener to my kind, I had to learn to love each word a little bit. I had to learn to bungee jump away from my own person and into the story and its possibilities. And wonderfully, it was most often myself that I found waiting inside of the syllable islands and at the end of the jump. As Crites (1975) argues, "The formal quality of experience through time is inherently narrative" (p. 43). I sought this honest coherence between the folkloral subjects of this inquiry and the narrative nature of their untelling.

In *Tay John*, the character Jack Denham contemplated that "to tell a story is to leave most of it untold. You mine it, as you take ore from the mountain. You carry the compass around it. You dig down—and when you have finished, the story remains something beyond your touch, resistant to your siege; unfathomable, like the heart of the mountain. You have the feeling that you have not reached the story itself, but have merely assaulted the surrounding solitude" (O'Hagan, 1960, p. vii). I chose the tellers of *The Folkloral Voice* not so much for their wide range in age, ethnicity and situation, but more because they honestly and with great humor, coherence and insight "assaulted the surrounding solitude." By their stories and the artistry of their telling, they seemed to willingly explore the secret places of childhood. They each shared in the Greek notion of truth, "aleltheia" or openness, by which I sense they lived and told their lives. Each in their Sparrowhawk fashion sought to name an unnamed country, to "unveil the darkness" by storying it (O'Hagan, 1960, p. 80). Each storyteller offered a connection between the personal stories and the mythological heart that beat within. And within each person, I sensed an important link between the kitchen table of their personal lives and the pursuant maneuvering and narrative sequentiality of their public personaes. Each brought me to the consideration of how it is that oral narrative speaks to our learning lives and joins the lore together. Each storyteller made my ears grow long. Like Polkinghorne (1988), I took story to refer to any "narrative production in general" and at its best a celebration of that which could not be silenced (p. 14). **Story to me became an oral and gestural engagement whereby pri-**

vately constructed thought was publicly shaped into mutually constructed sounds and silences.

I wished the conversations, all the mouth filling words, to resonate in my researcher bones. To that end, I listened and then responded with prose and poetry and deer hide paintings. Sometimes that order changed whereby transcription and field notes followed the aesthetic. And although I recorded the storytellers' words, my intent was not to quantify the syllables but rather to encourage an oral latitude in the telling. Each conversation, as both creation and performance, suggested its own form of "active recording," the manner in which the shadows were named and the stories retold (Connelly & Clandinin, 1990, p. 5). In the inquiry, I chose not to lean on any one methodological domain but rather to remain awash in a multiplicity of qualitative techniques and in a variety of different theoretical perspectives. I wished to remain awash, enabling the stories to suggest their own handling. I wished my storytellers to remain breathing after the labor of interpretation.

Neilsen (1989) describes the trend of educators to bring the research home, the surprise and the joy of educators "who find one another important" (p. 588). It is this celebration of life as a "dialectical balancing act in which one strives for various perfections, always falling short, yet sometimes achieving a livable harmony of competing narrative threads and criteria" that I sought (Connelly & Clandinin, 1990, p. 8). In that spirit, this study attempted to weave descriptive theory and recollective biography around the linguistic realities of several important people, individuals who return home daily in stories as high as the stars:

> I will give you the wind and a sense of wonder
> At the child by the river, the reedy river
> I will give you the sky wounded by thunder
> And a leaf on the river, the silver river. (Ryga, 1970, p. 83)

THE PURSUIT OF ETHICITY AND SIGNIFICANCE

> Methinks we have hugely mistaken this matter of Life and Death. Methinks that what they call my shadow here on earth is my true substance. Methinks that in looking at things spiritual, we are too much like oysters observing the sun through the water, and thinking that thick water the thinnest of air. (Melville, 1930, p. 33)

I have now been a part of four curriculum building projects in northern Alberta, and each project brought us to the round table of the storyteller. Each time we were asked the same question by parents, elders and fellow educators:

Is this for the children? I take that concern to be of the first ethical import. Is there something original for Mary Ann, Johnathan, Agnes and Angela and Grandpa Willie in this thing I do? I believe there is, and I believe the assurance of those uncommon combinations lie more in the nature of my storytellers than in the precision of my research methodology. I take full responsibility for my craft to celebrate their stories in a manner both aesthetically and ethically pleasing.

In sharing the oral narrative of their experience, my storytellers have shared a deep sense of person. They have allowed a voyage to the island of syllables and self. Thus, both the conversations and the ensuing transcripts have required an ethical handling. Anonymity and confidentiality were provided. In addition, all of the storytellers have had the opportunity to review and delete, as necessary, the substance of our conversations or withdraw from the study at any time, had they wished. Subsequent interpretations were made available for perusal and retelling.

Given the oral nature of the inquiry, a particular sensitivity existed in the area of language. The storytellers represented a wide range of linguistic backgrounds. For example, several members of the conversation spoke a different first language than I, be it Korean, Cree, Hebrew, or Swahili. Most often we met in the buffer state of English and friendship. Where necessary, we approached and utilized a participant translator. In these instances, the translator's presence certainly added to the hoopedness of the storytelling act. It is also common storytelling practice in many cultures that gifts be given to a storyteller at each sitting. I observed that custom. Gifts ranged from cans of tobacco to snippets of poetry to deer hide paintings to restaurant luncheons to bubble gum in a snuff can. The nature of the storyteller always suggested the gift. There were also particular times in the cultural life of the person and the community when the storytelling performance seemed most appropriate and ordinary. I tried to observe such practices and made every attempt to reflect respect and sensitivity to the "ways" other than my own.

In describing the shining days of his youth, Black Elk said, "I do not have to remember these things; they have remembered themselves all these years. It was as I grew older that the meanings came clearer and clearer out of the pictures and words; and even now I know that more was shown to me than I can tell" (Neihardt, 1932, p. 41). Ethically, I believe I have a responsibility to my storytellers to let the stories continue to bubble and resonate and retell themselves, to live beyond the frozen moment of transcription or interpretation. The storytellers gave me much more than I can tell.

Babbitt (1975) writes that "it is annoying in the extreme to find that one's work, struggled with for so long and finally finished after trying and discarding numberless bits of detail, can be found to have been summed—parts of it anyway—by a scholar years before one even began, and described as typical" (Preface). That may be as it should be. We need other ways of being original. Folklore is all about circles and stories and geese that repetitively blacken the sky each year. As much as the literate "we" struggles for single authenticity, the oral "we" is more satisfied with campfires and group personhood. It is not the intent of *The Folkloral Voice* to copyright the previously unmentioned or even unthought, nor does the study depend on CD ROM and a technological sense of "on-lineness." It was the storytellers, their richness and celebration of the folkloral, who gave pause and ethical significance to this listener. How does the metaphor of the story and the person and place of the storyteller inform our classroom practice? The significance of the answer is found in the crosscultural weave of researcher story, subject story, and the theoretical tradition of oral narration. The storytellers remind us that we need not look for truth in exotic places. Campbell (1989) suggests that "the Holy Land isn't some other place" (p. 30). Significance lives in the daily as does the holy land of educational inquiry. It is all part of a dreaming time. I wish to suggest also that poetic language, even poeticized narrative, can, as Gadamer (1986) writes, enjoy a vital relationship to ethicity and truth. Truth finds strength in the power of suggestion.

Finally, this study sought to know the dynamic nature of the folkloral voice, the shape of a classroom that could celebrate our oracy, one that could honestly and holistically facilitate the young lives in its charge and the nature of those traditional moments that exist between people (Toelken, 1979). These teaching moments are suspended between the contraries of sound and silence, and they smith us gloriously by their presence. I invite the readers to listen significantly where they will:

I see the folkloral as a time-slip talisman
And when I wear my storyteller's necklace
I belong to a planetary village of rawhide drums,
Frail spidermen, slow moving Chinese junks, Bambuti grins
Chagallian story winds and Korean spirits.
I am able to slip to shift with each story
Like a bit of lard
On the hot frying pan of experience.

I am able to move my heart around
During those ethical times
In the white calabash of wakefulness
And climb trees to the very stars.
And by it all I find honor.
I find honor.

Deer Hide Painting:
Bear Don't Live Here No More

Chapter 2
Orality

THE CONSTITUENTS OF ORALITY

A disciple secretly wrote down all the teachings he had heard from the Baal-Shem. One day the Baal-Shem saw a demon going through the house. In his hand was a book. The Baal-Shem asked him: "What book is that you have in your hand?"

"That is the book," the demon replied, "of which you are the author."

Then the Baal-Shem knew that someone was secretly setting down in writing what he had said. He gathered all his people around him and asked: "Who of you is writing down what I teach you?" The disciple who had been taking notes said it was he, and brought the Master what he had written. The Baal-Shem studied it for a long time, page for page. Then he said: "In all this, there is not a single word I said. You were not listening for the sake of Heaven, and so the power of evil used you for its sheath, and your ears heard what I did not say." (Buber, 1964, p. 66)

Some scholars mean to blow out the candle of literacy in an attempt to encourage the candle of orality to burn brighter. The opposite is also true. As Buber warns in story, even though we write of the oral, we must still listen "for the sake of Heaven" to the telling. To be in the service of one is to be in the service of the other. In a discussion of literacy and orality, it would be the utmost arrogance to denigrate the one while utilizing that same one, or even the other. My storytellers tell me, particularly when I listen "for the sake of Heaven," that the convenience of that duality, the oral and the literate, are just a scholarly convenience. Things are seldom that neat. What has often been held up as separate conceptual canoes are more metaphorically correct, a catamaran, two hulls, or more, to the one conceptual vessel.

My storytellers have brought me to this discussion of orality in story through the magic and variety of their collective person. Sparrow speaks and lives English as a first language; however, her grandparents represent and reflect both a French and a Ukrainian speaking background. Dafna speaks English with passion, albeit self-consciously at times; but her first language, both written and spoken, is Hebrew, and she modestly admits to a further scholarly acquaintance with Yiddish and French. Rattler, our grandfather of good humor, lives and speaks in English but also has a knowledge of oral Cree. Tololwa speaks and writes in wonderful English, like Dafna, but it is a second or third language. Our Masai friend first spoke Swahili as a child, then later learned the Arusha Masai tongue of his grandparents' village. Mosum, Sabochees, and Pesimwastches, our elder friends of the northern kitchen table, all live and speak in Cree. They each know and use some English, depending upon their ages, background, and inclinations. Mosum, for example, prefers to relate both story talk and story tale in Cree only. He speaks what is considered by others in the community as "High Cree." Sabochees will, for a good friend, visit in English, but under no circumstances will he tell a story in English—his art prevents it. Sabochees is similarly regarded as a speaker of "High Cree" and takes an active interest in both the oral expression and syllabic writing of his language. Pesimwastches, our tricksterish teller, seems at peace in both English and Cree, although as a long-time residential student he spent many years relearning his mother tongue. Je-Nee is learning to academically navigate in English and studied English as a young student in Korea. Her first language, however, is Korean. She uses the expression "my language" and "my culture" with particular and synonymous pride. There you have it, a wonderfully diverse linguistic and oral wash to the study, storytellers collectively connected in some fashion to English, Hebrew, Yiddish, French, Cree, Ukrainian, Swahili, Arusha Masai and Korean. In terms of literacy, my storytellers similarly ranged from strictly inhabitants of an oral culture to writers of multiliterate proportion. Like Ong (1982), I will not use the term oral literacy as I agree that it is impossible to define the primary term in the use of the secondary. A dog team is not a ski-doo with legs, nor is a ski-doo a dog team without legs. To press oracy into the metaphor of the written is to deny our ancestors their first voice.

I have chosen to "listen for the sake of Heaven" and then to write for a more earthly purpose. By their many, many stories, my storytellers have eased me into a consideration of orality, a study of those oral characteristics that are perhaps common to all tellers of story. In their orality, my storytellers came figuratively to one kitchen table. I suspected that at times the stories and the telling said as much about the culture of orality as they did about their specific cultural ways . And like a good storyteller, I as a writer must appreciate that there are those oral dimensions fully elusive, impossible to capture in chirographic or typographic print. Tololwa said it this way:

> But there's a lot of oral culture which will never be captured by the (laughter)…which will always be there, and it doesn't need to be captured and, you know, because the people who live that language…are leading their lives.…They don't need that life to be validated (laughter) through the culture of literacy…and what can you say?

There need then be no apology for that which eludes descriptive capture. Instead, I take the writing down to be itself a primary act of a primary reality, its own kind of life and one that participates in the full power of the communicative event. There are those, however, who practice the writing down as an objectification of our words and thoughts. They prefer to freeze the storyteller's breath into paper symbols. Writing need not always capture, need not always separate, need not objectify. Strangely, my storytellers have taught me that. In their loops and backloops of the expressed word, they have given continuing intimation of the power of language, be it spoken or written or other. It is going to take a story to explain this:

> One terrible day when the earth was frozen, the ground shook. The ice pack cracked on the sea. The floes piled up, grinding and crushing as the huge slabs of frozen ice heaved up on the shore. The ice smashed the igloo houses of a little fishing village on the frozen shore. The frightened people fled. In their hurry they forgot Agayk, their medicine man, who was too old to run. That is, all forgot him except the boy, Niklik. (Edmonds, 1966, p. 216)

And as the Inuit tale goes:

> The old man and the young boy were left to their hunger and each other. Although the medicine man was a friend of Raven, he was now

old and weak. He could only suggest that the pair move across the mountains for fish. The youngster was afraid of the people of the bay there, but the old man soothed the lad. "I will teach you to throw a magic spear, a spear made of words," said the elder. "There is more magic in words than in anything else in this world." Long days later, the weakened pair managed to cross the mountains and reach the bay. Immediately they chopped a hole in the ice and dropped an ivory hook into the Arctic water. But just as suddenly the two mightiest hunters from the nearby village rushed out to kill these stealers of fish. When they arrived, the old man referred them to Niklik as to one who had great and secret power over the seal and bear. "Tell us your secret," they demanded of the youth, "or you will be killed." And the lad haltingly replied, "I can only give the secret to one, to the mightiest amongst you." The two hunters each thought themselves the strongest...old rivalries and harsh words led to their fighting and within moments each had driven his spear into the other. Both then slipped into the ice hole and disappeared into the sea. When the other villagers arrived, Agayk warned them of the lad's medicine and his magic spear of words. The villagers were only too happy to leave the old man and the boy to their fishing in the bay. And so it was that Niklik learned of the magic in words and having so learned, became a strong man among his people. (Edmonds, 1966, p. 216)

In their story art, each storyteller has crafted a spear of words that when verbally thrown goes to the heart of the listener. It is that craftsmanship that I seek to describe for I have had the pleasure of tale upon magic tale. First, in my listening "for the sake of Heaven," I was initially struck by the connective nature of the stories and their telling. Everything connected: words to words, sentiments to sentiments, stories to stories. And regardless of the storytellers' own literate experiences, when they threw their oral spears of words, I, the listener, was also struck by this oral constituent of connectivity. They did not talk writing, although probably most were under the inevitable influence of their own literacy. Story talk and story tales both had a wandering way of taking their own shape, and that was seldom if ever the shape of the grammatically correct. Thus, in my transcriptions, I have leaned heavily on the "symbol of" to portray a connection between the puffs of narrative. Transcription itself did not lead inevitably to prose; rather, I thought, the storytellers in their Joycean stream of consciousness spoke poetically as much as they spoke prosaically. I mean that their stream of narrative did not by any means carry the stamp of their schooling. It wandered and looped and certainly did not possess the linearity that so characterizes the written word.

Storytellers often began "aux mideaux rez," middlemost, and did not always depend upon the familiar narrative triangle of beginning, middle, and end. Thus, my storytellers, for all their varying degrees of print experience, seemed to naturally slip into the additive orality of the kitchen table. This may be an equal reflection on the orality of their ancestors and the unsung orality of their own generations. At times, even the stream seemed less a spear of words and more a whole. For example, when Rattler said, as he did over and over again, "youknow," it was more of a piece, not two words connected; or when our Sparrow exclaimed, "ohmyGod," the listener was in the presence of the additive phrase. I have taken the time to consider those additive words or expressions that my storytellers most depended upon. Their meaning has come not so much from linguistic structure as from the entire context that surrounded their storytelling (Ong, 1982, p. 38). These following expressions most commonly formed the conjunctive points of narrative. First, our "littlest storyteller" Sparrow:

> Then, like, kindofneat, cuz, so, andthenuh, stufflikethat, sortof, I'mnotkidding, we-um, firstofall, sothen, andso, orsomething, and-souh, weird, youneverknow, andeverything, infact, ohmygosh, ohmyGod, wellyouknow, ohyeah, butalsobut, I-betcha, well-Iheard, totallydifferentstuff, ok-firstofall, likeIsaid, orwhatever, andsoandthen, bytheway, andlikefromthere, uhm.

The conjunctives for Sparrow gave a special narrative joy, a special pause in the oral movement. These connectives not only brought word and phrase together, but also seemed to fine-tune the wonderfully rhythmic relationships of speech to breath. In Sparrow's own joyful rush of story, the connectives certainly took the onus off the grammatical and situated it instead on the contextual performance of eye and hand and sound. Story and body were inseparable.

Grandfather Rattler, too, languished in a great sea of oral additives. They included:

> Yousee, that'sright-yes, atanyrate, andanyway, soanyway, youknow, Iguess, andso-on, anduh, butuh, yehpp, butanyway, sothis, ofcourse, so-ah, but-thee-uh, loandbehold, onthis-particularday, soreally, apparentlywhathadhappened, inotherwords, generallyspeaking.

To Grandfather, these conjunctive bits of storyteller glue were old friends. They seemed to roll out at will and facilitate his amazing confluence of narrative. But the additives came not only in word or conjunctive phrase, but also in his sprinkling of the drops of laughter. The laughter was a kind of additive that brought things together and made the next part of the story possible. Rattler also used silence, which Schafer (1969) describes as the only perfect sound, as a kind of conjunctive. I realized as listener that our Grandfather's clever, clever use of silence tied me into the "about to be said." The silence was certainly not empty space. In a similar fashion, Rattler used opinion as he paused to comment on the story or even the story of the story. Thus, he would slip into the additive space of commentator, omniscient narrator. By gesture, our Grandfather would give a throat clearing cough, not so much for physiological reasons as it was a gestural method of joining things together quite independent of grammar. Clock ticking in the background, there was the wee sip of hazelnut coffee and the spoon stirring, again and again. That clockwise stirring seemed to wind the tale up and was an additive and integral part of the telling.

Although Dafna's narrative journey through the colloquial and the ritual was a second-language sojourn, it, too, was characterized by the additive nature of its telling. Conjunctive words and phrases included "exactly, youknow, so, because, anduh," to name but a few. Just as Dafna spoke of the conversational passion of her own family and her people, it was often this passion that, like Niklik, threw her spear of words, passion that connected the last comment to the next. Dafna's storytelling helped me understand that just as words connect to words or add up, so stories connect to stories and add up. For example, in a single conversation, or collaborative telling time together, Dafna and I took the following kind of connective journey:

> The sound of our voices on tape…sacred nature of Jewish writing…the evidence and relationship of gender to text…shared knowledge in marriage…a beloved student…images of God…sacred scrolls…relationship of oral to sacred text…Torah…the Jewish holidays…harvest…life as ceremony…life as sacred…honoring the body…the body in death…symbol of Jerusalem as a city of good biblical stories…beach people.

What began as a reflection upon the sound of voices became indeed a celebration of the sounds and sense of the human life. The conversation was thematically additive, and in a similar fashion, our many conversations did indeed add on and add up, backloop jumping all the while. In the aggregate of story, I found the storyteller Dafna. The student of orality can take insight from the smallest part, the syllabication of sound, or from the syllabication of story and a larger context. The additive nature of our stories demonstrated, too, the oral means by which the storyteller found and promoted understanding. Thus, all my storytellers were somewhat formulaic and patterned in their telling. They told in an additive way that lent itself to retelling. The current seemed to situate itself in the context of the recent and just past. They told in a compounding way that allowed for the recovery of their narrative and person.

Pesimwastches, by tale, and Sabochees, by talk, together and further illustrated the additive "rather than subordinative" nature of storytelling (Ong, 1982, p. 37). Their second language conjunctives included:

> Something, likethat, ohyeah, youknew, likeIsaid, andallthis, anduh, theotherthing, youknow-whatImean, sowhathappenedwas, becauseuh, whenyoulookatit, allofasudden, yeahp, likeIsay, likeformyself, asfaras-Icanremember, inmymind, sotospeak, backthen-asakid, matterof-fact, fromthere, theway-Iseeit, those-kindofthings, inthat-generation.

That sense of the additive was found again in both word and gesture. There was the ever bubble of laughter, the clearing of the throat, the wrap around of tea and tobacco, and the evocative double dance of the hand. Our northern elders told with similar Dafna passion as "a man with his hair on fire looks for a pond" and told in an additive way. Just as the words formed relationships one to the other, again and like Dafna the stories offered profound relationships to yet other stories, other people. Insight surely comes from this study of the small parts. Some philologists suggest that words originated in whole and as an ancestral imitation of the forces and sounds of nature (Shanker, 1965, p. 12). Our love for onomatopoeia, for example, in Cree birds were named for their sounds, supports this notion. Other philologists argue that our words grew from the small parts, from the suffixes and prefixes and roots of our oral ancestors' language. This is an originary concept of language being "added to" (Shanker, 1965, p. 12). The storytelling in this study, I believe, supported both schools. The tale Pesimwastches told, *The Spirit Moans*, was wonderfully full of sound, within word and action, but it was an agglutinated sound, ever building one phoneme upon the other.

Thus, the stories were indeed additive in composition and associative in their interrelationships. Their recovery, however, very often depended upon their repetition or what Ong (1982, p. 39) calls redundancy. Because our words disappear as quickly as they appear, repetition was essential to the memorability of each story. As Mollel suggests, story "is what we make of our experience." There exists an obvious originatory relationship between the doing and the telling of it. Life may be an act of agglutination, the experience by which the new parts adhere to the old and become memorable. And not surprisingly, that additive process, both in the living and in the telling, required repetition. Learning and life to my storytellers was an iterative business. Story was the power that used them as its sheath. Dafna suggested that as much as a technological society, in appearance, moves on in a forever linear quest of the "next," it, too, plays out an iterative hand through story:

> It's wonderful to just open the invisible doors and pull [the stories] out. I thought always that it was very important for a teacher to be deeply situated in her culture....Whenever it presents itself, you can give an example from the past, and also it shows that there is "nothing new under the sun." Our human endeavor, you know, has been going on for so many years....They say Solomon wrote it...this is the Book of Wisdom, which he wrote when he was older.

Memorability then, at the heart of narrative, comes in large part from repetition. Orality builds upon itself as there is no written text of the tale or talk to which the listener can later refer. I believe my storytellers in their repetitive way gave further evidence of the importance of context to oral meaning. And although each storyteller had some form of access to literate expression, everyone sought to tell memorably, and that meant artful repetition. Rattler in his eye-twinkling way slipped naturally into the redundant:

> But somewhere in this vast clearing before they got to this little bridge, someone had tackled this miner with an axe, clove in his skull, and stole the money belt, killed him you see, stole the money belt.

> These waving trees, moaning and groaning trees and strange noises and little clouds passing the sky and the moon was coming in and out, ghostly shadows...and we climbed the hill, and we sat down, and we waited and we waited and we waited.

> You can make such good time on snowshoes once you get that pace; you just keep going and going and going, and you can see why a tracker made really good time.

> And every night they formed a circle, you know, with their wagons and they moved on and on, day by day and day by day.

> All the others had gone by, walked on the other side of the road, made no attempt to help as they passed him, you see....He stopped and bound his wounds, treated him.

Rattler's telling was a many looped affair, and the listener gained through repetition not only understanding and clarity, but emphasis and a wonderful sense of the poetic in orality. Words were repeated, thoughts were repeated, and indeed even entire story segments were iterative in the telling. Rattler's "youknow" and "yousee" simply gave pause and confirmation to the listener's attendant understanding. Thus, the originality of the storyteller came not so much in the composition of new tales but rather in the way the story was slipped into the context of the visit, lesson or conversation (Goody, 1977, p. 29). New elements, the foremost being the person of the listener, were continually and ingeniously built into the Rattler retelling. It made it impossible to hear the same story twice because the redundant nature of the telling swept new context into old stories.

Scholars have suggested "the echo principle" as a means of repetition by which the telling of great lengthy epics could be facilitated. Repetition then is a mnemonic aid that rhythmically brings the story home. In Sparrow's storytelling, for example, repetition was very often constructed on the folkloral notion of the oral triad:

> I'm getting really, really, really tired, and I'm getting sick because I'm so tired of school.

> And I went into this deep, deep, deep snow, and Dad had a hard time getting me out.

> At the school we have skis, these really nice white skis, cross-country skis, that we can go every, every, every noon with ski shoes and everything, and we go every noon and ski poles.

> And so then he went to the Plaza Hotel, and he stayed there, and it was a really, really, really nice hotel, like it was the nicest hotel in New York, maybe even in Canada.

Our Sparrow's delightful triple phrasings gave an indication of her passion for not only life, but for the telling of it. Within the repetitive, Sparrow's voice would concomitantly grow more impassioned. Thus, it was not the grammatical that gave meaning to the voice so much as the voice itself from within the context of both the accented story and the entire conversation. Our "littlest storyteller," in her iterative loops, shared both the story and everything else the story conjured up. At times, Sparrow simply loved the word, and in that soulful affinity to sound, repetition brought its own exuberance:

Oh I knew that was going to be it! I just knew it! I knew it. I just knew it was going to be truth!

In her exuberance, Sparrow spoke "for the sake of Heaven," while Pesimwastches brought solemnity and conviction to the story through the iterative:

I have heard that it was created, created earth through Wesakychak, that's what I heard, that's all I heard, I don't know how, but that's what I heard.

And the first day he travelled and tied up his horse now and then stopped and hunted in a circle, you know, hunted in a circle...tied up his horses. Nothing, no tracks, no animals, nothing...couldn't even kill a chicken or anything, you know, no rabbits, nothing at all.

When you think about it, you look at the dogs, wherever they go, they're small, they're small little things, small even, even small, smaller than you think.

Grandfather Pesimwastches repeated the old stories, examples being *Wesakychak and the Creation of the Earth, The Mourning of a Hunter's Spirit, The Exchange of Powers Between the Wolf and the Dog*. In doing so, our trickster teller brought out the old tales but again into the new context of his own life. And just as the old stories repeated, so the words within the stories repeated, giving the conservative authority of elderhood to the retellings. There are echoes of this as well in Je-Nee's stories:

There is a tiger and a grandmother, old, old woman, old woman, a grandmother....In my country many old people bent over, yeah bent over. I don't know the reason why, hard work or their position...was not good when they were young.

They always told, not read it the story and at the time it was so live, it was just real, real. I felt that real things was happening, was happening like when they told about tiger, they just imitate tiger's voice, and everything was just vivid, vivid, yeah.

As innovative and quick as our society becomes, it is apparent that the expression of that innovation is itself highly formulaic and traditional. My storytellers have also taught me something of the "vivid" nature of this repetition. Although many of the storytellers enjoyed a highly sophisticated literary expression, by way of practice and appreciation all slipped naturally into the additive and repetitive nature of their storytelling art. As much as the storytellers were able to access the sometimes separative nature of the written, they most often preferred to tell of their own living person and immediate circle of family and friends. Perhaps spirit lived first in the story of their personal lives. These personal tales promoted not only traditional values, but the traditional and repetitive expression of those values as well.

Both constituents of orality, the additive and the repetitive, imply much more than the mnemonic nature of our tellings. The storytellers added on and repeated for the purposes of power. As Malinowki suggests, among aboriginal peoples "language is a mode of action and not simply a countersign of thought" (Ong, 1982, p. 32). By their many stories, all the storytellers gave clear evidence of their belief in the oral word and its power. This was particularly apparent in their concern with naming and in what I prefer to call the denominative constituent of orality. Perhaps a story is in order.

Jennifer was my single Grade 3 student in Nose Creek, a one-room school in the colored mountains of northwestern Alberta, a little blue school on the banks of a spruce-lined creek. She was a joy. Jennifer met my every teacher-friend suggestion with the smile of the well-loved. Her notebooks were a particular point of pride to both her and me. The cursive writing was impeccable, flowing and expressive, the stuff of Japanese calligraphy.

After several months in the classroom, the grandparents and Bear and I decided to take the students in to the city, "otinow," for routine visual examinations. And it was then we discovered an awful truth. Jennifer was suffering from a progressive blindness. She apparently had some vision, but it was of a world quite unlike our own. Glasses would certainly help in the short term.

One spring day, not unlike today, and several weeks after our return home, the glasses arrived. It was my task to pass them out. And I can still hear Jennifer's initial response: "Mr. Sewall, there are trees on the other side of the creek. All this time I thought it was just green. There are trees over there":

> *I have long thought of this child*
> *Her writing finger winding black hair into knots*
> *Her yellow pencil bleeding graphite words*
> *Into robin's wings.*
> *I have long thought of this child*
> *And of her day when just green*
> *Became trees on the other side.*

The story of Jennifer and "just green" provides us with a powerful metaphor for human language. For just as the spectacles brought out the trees from the green, so naming brings out the particular from the general. Thanks to Shakespeare we have *Romeo and Juliet*, with Juliet's wonderful question "What's in a name?" As Shanker (1965, p. 33) suggests, we are all of civilization. By our naming acts, by our acts of denomination, we have identified places, people, things, even our time. Ostensibly, in this denominative act, we have created our own relationship to the named, and it, in turn, takes its place and meaning in our world. The power of naming and in naming goes to the heart of storytelling. Good storytellers bring the trees out from the green. By their words, they give the listener relationship. But just as the name binds, so it separates. Just as story binds, so story separates. Travers (1989) writes that "if one asks the question—'When was it that the lion lay down with the lamb?', the answer inevitably has to be 'Before they were named by Adam'" (p. 120). For once they were named, their fates were sealed, and their behavior became typical and appropriate.

Grandfather Rattler demonstrated a particular sensitivity to the denominative art. Perhaps to the storyteller being able to call the names is tantamount to giving the lion and the lamb life:

> I have a strong belief, that is why I put words down when I start interviewing these people because I think key words is tied in somewhere in your synapses, your keywords, you know, because they'll start it moving.

Even a discussion of "key words" triggered a telling:

> I used to use it a great deal in teaching. I'd put key words up on the board when I was teaching...and you know at the end of the week or the end of the month or whenever it came, I'd just go down through them. The kids would remember perfectly about each word and tell you the stories connected with each word.

Words were the denominative way into other words. They started the thing moving. And without the words, Grandfather felt particularly powerless. For example, on that always memorable first day of teaching:

> Names will certainly vanish from my memory, people I have known all my life, my mind will suddenly blank out and-uh this is the first week at this school....Well the farmers were coming in, picking up the mail, various people, there wasn't room in the little area....I got in the line-up, so I got in the line-up, I finally got to the wicket, and the master

said, "Yes, what's your name?" That's when my mind went blank. I stuttered and I stammered, suddenly realized I had no documentation, in case...I didn't have a driver's license, no charge card or anything like that in those days. She must have thought I was crazy. Finally I stood back and let the other person through. Embarrassing part was having to go to the back of the line...but I guess years and years later that lady...still talked about this crazy young school teacher who forgot his name.

It is perhaps only storyteller justice that such a state of helplessness could result in such a fine tale. Often in our visits, Rattler would look to the ceiling for a name or call upon his son in the next room. His stories were all about people, and so it was their names that brought them out of the green and into the particular. The names were much more than tags. They were the key words and the places where the people lived. As Norman (1982) writes, the names were filled by the people, by their stories. Again, "a power superior to man," says Plato, "gave the primordial names to things in such a way that the names are necessarily right and the rightness of the names makes the nature of things visible" (Travers, 1989, p. 120).

Thus, it is this denominative power that connects us to the Creator. To be able to call up a name, for example, "Rumplestilzkin," is to gain hold of the unnameable. It enables the story to continue and when necessary end. Similarly, Tololwa's grandfather gave characteristics to a name during the story performance:

> There would be sound effects throughout describing the passing of the planes (TOOOOOO) and then the dropping of the bombs (TU! TU! TU!), like then he would really take his time describing everything, and then he would see those people, like the British....He would describe the British as one person....It's not the British but the Englishman or the Russian or the German, and each one of them would have their own characteristics....The German would assume a life...become a kind of a personality.

In gaining their name, the old grandfather took possession of the story. In my own northern community practice, I have learned of the perils of naming and of the role of the unnamed in decision making. To avoid controversy and confrontation, it is often vital that the names be kept out of it. It is usually enough that one refers to one's sources as "a concerned parent," "a friend," "an elder," "a community member." To name the individual is to deny the conversation its general airing. In many cultures as well, it is important that one not name the recently deceased. To name them is to bring them back, and it may be too soon for that. Again, it is enough to refer to them by relationship (for example, "we lost our grandmother, you know, Old Henry's wife"). In this instance, the lesser word euphemistically takes the place of the more powerful word, the name. By the denominative act then, power is accessed. Trappings of this practice exist in the written as well whereby the highest academic honor one can pay one's colleagues is to name them in print. To name a scholar is to recognize his/her power and to draw relationship to it. In the naming of our children, both through ceremony and law, we situate them into a context, a life. Similarly, stories are the means by which we denominate our experience and passing. Thus, the Arusha Masai grandfather gave personality, through story, to the names. Pesimwastches, our trickster teller, gave this denominative story of his birth:

> When I was born my grandpa and my stepmother was there and my grandma was there. When I was born, the old timer took me up....Like in the old days when kids were born, the elders took them, and the elder took you, and he gave you a name. And that's what this elderly man did to me. He took me when I was born and...he said, "Pesimwastches." As it was, the sun was just coming up in the summer where I was born, near Moose Lake. The poles my mother used are still brand new. My stepmother changes the logs every fall.

The naming and the birth, in this instance, came together. The world has gained both a child and a story. And as we travelled about, Pesimwastches and I, friend and listener, he talked of the land and how it too became named:

> Where we're coming down, things have happened, you know we went through that. There is a story of the special route. Example, we came through Poplar Creek, and Poplar Creek just happened to be inside the reserve. There at Poplar Creek, back in the old days, there used to live a Medicine Man, and he was sent a lion there on his track. Somebody teased him, another Native person, and didn't allow him to cross the Poplar, could not go to the other side. That's...that's amazing, where could a lion come from out here? So that's where Poplar Creek got its name. And when you came further down it's called "Whyapskask," it means—there's a little cliff there, a little sort of a tunnel—When they were cutting this road, they didn't see this hole in the ground...they came to it with a horse, and it fell into the hole, so they called it Whyapskask. It's just a stone cliff.

Thus, we see the denominative power of story and how a land becomes visible in its names. With Dafna, too, the particular stories emerged from the green and became refilled with each generation and with each retelling:

> Everywhere we go in Israel reminds us of something that happened in this place. It's not an abstract place. If you go in the Valley of Galilee, it reminds you of a particular war that took place 2,500 years ago. And it did take place at this particular place. It still has the same name that is used to have then....They all come to life....It's a lived story if you want to call it that way....It jumps into your face.

That, I believe, is the power of orality. It can name the place and bring it "into your face." Thus, the additive and repetitive expression of orality enables the speaker to speak and the listener to listen, "all for the sake of Heaven."

All of my storytellers had also the wonderful gift of impelling themselves into the personages of their story and, in doing so, becoming one with the people. That sense of projection into the feelings of another is what I wish to describe as the fourth constituent of orality: connective, repetitive, denominative and, finally, empathetic. As Ong (1982, p. 46) writes, the oral individual is not simply a subjective commentator but rather one who moves into the communal soul. The storyteller and story characters and story listener(s) become wonderfully bound together in the oral performance. Traditional and somewhat formulaic expression facilitate this dynamic. Pesimwastches intimated this sense of the communal soul with:

> I thought about Grandpa Julian, when he used to live there....He used to have a dog team, beautiful dogs, raising his children, he had his own garden, his own stable....All these things I thought about by that stove, sitting on the bear rug, I wondered what he thought about when he sat on the rug, what stories he told. You know what I mean...but I was still talking with you. In the written word, you're directly where you are. In the oral, in the oral you could be three places all the time.

Pesimwastches was able through narrative to project himself into the story of his people. He was able to slip into the narrative personae. For example, during the recounting of his mission school days, Pesimwastches said,

> Old Johnny said, "Sometimes people cut their life short with their own doing, and sometimes it is cut short by other people's doing." And this is what happened in my case. Yes, sir.

Thus, in story, the trickster teller was able to bind together the past of the elder with the past of the school child into the present of the retelling. By the process of orality, the narrator, story character, and listener were each projected into the common world of the other, into the "communal soul" that is. Similarly, when Dafna told of the Biblical Samson, she remembered first the story's presence in her own teaching. She told also of Samson's wife, the unnamed, and in doing so grew wonderfully empathetic:

> So Menoach ran home fast and he told his wife, "You know what, I saw...God appeared to me, and He told me that we are going to have a son, and I'm going to be dead because I saw the sight of God....I'm definitely going to be dead." So she says to him, "Stupid you, if He wanted you to be dead do you think He would tell you this story?" (laughter) I just love it, I mean I just love it, the wisdom of this woman. (laughter)

Our Israeli storyteller danced the narrative shuffle from the "I" of Menoach to the first person of the unnamed wife to the school teacher in reflection to the teller participant of the moment. She was fully participative in the narrative tradition of her people as demonstrated by her ease of personae. As listener, I was brought to the face of Dafna's shifting place in the story. I knew by her telling and my listening that we were confirming the situation of things. We were important both to the continuance of story and to life. We accepted our responsibility as authors of the moment.

Perhaps for Sparrow, the participative celebration of story was most obvious in her most spontaneous telling. This little bundle of fanciful teller would spontaneously spin the narrative in the finest "pourquois" tradition. In doing so, she would enable one grey-whiskered listener to better appreciate the invisible hand of nature:

> Okay, one day the zebra...he used to be a plain old white horse...and then one day he went to jail for—racing. It was illegal to race other animals that weren't his, and so he raced them, and he got...sent to jail for one day, and they were painting the jail that day black. And so they started painting over the bars, and they didn't notice that the zebra was there, and they painted over the zebra, and then there were black stripes on him.

Sparrow had this delightful and empathetic gift of sensing the story in both things and people. Within the time space of sometimes brief moments, Sparrow could slip from the inside of stories like *Beauty and the Beast* to "frozen kidneys on the lawn" to Whitney Houston to "octopuses." In all of it, she was fully present. From *Honey I Blew Up the Kids:*

> Baby went behind the laser, and she got bigger....She was humungus, and she walked....They're trying to stop it and everything, and then it was really funny...and the baby passed the place we were staying at when we went to Los Vegas, the Circus Circus Hotel.

Our sprightly storyteller shifted with ease from her captain's chair at the kitchen table to landscapes storied with bats and air guitars and Charlois calves. There did not seem to be the firmly definitive, the tidy ordering of appearances and realities. Those story places most inviting were appropriately most told about. For Sparrow, synonymous with empathy was imagined adventure.

Rattler, too, gave continuing evidence of this empathetic nature of oral story. In the tale *One Room Knife*, for example, Grandfather told of a teaching colleague who faced his first rural class with tellable creativity:

> They'd go through three or four teachers a year....They were a rough bunch....Anyway, this little man, this little runt of a teacher came out the first of September and-uh I guess walked into the classroom. He had big cowboy boots on. He walked like a big cowboy, flopped the hat down and he reached in....All the children were sitting in rows as they did in those days....He reached into his thing [satchel], and he said, "I hear some of you fellows think you are tough guys, eh?" And I guess they looked tough and sort of winked at each other and thought...and so anyway, he pulled into his thing [valise], and he pulled out this big knife....It was about this long, and he threw it! The whole length of the [room], and it went Zaaap! Went right into the wooden door and split the door. There was a great crack and the door was split open, and then he looked down at them, and he says, "Got another knife here, too!" (laughter) And I guess it was a perfect class....He'd done all his school there, no problems....Years later [a student] ran into this teacher, and he says, "I'll never forget how you did that," and the teacher says, "I'll never forget it, too....I'd been practicing that throw all summer," he said, "that's the first time I ever stuck anything!" (laughter)

Through the artistry of the Rattler telling, the listener grew empathetic to the plight of the green-as-the-grass runt teacher and his first day with "a rough bunch." We fly with the knife, split with the door, and rock, too, on our cowboy heels in the full glory of the unexpected. Like both Rattler and his innovative and cowboy-hatted character, we, too, have "another knife," just in case.

But that other knife is another story, and for the present, a beam of laughter light has fallen on a colleague's "heart of darkness." The story of our species has been delightfully repeated, and each of us has found further connection through our enlisted participation in the narrative. As Achebe advises, "Where one story stands, bring another one to stand beside it, and if that's a better story, then it should displace the bad one" (Baker & Draper, 1992, p. 27). Thus, each story invites further participation, more stories, which in turn give further empathetic celebration to this engagement called life.

I am gently reminded of my first year teaching, art, Grades 7 to 11, rural Southern Alberta. Each morning I drove my old Triumph, TR3, top down, from our farm and ceramic studio to the consolidated junior/senior high in a nearby town. And each day that teaching year, the students and their green-as-the-grass teacher participated with the muse of aesthetic expression. Each day we conscientiously kneaded and rolled out and centered and shaped the Plainsmen clay. And each day the clay pile of discards grew, the unloved and the unclaimed. These were the wonderful ceramic expressions of misadventure, misfired and misthrown, and by year end, the pile was considerable. We talked, the students and I, wondering aloud if accident could become adventure and ceremony. The pieces were deserving of something. And finally, in the past-crocus season of early summer, a decision was collaboratively reached. Later that week, the Grade 7 class and I went on a dig, not to uncover but to cover. We dug out a home for the ceramic unloved beneath several feet of prairie coulee. We then covered the hole carefully, voiced our sentiments, and quietly returned to our ordinary lives. We hoped that future archeologists would be kind to us and one day greatly treasure those accidents of clay birth. Many of us listen to the radio news, even now, for word and announcement of their find.

Perhaps the unloved, most of all, need the participatory ritual of oracy. It enables us to listen for the sake of Heaven, to bring the trees from the green, to survive, even in the sight of God. And be our stories repetitive, connective, denominative or empathetic, they are sometimes the only thread that joins us back to ourselves.

Deer Hide Painting:
Coyote Howls to the Void

PLACE: THE HEARTHSTONE OF ORALITY

There is a wonderful Spanish story told of the creation of the earth and of the four elements which combined to make it all possible. These were the elements of Water, Fire, Wind and Honor. And not only did they accomplish the feat of creation but can be found, even today, in each human being. Having completed their collaborative task, the elements decided to each go their separate way. First spoke Water.

"My work is done and I'll leave now. However, should you need me in the future, I can be found in the streams and oceans."

The words of Fire then followed: "Yes, I, too, shall leave. Should you need me, I can be found in the sun and in steel."

"And I," added the Wind, in a whisper, "can be found in the Heavens above."

The last to speak was Honor. "If I am once lost, do not trouble to seek me, for I am forever lost." (Y Maestas & Anaya, 1980)

I would suggest that it is these same four elements that individually and then together most characterize the place of story, be it hearth or kitchen table, candle or campfire. Fire for warmth, for the gathering round, fire to illuminate, just barely, the storyteller's features; water in every holy place, water in the teller's and listener's tea, water as inward mist when we tell of the heart; wind in the words and laughter of the circle gathered, wind accompaniment on storyteller window late at night, wind that causes fire to dance; and honor, in the combination, honor in the conversational spaces that celebrate our species, honor in both the local and the ritual, the honor of telling, the place of honor.

Great energies have gone into the why and what of narrative but little into the where of the matter, the geographical place of story. Sheridan (1991) eloquently suggests that "earth becomes taken for granted as the point of departure from which we blast off into orbits of distraction from the guiding forces of Earth" (p. 25). And as he goes on to write, distraction creates yet more distraction. It may be the task and joy of the storyteller to remind us, on the living side, of the primary reality of earth, remind us of the wind, fire and water. We tell around hearths, campfires and kitchen tables and in doing so bring honor to our ordinary and undistracted places. As "Kitchen Talk" (Alford & Harris, 1992) suggests, home is where we must and forever return. Although we excitedly pursue our professional and linear distractions, we always come back to the fire to tell of our darings. Around the table we defend our writings and the separate expression of our lives. We have lunch together so that we might endure our solitary afternoons. We have tea that we might include ourselves in the blimp of collected consciousness that floats by. Where there is no hearth, we try to create one. We try to find a place where story can live. It may be the campfire, the hearth, the kitchen table, and it will inevitably shape the evolving tales. Although we go to great educational and professional pains to air brush out our footprints, the perceptive listener will always hear the fire crackle and the drip of water in the wind of the storyteller's words. Enunciation alone is a kind of rare honor around the hearth, h-earth. Le Guin (1980/1981) asks the question "why do we huddle about the campfire?" and concludes that our ordinary gathering together in circles and in stories is probably as close as we will ever come to a perfect circle and a life without end (p. 190).

The Tanzanian storyteller, Tololwa Mollel, told me of the hearth he grew up around:

> I went to live with my grandparents at the age of 9, 8 or 9....At my grandparents' house, there was no table really....The centre of the kitchen was the fireplace, which was the hearthstones, and then you have some small stools a little higher than that, that everybody sat on....There is a particular one for Grandfather, like a kind of big one.

Should guests arrive, they would be served at a table in another adjoining room. Daily life, however, took place around Grandmother's fire stones. Even Grandfather, as elder, head of the Arusha Masai compound, owner of his own house, came each day to Grandmother's hearth:

> Grandfather would come to the kitchen, too, and then after food and so on and sit there and talk with Grandmother and exchange the news of the day, what they have heard.

Thus, around the hearth informal story took the shape of everyday talk, the news. At other times, however, story became more formalized and took a folkloral shape:

> Grandmother told folktales usually around supper time because supper took a long time cooking cuz cooking was done on firewood.... Everytime that you'd be there waiting for supper and a lot of kids

would be nodding off, of course, so maybe that was one way of keeping the kids awake, waiting for supper.

The hearth, the food and the stories were all part of the evening ceremony of the meal. Grandmother's stories lent themselves particularly well to the sense of closing day:

> So she would be telling stories about folk, about monsters, mostly about monsters…and she liked to tell stories, joking stories, about…a section of the Masai people who are hunters and travellers…and they are the butt of many jokes among the Masai and Arusha Masai…the Dorobo.

Heated hearthstones, food cooking nicely albeit slowly, little ones wide eyed then belly laughing at Grandmother's infumated words, that is both the storyteller's memory and the listener's vision. The hearthstones carried the spirit of the place and provided foundation both to the literal and metaphoric treats that followed. A living fire lent itself to a living conversation in a way that the speed and efficiency of a microwave strangely denies. Perhaps it is impossible to be a stranger at a living fire. The sun has come to visit us in the guise of a cooking flame. It is among us. The fire belongs to all, not just the storyteller or the listener or the stirrer of sticks. The fire and its stories belong to us all.

I am reminded of my own little boy days and our branding fires. Steel branding irons would be knowledgeably set and turned in the flames of an old cedar fencepost fire. Too young to wrestle calves, I would add sticks to the fire and glory in the cowboy-booted company. Cows and calves would be bawling, heelers throwing out their loops and dragging Hereford calves to the waiting wrestlers and irons. Stories were told cryptically, wryly, shot out like tobacco juice from a whiskery cheek, stories told from within the action. Later, calves all branded, mothered up and kicked out, sore knees would bend around the fire and the more formal tellings would be dallied out, the words leisurely and chased out with a swig from a long-necked Calgary beer bottle. The branding fire cinched us together, the rheumy eyed, the old and beat, the young and freckled. Conversation was often rough in the telling but gentle in intent. "Guess we better snuff out the fire," Grandfather would say, and the prairie ceremony would come to a close for another year. The branding crew, those who a moment before were studying the crackles, now separated off to the round corral of their own lives. Like Tolowa, the flames, for a time, had turned strangers into family into an oral testimony. And like Grandmother's stories, our branding tales took time to fully reveal themselves. The better ones always put the felt-hatted listener on a trail that took them back home. Branding fire stories gave direction, themselves fireflies in the nights of privacy.

Je-Nee takes us home as well with her stories of a South Korean childhood, home to the story place of a "floor culture." Again, it was a retelling in which the gentle and lively person of Grandmother figured largely:

> It's very interesting because as I said to you we have the floor culture and then we have special things to make the floor, you know, we make it with cement. On the cement we put some paper, dahk, made by dahk tree....It's a kind of wood, but it's very light and durable.

In what Je-Nee described as the traditional way, first came the cement floor, then the dahk paper, and finally several coats of lacquer. The result was a floor shiny and durable, with colors that greatly pleased the Korean eye:

> Beautiful...color is beautiful, and then feeling is very beautiful. It's always clean, always clean, compared to these carpets!

Je-Nee went on to describe the wonderful warmth of the traditional lacquered floor:

> We make it warm in the kitchen because it is connected with the kitchen....There is a hole to make the room warm, and then we can cook there....Coal, the black one, we use that....We make it in a special shape, special shape, when we use it....Now usually they have very westernized house, but my home is not, so far.

Je-Nee's first story place, the clean lacquered dahk floor in the living room, wonderfully warm from the slow burn of coal in the kitchen, was made complete by the presence of Grandmother:

> How wonderful it is, sit on the floor, it's very warm...feel very good and then we put the blanket...and I usually sat on Grandmother's knee and listen to the story....I, my younger brother and younger sister listened to the story together.

There were times, however, when Grandmother and her stories moved out of doors, from the place of the lacquered floor to the place of the straw mat. Grandmother made possible a connection from the elements of earth to the figments and fantasies of a child's mind:

We put the [straw] mat on to the yard, and then we sat around and we listened to the story. I usually put my head on my Grandmother's knees and lie down, and sometimes I fall asleep listening to the story and-uh dream the story which I listened to from my Grandmother....I can be a fairy, I can be a tiger, or any animal, I can be a mountain guard....Mountain guard always punishes the bad men and give good things to the good people...and then I can be a princess.

The coal fire of the Korean home was exchanged for the wood fire of the Asian night, and Grandmother's words gave a special clarity to the very stars above:

I remember the sky was so clear, you know, and the stars were so shiny, stars were so shiny...because we sat on the mat we cannot put fire in the middle, just put fire beside our mat...to eliminate the mosquitoes.

There is that sense of conspiracy, synchronicity perhaps, whereby small wood smoke and Grandmother's words of mountain guards and shiny stars all conspire to set the story in one child's narrative memory. Like Tololwa, Je-Nee sat close to the earth and in both the coal fire and the small wood fire found family and story:

[She would tell] old, old stories, and it just started from once upon a time...old, old time. I think sometimes she made the story....The story gave me dream when I was young...it makes me comfortable. My grandmother's voice is very soft, and after my grandmother died, I remember that time when my grandmother told the stories.

There would be other storytellers and other story places in Je-Nee's well-travelled life but no one or no place with the first recall power of this. The first stories would always come from the lacquered floor and the straw mat of a Korean night. And by each retelling, by each narrative recall, Grandmother would continue to celebrate the oracy of the folkloral. Through her soft voice, story was able "to set the inner life into motion again" and again (Estés, 1992, p. 65). Surely there is something universal about the bedtime story, a kind of intense life before death. It seems that every child needs a drink and a story and a hug before this nightly dream voyage. It may be the final daily dress up of tiger or princess or mountain guard. Through the hearth of Grandmother story, both Tololwa and Je-Nee were able to meet this childhood night.

To the Israeli Dafna, the hearth, the kitchen table, the campfire were equally important. They, too, were the first story place. In fire Dafna found a special sense of togetherness:

> Many activities that took place in classroom or in the youth movement that we used to go or we used to belong used to take place around the bonfire. We would build a bonfire, and we would sit around, roast potatoes.

Food, fire and story, echoes here of the Arusha Masai Grandmother. And it was no coincidence that as I listened to Dafna's story of her early narrative places, we shared homemade soup, olives, cheese and "sambusak." Gathering around food and fire was as old as the story of her people:

> We used to roast potatoes and sing and talk and play games around the bonfire....This started with the settlers who came to Israel. They used to sit around bonfires, dance around it, sing around it and have this togetherness feeling.

In the fire, in the flames, Dafna found continuance. Just as Je-Nee recounted her shiny stars, so Dafna made narrative time shuffles as well and slipped by storyteller license to other times:

> And I remember dozens and dozens of bonfires like that...ever since I can remember myself until, and you know what, even as an adult sometimes, we still make a bonfire and sit around it...and my children do the same....It brings you together, you sit by those wonderful flames. It's so beautiful....Sometimes in the winter we used to bring blankets and cover ourselves with blankets and just keep warm...sometimes until the morning....It was a wonderful sense of togetherness, and many friendships grew out of this closeness.

If someone brought a guitar or an accordion, then for Dafna the night was complete. Again, there were no strangers in the story place of fire. After describing the bonfire to me, Dafna sighed and filled the ensuing silence with the meaning of her inward looks.

And in the conversation, it was a natural shift for Dafna to slip from the localized story of the bonfire to the more ritualized tale of the candle and its importance to Jewish people:

> With the lighting of the candle you bring the holiness to the Sabbath...candles symbolize the entering of the Holy Day, and candles

symbolize the exit of it on Saturday eve. On Friday night we light the candle to welcome the Sabbath, and Saturday night, after the sunset, there is another type of candle that is lit to differentiate the holiness of the Sabbath and the, how do you call it, the everyday life of the other days.

The flame of the candle, Dafna explained, had both religious and cultural significance. Even for those not especially devout, the candle was an important symbol of home and togetherness. It was a burning symbol of the people:

> This is done mainly by religious people…but on Friday night many people light the candles welcoming the Sabbath, even if they are not religious because there is so much symbolism in it that you cannot give it up.…Many times I do it, especially when I am not in Israel.…This brings back the Holiness that you can feel.

All of us who have gathered about a flame, be it candle or campfire, know of this holiness and the elemental spirit that you can feel. It is no wonder that fire is such an important symbol of spirituality. It is no wonder that storytellers the globe over often begin their tale spinnings with a lighting of the candle. In that flame lies transformation, a universal theme. The everyday is able to intimate the immortal (Estés, 1992, p. 492). By fire we change states and are able to transform our separate lives into a hoopedness. Perhaps story is itself a kind of burnt offering to the ancestral gods.

Thus, in the Israel of Dafna's remembered childhood, whether it was the Sabbath or "the everyday life of the other days," the people daily gathered around their tables. This was the story place of the indoors:

> We probably lived around a table, but it was not so much a kitchen table so much as a dining room table because that's where we used to eat.…Our kitchen was so small.…It was not a giant table.…Most of the activities that took place in your life took place around this table.

The family's dining room table was a place of revolving friendships and the intimacy of shared sustenance:

> The most important activities I remember were a lot of having friends and family around, a lot of it. There were always people coming in and going out, coming in and going out…and they were all sitting around this table in the dining room.…People never just came.…They always ate, no matter when it was, they always ate.

Years later, when Dafna and her husband started their own family, the acquisition of their dining room table became part of the young family's ceremony and story:

> We were quite poor, but I really wanted a nice dining room table, so we went and we bought the table of really good wood, made in Yugoslavia. And you know the funny thing is, first we bought four chairs, and then when we bought the four chairs, I looked at them and said, "Hmmph, this is not enough." So we went back to the store and bought two more. I'll never forget it. I had to bother my sister-in-law because we didn't have a car to go again and bring two more chairs....So this is something that stays with you...yes...and that's all we had. We didn't have anything in the living room, but we had a wonderful table with six chairs.

Dafna's table meant tradition. It ritualized the daily. This Yugoslavian table symbolically brought the mutuality of food, fire and story into the home:

> I still have it, and everytime I want to change because it's not wide enough....Then I look at it, no, it has too many memories, you know. I cannot give it up. I can't and I won't.

Like a Korean mountain guard, Dafna protected her family and in doing so protected its symbols. Her heroes were those who also gave protection, for example, her pioneer mother-in-law's decision not to enter an agricultural kibbutz:

> She didn't mind the hardships, didn't mind the work, she loved the work on the land...but this communal life, she could not. She said, "When they asked me to give up my mother's tablecloth, I couldn't, I couldn't."

The celebration of the hearth, by bonfire and candle and dining room table, was not only a celebration of a family, but of a people. A Jewish past shared the transformative table with an Israeli future. And the medium of this transformation was that of passionate story, be it a ritualized tale of Solomon and the cooking fires or the more localized magic of one's own pioneer ancestors and their tablecloths. Perhaps it was in the flames that for Dafna place was most vividly transformed into story.

Good relationships and good conversations take time, both privately and publicly constructed time. More traditional hearths, fireplaces and campfires provided that time. During the slow cooking of the meal, the day had time a plenty to story itself. That was apparent in the Arusha Masai hearth fire, the Korean specially shaped coal fire, and the Israeli bonfire. Technology and its people, however, have now secreted fire into 100 watt bulbs and electric stove top elements. As a result, both the food and the story are often hurried up and the relationship of the circle nonexistent. And yet, inspite of that technological propensity to separation, humankind goes to sometimes incredible lengths to find a campfire. In western society, it is the quintessential element of the successful holiday, the hunkering down over the marshmallow fire. Only the very best homes sport the open flame, the triple A chimneyed fireplace.

Our stories need a fire and the inward looking, listening circle, which it always provides. Through the flames, we are able to discern the shadows of one another, what we each are and are not. As a young teaching couple, I remember our family's move to the northern community of Garden Creek. It was my task as teaching principal to maintain the power plant, two Deutsch diesels on an electronic panel. The power supplied the four trailers that we called our school and the two mobiles that we teachers called home and the trailer nursing station. Thus, our professional and private lives were in the care of a diesel generator and a propane tank, both more remarkable for their whims of misbehavior than their dependability. The rest of the community, however, the other 30 homes and their occupants lived their lives around the rhythm of a wood stove and coal oil or high-test lighting. Nothing could more accurately describe the wide gulf that separated these two worlds: the story and unhurried culture of the wood flame of the one and the diesel rhythm, the propane efficiency of the other. Imagine the feeling of separation and difference as you sit by your evening table and fluorescent light, silently heated, while in the midst of 30 wood stoves and their crackling laughter.

How many times at 40 or 50 below did we proponents of the new and technological way seek temporary shelter and comfort in the homes and mint tea cups of the community? Imagine our sense of belonging when we delightedly installed a franklin stove in our teacherage. We still talk of the many wonderful visits around that Garden Creek stove, of the slow cooking of gifts of moose, of the frequent warming of river chilled body parts. I think now that when we installed that "inefficient" wood stove we crossed the line from fly-in visitors to community members. We became full participants in the story circle of the flame. The going for wood, the splitting, the hauling, the making of fire were all part of the ceremony that we called the north. Our wood stove hearth eased us symbolically into a context of northern life, a lifestyle of fall and spring hunts, ski-doo carnivals, handgames, and old sled dogs howling to the void.

This context of the hearth can be found again and again in the striking tales of Rattler. Perhaps the most memorable day in every teacher's life is that first nescient day of class. Such was the case with our grandfather, and it was made all the more remarkable by his side-splitting sense of story. It was the first of February, 1946:

> But I certainly remember my first week....Did I not tell you this before....How absent-minded I am....Farmers were coming in, picking up the mail, I get in the line-up, I finally got to the wicket, and the master said, "Yes, what is your name?"...That's when my mind went blank....I stuttered and I stammered...embarrassing part was having to go to the back of the line.

With great joy, savoring each detail, Rattler told me of his first day, of the terrible blizzard the week before, and of his tractor ride to school down a narrow lane between six-foot snowdrifts:

> School was only about 3/4 of a mile from the place where I was staying, but they said, "Don't bother." This little boy who was in Grade 1...he said in weather like this his cousins came along...."They've got a heated cart, a box heater in it, coal heater, and they'll be coming by. You ride to school." It was kind of a crowded cart because it had been picking up kids all the way. (laughter)...So by the time I got to school, I knew an awful lot of my kids quite well. (laughter)

This fellowship of the box heater continued when they reached school but with a twist:

> There was an older girl. She was about 13 or 14, but you know very efficient. She had complete control; she was the teacher. Someone came in and started the fire...and she grabbed hold of their lunches because most of them were frozen and remember setting them around [the stove]....She had everything all organized.

Not only did the fire provide warmth, survival, but it also provided a young green-as-the-grass teacher with subtle clues to classroom management. Each had his/her part to play:

> And the kids sure listened to her, so I knew all I had to do was get her on my side. (laughter)

Thus, Rattler's earliest and perhaps most poignant recall of his teaching life was situated around a coal box heater and the wood stove of his one-room school. This sense of the circle and hearth repeated itself years later when he described in story his "ideal principal":

> Some of my fondest memories of teaching goes back to there because our principal was like an old grandfather. He was silver haired. He's still living....After he got his class going and he'd say, "Go have a cup of coffee, Rattler, I'll look after class."...You know, they got to know their principal well. We always ate together. Around noon he'd send a couple of his Grade 8 girls out to put the soup on. We had soup every day at noon and tea, you see, we had tea.

As technologically sophisticated and busy as education had become, it was this hearth time that Rattler most vividly recalled, the fellowship of soup and tea together. The attitude of the principal was calm and caring, above all relaxed:

> It used to be different, you know, we had much more relaxing times, and education was no worse, you know....My early years of teaching, we were teachers just as much and in many respects more, I think, than what's been [taught] in this super-heated steam pressure that they are under now.

At both the staff room table and the one-room school wood stove, Rattler became at one with the others and took his place in the circle. Professionalism had everything to do with the shared intimacy of food and story and laughter and others. As André Gide said,

> When I am alone I feel that my life is slowing down, stopping, and that I am on the very verge of ceasing to exist. My heart beats only out of sympathy; I live only through others—by procuration, so to speak, and by espousals; and I never feel myself living so intensely as when I escape from myself to become no matter who. (Ashton-Warner, 1986, p. 212)

Rattler, as one who lived with such joy in the "no matter who" of the storyteller and historian and in the espousals of others, shared this incredible image of another people, pre-Albertan, who also shared in this fellowship of the ring:

> They avoided the bottom along the river....They'd camp up above, catch the breezes, this is where you would find the camps....This sacred spot was a death lodge site, you can still see....I counted....It was a very dry year....I counted 70 lodge circles all closed, in other words, they were death lodges, camps....They didn't have the opening for the entrances, stones were completely closed....It was all death lodges.

The closed lodge ring, the circle of stones without entrance, signified death. The metaphor of the open circle, one that admitted and allowed entrance, meant life. Rattler's stories, spinning inward and full of introspectivity, were like that. They lived and so allowed you in. Reciprocally they became completed by the warm attendance of listeners, be they students, colleagues, or grandchildren: friends all. I mean that this theme of hearth was an open circle theme, and it repeated itself throughout the stories and espousals of Rattler's life: for example, when he spoke about his Spirit River homestead days:

> I remember 10 inches of snow on the tenth of August in 1950....I'll never forget that. We were sleeping out under it. (laughter)...You know there we were, trying to get a fire started...and of course the wood was wet, and we were having an awful time....Finally, we heard this truck roaring....One of the people that knew we were back there worked his way in...rescued us and got us in the truck, got us to his wife, and she had the fire going, the coffee pot going and the porridge going. (laughter)

There was always room at the hearth of a good neighbor. There was always room in the open circle for another plate. For Rattler, the earth of wind and lodge circles and box heater flames remained his primary reality and storytelling his chosen expression of that reality. Box heater and staff room table and homestead neighbor kitchen simply provided the place where earth and story most comfortably met, the place where reality and its representation most naturally lived. The telling of the hearth came not from photocopier or fax machine. It came instead from the ritual of the flames and the porridge and the tea. It came from the bones. As Campbell (1972) writes, this ritual of the folkloral survives "not only in the decorum of courts and regulations of military life, but also in the manners of people sitting down to table together" (p. 43). The individual life is itself a lodge ring born open to the espousals of one's kind. Rattler's stories taught me that. On the living side, and as Rattler would tell of it, the first place of life is itself an open circle, with story the viand of that first table.

Around the northern table, I was given also a wonderful intimation of story place in the Woodland Cree culture. Sabochees, straight-backed and wrap-around moccasined, liked nothing better than to tell about what he had seen in his life. And as he softly spoke and laughed, there was always a child on his blue-jeaned knee. Little ones always sought him out, and Sabochees always let himself be found, as had I:

If it was summertime, they sat around the fire, but if it was wintertime, the storytelling happened in the cabin. It doesn't have to be with bright lights, maybe two candles. That would be good. That's what I remember.

At these times, even the candle was of the traditional kind:

> We used that kind, "the bitch." It's not hard to make one like that. It's a good light, lard and a piece of cloth twisted like that. Melt the lard and put that cloth there and light it up.

Even "the bitch" or candle around which the ceremony of story unfolded provided a tale. Sabochees also spoke of the mud fireplaces that predated the modern airtight wood stoves:

> I think I know what they looked like. I've heard. My Dad told me about it, what they looked like....Not just my Dad but some old people. They told me what it looked like [willow ladders and mud]. I think the willows had to be green...right in the corner, not in the middle—yeah, it was all the way up, like a chimney, so you can look at the fire inside. There doesn't have to be any light or candle, nothing, no....The light is all over, and you can cook something there, bannock, everything.

Through his father, Sabochees was able to witness not only the traditional willow fireplaces, but also the countless stories that hovered about their flames. As in the Arusha Masai hearth, the Cree candle and fireplace gave not only warmth and nourishment, but also time, a cooking time, a telling time. I personally have had the pleasure and honor of many a tea fire in the northern bush and languished greatly in the privately constructed narrative time of spruce flame and muskeg tea. My own children, when still small enough for their father's wishes, prized above all else these journeys out for fire and tea. They probably knew that their stories would always be heard by those fires. I have watched, too, our elder Sabochees by the hunting fire. His building and tending and cooking in the flames are always done with grace and efficiency. Different needs require a different kind of fire. His movement about the fire is never unsure, and there is always something about the meal, the tea, and the stories that gives back to the flames. When Sabochees is at the campfire, he is not away from somewhere else. He and his stories are at home. It is no coincidence then that for Sabochees and his people fire and ceremony are inseparable. One naturally gives thanks to the flames. They make the ancestors possible. And like Je-Nee, Sabochees described the night as the special and traditional time of story:

Anytime at night, in the winter, same thing in the summer-time...that's the best time for stories and not in the daytime. You never, especially those old legend stories, you never tell them during the day, only at night.

As Sabochees told it, the ritual of storytelling was part of the rhythm of a travelling people. The local or clan tales would be shared on occasion at the larger hearths, at the gathering places:

> Anytime in the wintertime, it doesn't have to be New Year's [Kissing Day], anytime they visit around and listen to stories....Some people used to visit the old people and listen to stories. In the summertime it was different. They came from...all over. All those people went to Little Red. People talked of all kinds of things....That was a time for lots of stories. People came from all over because people lived all over, all around here.

In the long summer nights on the banks of the Little Red, the people played handgames, exchanged the news of their survival, laughed and shared the gifts of story. Always there was fire: at times for cooking, at times for warmth, at times for ceremony, and at all times for story. And upon this theme, Sabochees's nephew, the younger Nitotem, remembered also the first story places in his life. It, too, was a time when the sun went down:

> It was in the evening....I've seen the tail end of the community when they used to send their kids in when the sun went down. That was the time I remember Grandmother lived in her house and we stayed overnight and then she was telling stories....It was in the evening.

Like Tolowa and Je-Nee, Grandmother was of vital importance to the youngster Nitotem:

> A lot of the stories that I know my Grandmother started, and then, somewhere in the middle, I fell asleep and never got to the end of the stories....You always wake up wondering what happened.

Just as Je-Nee dreamt of fairies and princesses and mountain guards, so Nitotem regularly slipped into a grandmother induced dream and fantasy. At other times, the stories were father spun:

> My father, when he was trapping, like when he came back...like there was always stories he can say to us, either experiences on his trapline or stories that he heard as a child...and it's usually in the wintertime,

long, longer nights....More stories used to go on back then, you know, longer nights and kids are in by 4 o'clock.

The early story places for Sabochees's nephew were again the ordinary places: Grandmother's house, the family kitchen. For Sabochees, this meant also the homes and hearths of the friends and extended family at Harper Creek. As Ong (1982) writes, "Oral cultures must conceptualize and verbalize all their knowledge with more or less close reference to the human lifeworld" (p. 42). The grandparents who so capably stored and then storied knowledge deserved everyone's respect. Just as sound leaves existence when once uttered, so the early story places were filled with word images that were continually slipping into and out of existence. The long winter nights provided the conversational space that a good story required, both to appear then disappear. They warmed the listener, like a sugared mint tea. The espousals were both in and about the "human lifeworld." Life was not characterized by lists or data banks or pin code numbers. Life told of itself where it happened, in the story places, in the hearths and in the dream reality of childhood. Like Je-Nee, Pesimwastches spoke of it this way:

> I take my drum...my little grandson wants to sleep in the evening. I start singing my songs, and I put him to sleep with my songs. It is the same thing with storytelling. Kids gather round you, and you start telling them a story, you know, and they feel good...a nice quiet voice telling them a story, that's the best thing a kid could hear before you go to bed...cuz it puts them to sleep....Then when the kids sleep they have dreams....Some of the kids take visions out of that.

As the stories circled the hearth, the spirits of the children were deeply touched by the storied lifeworld:

> Your spiritual world expanded because it was looking, seeking...the place where you are or the thing you are because you're as your spirit.

Dafna and her Israeli bonfire, Je-Nee and the Korean coal fire, Rattler's Alberta box heater, Tolowa's hearthstones, Sabochees and Pesimwastches with their woodland tea fires, all speak to the place of story. They tell me that story is not independent of the elemental realities of wind, water, and fire, and that story that only lives in a secondary reality is, indeed, a more distant story. It becomes story that enweaves a child to family and "human lifeworld," but it is candle and campfire and kitchen table that provides the requisite space. Those places, Pesimwastches would argue, are indeed particular and far from nonchalant. They are where the elements meet; they bring the wind and fire and water together in an honorable way. It is these hearths that provide the co-ordinates of immediate personal experience. It is the candles and the box heaters and the tea fires that enable the subjective individual to later negotiate when away from the flames. The fact that our ordinary stories are situated around the ordinary hearthstones of our lives in no way denies them their power. If anything, they burn brighter and thaw out in the flames. Norman (1982) gathered and translated a Swampy Cree poem that for me beautifully expressed this relationship between the hearth and the words that thaw out in their presence:

The goose is frozen in the lake.
I'm going to thaw it out.
The goose was hurt in the wings.
The ice came fast.
The others left without it.
The ice came fast.
I'll build a small fire
by the goose.
Frightened look in its eyes.
See, its neck is stretching
the way the others went.
It's got the south in its neck,
stretching that way.
But the wings kept it here.
The broken wings.
I'm going to thaw it out. (p. 102)

And although we look south to those who have left before us, our wings keep us here. Our wish is in the thaw, in the light and flames in the ordinary story places, and not in the Greek ideal of end that marries back to beginning. Our neck stretches, not only to the south, but to the slow burn of the storyteller's words. Even then, the ice comes fast without the light, or as Sparrow tells it:

I turn off my light and I'm wondering if something is going to jump out of my closet, soon, or if something is going to crawl out from underneath my bed.

Closets are to be visited, Sparrow would say, not lived in. We need the light for that.

Deer Hide Painting:
Knots: Combing Out The Sound

SILENCE: THE INTERSTICE

> The silence is all there is. It is the alpha and the omega. It is God's brooding over the face of the waters; it is the blended note of the ten thousand things, the whine of wings. You take a step in the right direction to pray to the silence, and even to address the prayer to "World". Distinctions blur. Quit your tents. Pray without ceasing. (Dillard, 1982b, p. 27)

To speak of silence is no less of an important contrariety than to write of oracy. The interstice of silence in storytelling both separates and joins that vibrated air we call human voice. As narrative researcher, I first captured the authority of this voice by means of a tape recorder, and as Schafer (1969, p. 8) suggests, I then journeyed within ventriloquized sound. Thus, I moved from the actual sound of the kitchen table to the ventriloquized sound of the recorded voice and then into the silence and separation we denominate as writing. My writing seemed to become a muted sanctuary, possessed in part by the eternal silence of beyond the ozone. At times I found the writer's alphabetical silence frightening, and I would flee into an electrical background wash of Pachelbel's Canon or the clothes dryer. Schafer (1969) mentions that "in Babylonian mythology there are hints of a specially constructed room in one of the ziggurats where whispers stayed forever" (p. 8). I felt this to be a wonderfully apt description of my educational research, a room where the whispers were kept. Thus, we seem to break silence that we might understand it together. We fill our world with vibrations of dissonance and consonance and then seek out river hills to escape them.

My storytellers taught me that when they talked and paused at their holy places the story, like the earth, came from silence and once told went into silence. They also taught me that each of us, all storytellers ourselves, came from the heartbeat of silence into the glare and life of sound and out again. There was always in their stories this telling relationship between silence and creation. Illich and Sanders (1988) write about Genesis and the beginning of silence, silence before it became the vocalization of history:

> When He hammered out the first gold foil (a word usually translated as the "firmament"), He separated the roaring waters below from the thundering waters above. With a three inch shard, or a glittering foil, silence began as an interstice, keeping the voices of Heaven and those of the Abyss apart. Silence was the first creature on the earth.

"Earth" grew from it. And that is the silence out of which, later, history took shape, as human voices made it vibrate. (p. 120)

For my storytellers, silence seemed at times to take the form of nonvibratory act or elliptical performance, and at other narrative times, it was much more object than act whereby silence became an opportunity missed. Characteristically then it assumed, like the first creature it was, both a negative and a positive dimension and a multiplicity of shapes. And on that resonant note, there is an African story that speaks beautifully about the white space or interstice we call silence:

> In the time of the first people, there was a man who fully loved his herd of black and white cattle. He gave them the best of his care and each day walked them only to the finest grasses. Each evening the herd was safely returned to its thorn kraal and in the mornings, he would be rewarded with their plentiful gifts of milk. One morning, however, their bags which should have been full were dry. The man changed the pasture again and yet again, but each successive morning their bags were again empty. Ultimately, he decided to stay up and keep an eye on his herd throughout the night. Imagine his surprise, when he observed a cord from the stars drop into the kraal, and the descent of several young women from the people of the sky. They lowered themselves hand over hand into the herd and then merrily began milking the cattle into their calabashes. The man, full of indignation, chased them in every direction but managed only to catch the last lovely young lady. She agreed to stay behind and become his wife if he promised never to look into the tightly woven basket which she carried with her. The sky woman's beauty was great and the man readily agreed. They did well together, these two, she to the fields each day and he to the herd of cattle. But each day the cattleman became more curious about the basket and its contents. Finally, he could no longer wait and while the wife was in the field working, removed the lid from the tightly woven basket and looked inside. He laughed at what he discovered. When the sky woman returned home that night she knew.
>
> "You looked, didn't you?"
>
> "Yes," he admitted, "but why get upset? There was nothing in the basket, nothing!"

"You saw nothing?" she replied. "Nothing?"

Slowly, the sky woman turned from her husband and walked into the mystery of the African sunset. She never returned. Never. (Van der Post, 1961, p. 143)

When I told this story to my own children, they insisted it was about not keeping one's word. But as the old woman who told the story said, Sky Woman went away "not because he had broken his promise but because looking into the basket, he had found it empty. She went because the basket was not empty: it was full of beautiful things of the sky she stored there for them both, and because he could not see them and just laughed, there was no use for her on earth anymore and she vanished"(Van Der Post, 1961, p. 143).

My storytellers have taught me that silence, too, is a tightly woven basket. And to some it is devoid of meaning, empty, worthy only of our cuts of derisive laughter. To others, however, silence is full of the beautiful things of the sky, deserving our celebration and praise.

When I listened to the talk and tales of Mosum and Sabochees, I felt this praise of silence. With the elderly Mosum, for example, the conversation was in great part silent, both in the telling and in the translation:

> (silence)....When a hunter killed a moose that was far from his home and he had to stay overnight, they used to use the moosehide (silence)...but you had to be careful, and you had to put little sticks, strong sticks, to hold up the hide, or...because of the winter cold, (laughter) the hide would freeze, and the hunter may not be able to escape from his blankets in the morning. They used strong sticks. (silence) He said it was very warm, and he had done it on a few occasions. (silence)...They used the bear as well in the same fashion after the kills but not often because the bear had hibernated. (laughter) They used to dry the bear skin and take it with them for a blanket....(silence)

Grandfather went on to describe the hunter arts of winter survival and in the telling generously situated his words into the interstice of silence or, perhaps, more appropriately, the quiet. Perhaps up to even a quarter of the narrative time was devoted to this one kind of silence: oral pause. At times, the story was indeed silent, a silent moire, yet rich with the subtleties of eye and hand and smoke that curled to the people of the sky. Silence for Mosum was an essential part of the story performance. There was no hurry.

Oral dignity forbade it. Indeed, the extended silences themselves extended invitation to the listener. When Mosum gave me silence, not nonsound, he gave me a space for reflection. For example, I was completely swept away by the possibility of a hunter, committed to the survival of his people, entombed in the very silent creature that meant life. Silence allowed the metaphor to take hold. It allowed me time to draw a connection from this story of Cree winter survival to the life I called my own. Mosum's oracy was like sugar in the mint tea of silence. He stirred it up, gracefully. And when I responded to the story with a similar silence, it seemed both appropriate and respectful. With other storytellers, my silence might have been construed as indifference, but with Mosum, a quiet response intimated thoughtful participation. I had the right to remain silent.

As always, the challenge for the research writer was to hear and appreciate the oral pause then somehow transfer that grandfather silence onto the page. To some extent, the alphabet allowed for just such an undertaking for there was space not only between the letters but also between the phrases and the transcribed sentences. Transcription and literacy built upon interstice just as Mosum connected the silences together into an oral story act. Our friend Je-Nee brought these polarities of literate silence and oral silence together in her story of Korean calligraphy:

> We have the same kind of skill to draw picture, and then we usually draw the picture in white on white paper...and then pictures black because we use the black color, watercolor...so the paper is white and the picture is black. There are lots and lots of white space, you know...and then we tell that space is room which we have inside....That's more philosophical. We use black watercolor and draw a picture with that....There are lots and lots of space, white space, so people say that that's room which we have inside....I think silence in a sense connected that way...silence.

It is fascinating as well that in Japanese literature silence is designated by a marker '.....' (Saville-Troike, 1985, p. 4). Thus, in Je-Nee's calligraphic white space, I was able to better understand Mosum's oral silences: they were a white space that allowed the listener to go to the inside. At times, the silences were only the subtle pauses in the stream of syllables, at times the narrative gaps between thoughts, but most noticeably, they were the longer white spaces that invited the listener in. I have witnessed those northern times when silence was the best possible answer to a question. In those instances, silence enabled the least amount of confusion to take place. It uncluttered the answer. Understanding can also live in the unvocalized places. When, for example, I asked Sabochees of the places too sacred for our presence, even our stories, he first replied with silence and only then said:

> (silence)....My Dad used to tell us not to go in there because there's nothing for us there...not for people. (silence)...They don't have to go there.

Sabochees enabled me to understand that there are times when silence is a sacred place and should not be violated with the vibration of sound. I am reminded of the community funeral of a cherished grandmother and of the son who stood by her side throughout the ceremony. As Grandmother slipped into the final northern mystery of the other side, friends and family filed by, giving their respects and shaking the son's hand. In the silence of that touch was a telling more vital than mere words. Similarly, the Japanese word "haragei" refers to a "wordless communication," a kind of silence beyond or outside of words (Matsumoto, 1988).

I am reminded of the landscape silencing of northern snowfall and our dog team days. Bear Woman and I ran dogs for 7 years. We midwifed, mushed, harnessed and loved those wolfy critters: Tse Ne, Tse Quain, Skimo, Genghis, Festus, Woodstock, N'Chilla, RIP, may they run in peace. Those seven pulled our old birch toboggan and canvas carry-all and little ones. They pulled us through the silent bush on snowy evenings and across the frosted landscapes of our ordinary lives. They pulled. There were the special trips as well, the "frozen left foot trip," the "followed by wolves trip," the "Lena fell on the fence line trip." A dog team ride was never just a dog team ride. It was a silent visit with the ancestors. And even today, I still feel the connection between these 100 pound pulling canines and my life. I cannot imagine being ever stuck for a metaphor. That team of seven taught me about the silent language of the cultural north. They joined Bear Woman and me to the bush and to the people of the bush. They taught us the joy of running together in a connected way. And they taught us that each quiet trail leads away then back to home.

Thus, Sabochees and Mosum confirmed by the act of their telling, the nature of silence, that the tightly woven basket was indeed at times hallowed. Maltz (1985), in his consideration of noise in Pentecostal worship, refers to this common "equation of religion with silent reverence" (p. 113). His study reveals that reverent silence contains a cultural bent. In the storytelling world of Mosum, Sabochees and Pesimwastches, the silence was a cultural event that reflected a particular view of the universe. The times of reverent silence, as Tannen (1985, p. 94) suggests, were positive and held the promise of something within. Even the length of the pause was culturally important, for if it became too long, the silence was in danger of becoming negative. Mosum and I would slip into an easy laughter in those times when both the words and the silence had been long enough. Tobacco also was important to the gathering and the telling and the pauses. Mosum taught me that silence and quiet, particularly reverent silence, was a mutual and joint production (Tannen, 1985, p. 100). It took both of us to create these sacred white spaces. It took both of us to see something in the tightly woven basket. Silence, too, was a corroborant act, an act of propinquity. We came near one another in the quiet for it existed only because of our sense of mutuality. My grandfather's silences did not need to be filled. His stories, both colloquial and ritual, were perhaps not given in response to the question "why?" Silences did not need to be filled with answers because they could communicate without words.

Dafna, too, brought a celebrative and cultural perspective to that reverent silence found in religion and prayer. She, too, intimated that such silence was positive space and held the promise of something on the inside. Within the ceremony of the Sabbath, for example, there was a silence of holiness:

> On Friday night many people light the candles welcoming the Sabbath, even if they are not religious, because there is so much symbolism in that you cannot give it up....Even though I am not religious many times I do it, especially when I am not in Israel because this brings back the Holiness that you can feel...in Israel Friday night. Even if you are strangers you feel that it is different because all the shops are closed, no buses run and most people are around their tables having dinner together, and you can feel it. Almost every house lights those candles, the Sabbath candles.

In the quiet of the candles and in the quiet of the Israeli Friday night, our Dafna found holiness. In the sound and silence of prayer, a connection was made to God, from the temporal to the eternal, from the mundane to the sacred:

> There is a prayer for everything in life, every single event in life a prescribed prayer...and you know when you go to a strange country...you walk and you say "shma Israel"..."Our God, this is our God and our God is one"...and this is the prayer the Jew will say just before he is persecuted, you know, this is his cry to God.

As Dafna pointed out, the prayers came before the written word and by their formulaic expression and oral repetition helped frame a holy silence. I found the reverent silence as well in Dafna's great love of literature and particularly when as a little girl she curled up into the separate world of the avid reader:

> And I read a lot as a child....I was a bookworm. I was one of those behind the book....I read a lot of Russian literature, a lot of French literature, American and English literature....This was my bed time....In many things I cannot be as articulate as other people, but I feel I have this with me.

In part, the consecrated nature of silent reading came directly from the cultural perception of writing as a holy undertaking. In her silence then, Dafna felt a great awe of those who could fill the pages with passion and make them live for her. This outside silence of the page was in clear contrast to the animated inside noise and the interiority of the enthralled reader:

> What was in The Count of Monte Cristo that made me go again and again....I knew it by heart, word by word....It has everything in human relations, love, hate, envy, revenge, terrible revenge...and adventure...everything in this one book. I read five times War and Peace, Anna Karenina, Victor Hugo, Emile Zola. I like Hemingway and Steinbeck...Chekhov....They combined poetry, art and literature because the way they wrote it you could see it...the battlefield....You could see the dead bodies lying there and the horses lying there.

I felt a great similarity between the formulaic silences of the Cree storytellers and the privately constructed silence that our Dafna found in these childhood readings. Yet in wonderful contrast to the earnest nature of the silent candle, the Mediterranean beach, the good read was the disquiet of Israeli conversation. Dafna often spoke, herself with fast pace, of her people's passion for animated conversation:

> With us, you cannot finish one sentence because 10 people will jump into it.

In this sense, silence represented an opportunity missed, a space of nonsound. An impassioned life was one that filled the silences with story and song and laughter. Indeed, silence could at times even suggest subordination. In describing the Passover, for example, Dafna said,

> We have a special book that is read on this night, and it says, "And the father should tell his son all that has happened in Egypt" so the story will go on from generation to generation....But it says that the father should tell his son...not the mother, not the daughter. (laughter)

Thus for Dafna, as for women of so many cultures, silence was often an expression of inferior status. Those with the authority were the ones who so frequently filled the silence with prayer and reflection. I am reminded of the Apostle Paul and his contextualized words "Let a woman learn silence with all submissiveness. I will permit no woman to teach or to have authority over man; she is to keep silent" (I Timothy 2: 11, 12) (Saville-Troike, 1985, p. 4). I, too, have often witnessed the sound and silence that occurs when people of different cultures first meet. Very often, the silence is what Tannen (1985) describes as a negative space, either when silence "represents the existence of something negative—the silence of seething anger...or if it is assumed to represent the omission of something positive—the omission of a greeting" (p. 95). The silence that in one culture may intimate agreement in a different culture may symbolize quite the reverse.

Sparrow similarly reminded me of those frequent times when the culture of childhood clashed with the culture of adulthood. Very often, this drama was played out in the dynamic of sound and silence: for example, when Sparrow described the upcoming comedy night at school, she expressed both pride and concern over her leading role:

> I never am going to memorize it, I know....I'm good when I say my lines....It sounds good...so I go "he's so handsome!" to Desperate Billy (laughter) and then I go "he's so ugly!"

This leading role meant a personal sound production and was in vivid contrast to that of her little sister:

> She's a chicken. She wanted to be a chicken. All they do is run off the stage and go "buk, buk, buk!" (laughter) She wanted to be a chicken when there are better things to be....She wanted to be a chicken.

Throughout her many, many stories, Sparrow described characters from the bat hero in *Fern Gully* to Bryan Adams to Whitney Houston to the child heroines in the Fear Street novels as those who filled up the silence with their lives, just as the Sparrow storyteller filled up the silence with the retelling of those adventures. Indeed, childhood seemed to be all about this act of replenishing the silence:

> I kept on talking and talking and talking, and [teacher] finally said, "Go on out of the classroom"...yeah, out in the hall for the rest of the period....Mom wasn't really mad at me though because I only talked; at least I wasn't bad, I just talked too much.

Saville-Troike (1985) examined this process by which "children learn when not to talk, and what silence means in their speech community" (p. 11). She discovered that those children growing up in a culture that applauded individualism, as opposed to group achievement, appeared to talk more. I have personally witnessed many children engaged in the learning of a second language. Even though these children have acquired new verbal structures, they very often retain their first language silence patterns (Saville-Troike, 1985, p. 13). Our Sparrow was learning when to be seen and when to be heard and the fine line that separated verbal silence from nonverbal silence. Interestingly enough, there was a parallel here to our Grandfather Mosum, who categorized his own stories on the basis of what he had seen and what he had heard. In fact, our "littlest storyteller" received the name Sparrow for the high energy with which she filled the silence. Sparrow's fascination with the theatre and public speaking, with music and improvisation was perhaps because of this freedom to fill the white space of silence with the calligraphic notations of her conversation.

Although Sparrow put such care and energy into the resonance of positive sound, she, too, was fascinated by the mystery of eternal and absolute silence. An example of this was Sparrow's prolonged interest in the Bermuda Triangle. She loved to talk then pause on it:

> They either disappear and they don't leave anything, like they don't leave no bodies washed ashore. (silence)...They don't leave blankets swept ashore or anything. (silence) There's not even an oil slick. (silence)...They just disappear in the air. (silence)

This was the imperishable silence of "Pascal's universe," not just the privately constructed quiet of a walk along a river shore, and not just quiet like a Christmas tree in early morning gift, but endless and mysterious silence.

It was the silence of what happened to Terry Fox, of what happened to a world when the last tree was chopped down, of what lived and waited under a little girl's bed. This was the mystery of silence, a silence of destiny, or as Dillard (1982b) writes, the silence that is "God's brooding over the face of the waters" (p. 27).

I, too, have felt intimations of Sparrow's eternal silence, heard the ziggurat whispers from Babylonian mythology. I am reminded of a Northern Alberta evening, several years ago now, frosted and full 40 below. The evening was young, albeit dark, as I stiffly walked the last few steps from my ski-doo to the house. Wanting to tease, I slow-toed my way up to the picture window and peeked in. There they were, my family and universe, just leaving the supper table, animated, full of gesture and purpose. We were separated by only a transparency, the inside from the outside. And it was I who was on the silent side, just out of reach of their customary lives, like a dancer in the Northern Lights. I tapped the window then, perhaps harder than necessary. Yes, I, too, have felt the intimations of Sparrow's imperishable silence, that silence before and after language. And when I asked Bear Woman if she had ever heard this silence, she replied,

> I heard it for the first time the day my father stopped breathing. It came after his last breath. I have heard it many times since. (Betty Sewall, in conversation).

Thus, my storytellers have expressed the shape of silence in a miscellany of ways, from the reverent and ritual silence of Mosum and Je-Nee and Dafna to Sparrow and the painful silence of subordination. Yet for all the storytellers, the meaning of silence was deeply contextualized and not found as a phenomenon apart. For example, for Grandfather Rattler, silence most often took the form of a brief hesitation in the telling. It was part of his elliptical storytelling performance. Grandfather's storytelling goal was certainly not grammatical precision but rather listener comprehension. Thus, he wanted you to get the picture. As Chafe (1985) suggests, "Pauses, false starts, afterthoughts, and repetitions" did not hinder that goal but were steps on the way to his achieving it (p. 78). Theorists of spontaneous speech have referred to this act of consciousness by which bits or "spurts" or "chunks of information" come to the retelling surface. Hence, it was the brief hesitations and silences that most demonstrated Rattler's technique as he conversationally moved from focus to focus. A good example was our Grandfather's retelling of his first teaching experience:

Four months...it went from, actually you see, from mid-September to mid-January...mid-Christmas and then a month, January, and you were teaching the first of February, oh yes, I had a choice of best....You know there were such few teachers, so few....My first school was just a little school...which was about 10 miles from where I was born....It was closer to...and I remember to get there....There had been a terrible blizzard....In order to get there I had to go in a Ford tractor, a rubber tired tractor....They're still talking about that.

Connotative hesitation, brief silences were a narrative way of knowing as our Grandfather moved from focus to storytelling focus. Chafe (1985) and others suggest that "speaking is not a matter of regurgitating material already stored in the mind in linguistic form, but that it is a creative act, relating two media, thought and language, which are not isomorphic but require adjustments and readjustments to each other" (p. 78). Brief silences allowed Rattler to negotiate his way, to shape his speech in a highly creative fashion. Thus, the hesitations came most often when the focus changed and not while Grandfather remained in the focus cluster. For example, when I asked Grandfather about indigenous dyes:

The iron oxide, which is basically what they used for their basic browns and reds, you know, and there was what they called the Paint Pots Coulee, they used to get a lot of it. David Fiddler, in his diary, mentions stopping off there, and I did actually find a couple of paint pots that were still, you know....They used a lot of vegetable dyes, too, of course roots and plants, the scarlet....It just seemed to grow where nothing else would grow...and berries, the silver berry, we used to call the wolf willow, and it's almost black, from the berry itself....They-uh mentioned the red willow, the bark of it was used, too, for three colors actually.

The apparent sequence of storyteller narrative was in fact a kind of creative necklace, beads of fours and gaps of silence. Hesitation was most often triggered by a change in character or location, time or event. And in some instances, Grandfather's silences came from the struggle to find a word that would embody the particular sense or concept being expressed. Whatever the trigger, Rattler's hesitation was an artful twist on the storytelling act. His brief silences enabled the thing to move.

There was perhaps one further and fascinating dynamic at work in the storytellers' use of silence. That storytelling constituent was the silence of gesture. It was visible in all the stories and in all the telling, although not ventriloquized onto tape or technology. It came within the relationship of storyteller to listener and at all times was an integral part of the telling, be it ever so silent and subtle. At times, the gestures were pronounced and deliberate while on other occasions a mere reflex of the unconscious. Although not syntactically driven, the gestures lived with the speech and were an inseparable part of the oral performance. When Sabochees talked about the moose hunt, his upturned hands came together in the cultural symbol of a kill accomplished. Pesimwastches told of his birth and naming, and while he did so, he pointed with his lips to where the place could still be found. Mosum's eyelids would move up dramatically, slowly from the floor as he slipped from conceptual cluster to cluster, and then suddenly, they would rivet on the listener, but only for a moment, a polite moment. During our delightful improvisations, how the animals got their shapes and colors, Sparrow's fingers would hold an imaginary paint brush and her eyes would grow wide with trickster wonder. Rattler sat coiled at the kitchen table, like his namesake, then suddenly he would full body relax into the laughter of the telling moment. His supple hands did their telling, shaping the storytelling air between us.

Dafna talked and taught with her body. When our dear Israeli friend talked about the movies *Of Mice and Men* and *The River Runs Through It*, her hands and eyes pointed to the people of the sky and a deep sigh slipped into the appreciative silence. And on another occasion, a fellow Israeli had recently returned from a trip and adventure to South America. This young man visited Dafna's school and eloquently told about his journey and did so in a narrative and somatic way that held everyone captive:

> When I looked many times in the crowd, it was just amazing, everyone just opened their mouths and were sucking in everything he said....He has to have the gift of...he has to be living in the telling, that is the important thing...and you have to be something of an actor....You have to have a special voice, no doubt about it...but the whole body told the story. It was not just [his] mouth. The whole body talked. Really, everything, the eyes and the hand, the hands and the feet, everything. So this you do not get from a book. It's just a flat piece of paper, no matter how wonderful the story is, it's just flat....The doors were open, and it was...quite cold, and it was at night. Everyone was freezing, but no one even thought of leaving or going to look for something to put on.

Words sometimes fall short in the storyteller's performance. Thus, gesture provides a way not only to illustrate what is being said, "but to add to what is being said, to convey aspects of meaning that cannot readily be conveyed in words" (Kendon, 1985, p. 232). Gesture was indeed an integral and vital part of the woven basket called silence, a way by which the story could go beyond itself and the storytellers beyond their stories. It is probably true that when the story was in the gesture, then it was indeed in the bones. If story is engagement, and I believe it is, then it is the full-body engagement, what Ong (1982) means when he says that "spoken words are always modifications of a total, existential situation" (p. 67). He also suggests that "oral memory has a high somatic component" (p. 67). The history of storytelling is rich and replete with example, from the Australian Aboriginal creation of string figures with songs to the use of storytelling beads on strings to the bardic use of stringed instruments to the bodily rocking back and forth during a scriptural oration. Even the body at rest, the nongesture, is wonderfully powerful. Pesimwastches, for example, would grow increasingly composed, as during *The Spirit Moans*, quieted by the somber events, quieted by the mystery of which he spoke. His quietude was all the more remarkable for its being so foreign to his usually jocular telling: the power of the nongesture. This somatic component then was evident not only in the person of the teller, but in the listener(s) as well. As previously mentioned, storyteller silence was always a joint production, an act of collaboration, and so, too, was the gestural. I find myself as aspiring storyteller taking my performance cues from the bodily expressions of my listeners. There often seems to be a gossamer thread from the telling to their persons, from the vocalized to the embodied. This thread was evident when Dafna described a particularly loving relationship with one former student and his family:

> He was just...ahhh...a wonderful child really! And we got very close to his parents, too. Very unusual child....I tell you, even if I only did this for him, made him feel better, the way he did...I earned my certificate. (laughter) And there were some others.

Dafna's eyes misted over with the memory, her animated hand delicately touched her heart in the telling. And I, too, felt the somatic warmth as the faces of my own former students appeared before me. Throughout the stories, I witnessed and participated in this sympathetic and somatic dialogue, this heart-felt conspiracy within silence. When Sabochees talked of Harper Creek country, his thin angularities softened, his eyes and hands danced as he told of the most recent hunt. As listener, I could taste the delicious red moose meat that hung dripping on green willows by the fire, salted and cooking lovingly. I could taste the fresh and sugared mint tea, just removed from the tamarack fire. And my cheeks ached from the grinning at the good parts. Indeed, my storytellers gave me much more than a telling. To the willing listener, they offered a full somatic engagement, a meaningful and natural silence, the aesthetic weave of sight and gesture to speech and sound. Hence, it was silence and not just the talk that structured our interaction. That silence itself varied in shape from the artful hesitancy of a Rattler to the reverent pause in a Wesakychakian tale. That elusive trickster silence was itself the stuff of metaphor as it bridged the knowns to the unknowns, the nonsilences and resemblances together. And nowhere is this metaphor more alive than within a good story:

> Have you ever been beside a lake in Africa at night and listened to the frogs? You haven't? Then you cannot imagine what the noise is like. And it's not just one kind of noise, it's several. Over there, for instance, are a thousand creaking doors that have never had their hinges oiled and someone opens and shuts them—and keeps on doing just that. Over there are a thousand fat men snoring and no one wakes them up. Then there are a thousand carpenters sawing planks and all the saws want a touch of grease, and a thousand little bells are being struck and a thousand corks are being pulled out of bottles.
>
> Noise! You can hardly hear yourself think.
>
> Then you go a little closer until you can just see the edge of the water and perhaps a reed or two and there is silence. Just the splash of a frog jumping into the water late because he was asleep and didn't hear you coming. Then nothing and you can hear the whole world breathe. There's a story about this.
>
> As the story goes, the frogs once lived a very noisy and disruptive life. Sick and tired of it, one frog with a very good voice called together a meeting of the frogs. It was decided that only a king could bring order to the chaos. One wise old frog was chosen to convey this desire to Mmumi, the Great God. The elder made his petition to a somewhat sleepy Mmumi and then returned. Some time later the Great God awoke, remembered the request and threw a huge rock, a rock the shape of a frog, into the noisy pond.
>
> "His name is Gogo, your king. Respect him," Mmumi commanded.

The rock king Gogo was quite a sight as he sat entwined in the weeds on the bottom of the pond. His appearance and his noisy entrance brought sudden calm and peace to the community of frogs. In time, however, the little ones began to take liberties with the stone king, jumping from his back as they did. And soon the pond returned to its noisy ways, perhaps even more so.

Again a meeting was called and again an elder was sent to Mmumi to petition for a new and more active king. The Great God awoke with displeasure and in an angry voice promised another kind of leader.

The next night, Mmumi gave Mamba the Crocodile to the pond. The new king did not arrive with a big splash, but silently, silently Mambo the Crocodile "swam, silent as a shadow, lithe and long and secret, his jaws grinning like a trap." And whenever the new king happened upon a frog subject, the jaws opened silently and brought a quick end to that frog. And so it was that the frogs learned to respect their new king and live quietly, their eyes very often turned to their backs. Although they still on occasion sing, they now practice also the fine art of silence. (Harman, 1962, p. 49)

In the storyteller's world of orality, there lives both the disinterested silence of the stone Gogo and the deadly silence of the crocodile Mamba. In our consideration of oracy, we are very often given over to such bipolarization, in this case to the apparent dualities of sound and silence. But even as we separate the phenomenon in an attempt to understand, it is equally important that we conceptually join things back together. We seem to refer mainly to the sound and silence of our own humanity. And try as we might, even our expression of the undying is less than a divine act. Our humanity, our sound and silence, is found in both our moments of loneliness and of comfort, in our confidence and embitterment, in our noise and dumbness. Perhaps the power of oral silence is finally a mnemonic one for within it lies memory and within memory is our humanity. By acts of silent memory we retell of the children who live in the space behind the curtains. We retell of the grandmothers who lie quiet and wasted after a second stroke. We retell of the little ones who take their first silent step.

It has been argued that the silences within our orality, whether primary or residual, are far different from the silences within our literacy. As Sheridan (1991) suggests, "Silence in education is conceived of primarily as the absence of words, rather than as belonging to realms of stillness and the unsayable. In the realm of the unsayable and in the silence of the human voice, oral culture still hears, smells, touches, and tastes the wind, waves and rain. Thought is not constrained to be lexically referential" (p. 24). Thus, just as the soundscape has so dramatically changed from predominantly natural sounds to one of motorized sounds so, too, have the silences. The quiet of my ancestors was similarly far different from the privately constructed silence I experience and that my storytellers experienced. Ancestral silence emanated from within an earth, an existential situation that no longer exists:

> The alphabetization of silence has brought about the new loneliness of the "I," and of an analytic "we." "We" is now one line in a text brought into being by communication. Not the silence before words but the absence of messages in a chaos of noises precedes the establishment of an interactive pattern. The pretextual "we" of orality, the ethnic "we" that has been transcended through conscience, has disappeared from reality. We know that the history of silence is reflected in the transition from the ethnic to the analytic "we." (Illich & Sanders, 1988, p. 122)

In an oral culture, it is human beings at the centre. Both the sounds and the silences come from the inside. And it is that sense of a silent "we" that gives expression to the community. Once our sounds were committed to script, however, our silences changed, too, and were given a shape in relation to that change. Thus, silence became much less of the "unsayable" and much more of the "absence of words." The silence of the stone king Gogo slipped into the silence of the lithe and long Mamba, the Crocodile. It was an example of the tool reconstituting the toolmaker, the story retelling the storyteller. The reverent silence of a Harper Creek country was to go in search of words and humanity, was to enweb itself in the secondary reality of presentation. It was not the land that called itself silent. Thus, language first recreated silence and then in the chirographic expression created it again. The words gave us a way to peek into the tightly woven basket, changing the basket and the story of it in the process.

Van der Post (cited in Travers, 1989), in his work on the Kalahari, depicts the ostrich practice of putting "one egg in front of her, outside the nest to remind her of what she was doing" (p. 105). In a strangely analogous kind of way, I believe that silence is sometimes to the storyteller what that egg represents to the ostrich. Silence is in front of the storyteller. It reminds the teller what he/she is really about, where the stories come from, where the tellers come from, to where they all return. And as artful as the performance of nonsilence becomes, it remains a wonderfully imperfect act, an act of contrariety even. The prophecy of silence, the ostrich egg, is the reminder, too, that knowing can only go so far. To the egg of story, the ancestral and the futuristic are prophetically and mysteriously one.

Mr. Bonnet, our high school English teacher, was tall, angular, even painfully thin, of British military bearing, with a white slight scar that ran from the bottom of his right eye to the top of his Royal Air Force moustache. His single tweed jacket sported leather elbow patches, and his greying hair was parted precisely. A poet himself, Mr. Bonnet had but one pedagogical failing: he was thoroughly kind.

And we students, in the mandate of our youth, abused that man. Erasers, wads, notes, even loud profanity were thrown at our Mr. Bonnet. For his part in the erudite drama, he would pirouette about from the blackboard, facing us with the terrible expletive "Now class!"

Until June of that year, until June of that year, by then Mr. Bonnet would have known of the Board's decision; until June when one particular prairie day and after a double period of abuse, our Mr. Bonnet twirled about. No gentle reminder this time, only silence, and a single tear that slid and shouted its way from the bottom of his right eye along the scar to the top of his Royal Air Force moustache.

In that silent tear, we came of age. And we found the sound of our humanity in expiation:

I am the silence
and all things mindful
when with somatic tuned, bended and cupped
story to full piped teller
I umbilical tie it together.

In the seashell of my audition
are the dreams of one day tellers
dreams of the one night tellers
and it is I silence
who bring the egg of sun to its rise.

It is I who one hand clap
for the grey
praise the sound of grey
and all that story gesture that lives
between the tight weave of first and last breath.

I am the ear of story.
I blackbird sit on telephone wires
and resonate to coyote howl.
I am where the voice goes, under the rocks.
I am childhood, the conveyor,
and the pause before each wizard word spell.

I am the silence
of interstice.
I am we…

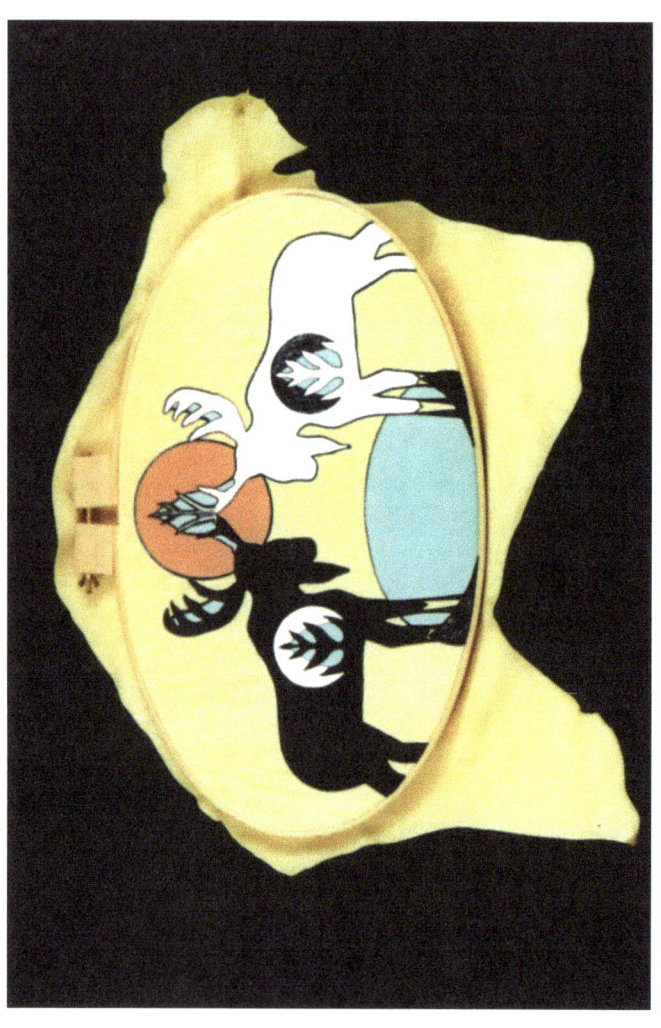

Deer Hide Painting:
Two Moose: One Moon

THE GILTHEAD OF LITERACY: TRANSUBSTANTIATION OF SOUND INTO SPACE

He thought: This is the last newspaper I will ever read. I won't buy another. I have skimmed newspapers all my life and never got the whole good out of one. Well, I will read every word in this one and when done I will know for a fact what was going on in the world on the twenty-second day of January in the year 1901. It is a damned important day to me. For a sizable part of it, I did not know I was about to die, so in a way it was my last one alive. (Swarthout, 1975, p. 13)

A young man, Wu Fang we shall call him, was out flying his kite when it became tangled in the branches of a tall willow tree beside the home of the Chen family. Being agile, as well as handsome, the young man climbed the tree in pursuit of his kite. Wu Fang then glanced over the courtyard wall and espied the most beautiful of all girls in the nearby garden. In profile, the young lady appeared to be physical perfection itself and Wu Fang fell madly and completely in love with her.

"I finally agree to get married," he later said to his parents, "and I know of the girl that I wish to wed." He then described the young lady who sometimes sat in the Chen garden near the old willow tree. A matchmaker was immediately assigned the task of making the inquiries and consulting the fortune tellers.

"The maiden is good and fair and rich, but there is just one thing you should know," the go-between later reported. Wu Fang, however, would not listen to any such talk and insisted that the wedding proceed. The girl's parents were delighted with the match and soon a card from the groom and a pair of fat red geese were delivered to their courtyard gate. The bride's parents politely returned one of painted geese along with their consent for the wedding date. Preparations were carefully made and a great number of wonderful gifts were exchanged by the families. At last the wedding day arrived. On that day Chen Lien set out for the Wu home in her curtained marriage chair. Trumpets and horns announced the procession and ceremony to all. The bride was veiled and dressed in a beautiful robe of red silk with gold embroidery and soon arrived at the courtyard of Wu. Head politely bowed, the bride was led into the family home and the wedding ceremonies proceeded. The young couple met in the Hall of the Ancestors and there they bowed to the Gods of Heaven and Earth, bowed to the ancestors and to each other and later bowed to the guests and parents. They then drank wine from the cups tied together with the red cord of joy and ate the wedding rice. And after the feasting was over the bride raised her beaded veil for the first time.

Wu Fang could not hide his surprise for Chen Lien had only one eyebrow! In the place of the other was an ugly scar. "Didn't you know about my poor eyebrow? Didn't the matchmaker tell you? When I was just a little girl I was playing in the garden of some family friends. A small boy threw a stone and I was accidentally struck on the brow. I wanted to be perfect for you…but this scar will accompany me even into the World of Shadows…"

"Were you playing in the garden of the Li family in the City of Pleasant Rest?" Wu Fang asked.

"Why yes!" Chen Lien replied, "How did you ever know?"

"Because I was that boy! My parents have often reminded me of the incident. It is perhaps no accident that our ankles are joined by the red cord of marriage," Wu Fang whispered.

The bridegroom, again on the will of the Gods, reached for his rabbit hair writing brush and black paint. Carefully, he drew a willow shaped eyebrow over Chen Lien's scar. It was perfect and now no one could tell the difference between the natural and the artistic.

And every morning thereafter, for the rest of their long and happy life together, began with the ceremony of the eyebrow. Wu Fang would artfully paint a willow-leaf eyebrow over the scar he had caused his beloved Chen Lien. "So did the Gods bring joy out of sadness"…and so did the people learn how the human hand sometimes improved upon the handiwork of the Gods. (Carpenter, 1937, pp. 56–65)

The Chinese folktale of the *Painted Eyebrow* speaks eloquently to the grammarian act by which talk becomes writing and sound is transubstantiated into space. Writing, it might be argued, is the human attempt to improve upon the handiworks of the Gods, or at the very least to describe it. Our writing also gives strong evidence about the ease with which we humans move from the natural to the artificial and back again. Both Chen Lien and Wu Fang were forever changed by the new willow leaf eyebrow. As a painted symbol, it stood external to them, but upon their first and then daily perception, the eyebrow indeed went to their hearts. An external act was internalized and by the process forever changed their view of themselves. The brush painted eyebrow was also an attempt to keep something in existence, something that had been lost through injury. The symbol brought its idea back. In a similar way, our writing is a contrivance, an attempt to recover what has been lost by nature. The oral, as Ong (1982) repeatedly informs us, is forever going out of existence. That is the nature of sound. Writing, however, recovers that sound by its almost magical conversion of sound into space. We can thank the Sumerians and their cuneiform script for that. And when that recovery takes place so, too, does the interiorization of the symbol. The artificial and the devised become the natural.

Very often, my own storytellers thought of the symbol and thought by the symbol. For those who were writers, it was probably impossible to do otherwise. Thus, there was in their stories a curious conversational interplay between the written and the oral and, subtly, between the written nature of their spoken thought and the oral nature of their spoken thought. They had been recreated not only by their stories, but by the media in which they were expressed. And to linger over the metaphor just a moment longer, our tales and our talks were also a ceremony of the eyebrow; all of us knowing well that at some point and in some alchemical fashion I, as the researcher, would transubstantiate kitchen table sound into the literary and educational space of a dissertation. Whether or not it is possible to improve upon the handiwork of the storytellers was perhaps not the issue. The act of research writing does enhance and promote an interiorization at the very least. As widely divergent in background as my storytellers were, they were each and in some manner profoundly touched by the ceremony of the painted eyebrow, by the solipsistic or self-endeared act of writing:

To give away yourself keeps yourself still;
And you must live, drawn by your own sweet skill.
(Shakespeare, 1966, p. 8)

For Grandfather Rattler, some of his earliest and most cherished memories were situated in the personal world of the reader. On one of my visits, he had just received a fascinating note from a former school teacher, and she had sent along a rediscovered letter that she had written on Rattler's behalf in 1936:

To the Secretary of the East Coulee School:

I know it's difficult times now, and we do have a better library than most one room schools, in fact we have 311 books, but [Rattler] has read them all. And he's just finished Grade 3! Is it possible for you to get a few more books?

Not only was the reply from the school board in the affirmative, but the 17-year-old school teacher received an extraordinary cheque in the sum of $100 dollars with which to buy books:

Which is just like a fortune then...but there were two wealthy farmers...farmers did quite well if you had a lot of land....Actually, they survived the depression very well because labor was cheap, and in our area, we never had crop failures, and anyway these two big farmers had put in $50 each so that I got some books. (laughter) And you can buy an awful lot of books for $100 then.

Grandfather laughed mid-story and admitted that of the 311 books only one proved beyond his grade 3 comprehension level and that was Charles Kingsley's *Water Babies*. That one-room school library, albeit limited, had a profound and lasting influence on the young Rattler:

These 311-odd books, many of them were science books, you see, which got me absolutely interested in science, and there was also a Green's Short History of England, which really wasn't short....It was about that thick I remember, (laughter) but I did wade through it. (laughter) You know, there was something for everybody, but I think this was where my early interest in science...cuz there was an awful lot of natural history...and I think I got really fascinated by the natural history and astronomy books....Then, of course, when I finished high school, I entered engineering, you see, and took two years of it.

Grandfather's own emergence as a scientist and historian had a "Kingsley" touch about it. Books were a natural part of the youth's prairie world and if anything facilitated the boy's fascination with the nonbook world of dragonflies and life's creatures. Those 311 precious books connected the inner world of one prairie lad to the very stars. The nonbreathing symbol of the written letter and word meant life itself. Yet for all of that, Rattler's paper world was not strictly demarcated by the analytic pen of the scientist for it included the pencil and brush of the artist as well:

I always loved to sketch and draw. My father was a great sketcher; he loved horses. The barn walls were loaded with sketches of horses. (laughter)....My Grandfather, the one who went up into the Peace River country and was a veterinarian, had a very artistic flair...and, uh, I remember my Grade 7–Grade 8 teacher really encouraging me. She bought me a set of oil paints. The first year she got me some pastels and told me how to use them. The next year she got me a set of oil paints and taught me how to use them. She was very, very artistic.

At a young age, Rattler became conversant in both paint and print and able to pursue his expressive interest in a wide variety of disciplines:

Most of my academic career was totally unplanned. I just took what interested me. (laughter) I did manage after all my years to get a B.Ed. and a B.A., but I remember my staff advisor said, "You know, you've got more courses and fewer degrees than anyone I have ever known!" (laughter)

Rattler's growing years reflected a dynamic interplay of the spoken and the written. Although he developed literary skills at a very early age, our elder seemed most comfortable when academic expression took a multimedia format. For example, of the memorable 9 years he spent as teacher in a one-room school, Grandfather remembered in particular detail this multidisciplinary project:

The school was way up on top of the hill there, so we made the map of Alberta, we carved it into the hillside. (laughter) And we dug down and ran water into the rivers, piled up rocks where the mountains were, (laughter) built the forts. You know they had a wonderful time. (laughter) Alberta was every bit as big as the whole school room. (laughter) A couple of parents were so impressed with it they brought tarmacks and covered it so it wouldn't get damaged....It was there for years apparently...a walk around Alberta, put in the towns, the historical points. We'd all gather round, and they'd dramatize various cities and towns I remember...and invite other kids out to watch these dramas taking place in Alberta.

Although D'Angelo (1982, p. 155) distinguishes between the abstract thinking that characterizes literate people and the more concrete and specific thinking associated with nonliterate people, Rattler demonstrated both. In doing so, his thought took on a protean shape. As a student of natural history, archeology, athletics, art and drama, for example, Grandfather's thought both created and expressed the situation. Yet that situational thinking was itself highly metaphoric and conducive to abstraction. Thus, he was able to both survive and flourish in a technological society yet also remain sensitive to the shortcomings of our motorized worlds. And although our elder devoted a great part of his heart and career to the promotion of literacy, he did not seem to take literacy as the final measure of humanity. As Davis (1982) writes, "If we are not careful, literacy may be misconstrued as the measure of a human being's worth" (p. 58). Indeed, probably the great majority of our storyteller's leading characters were nonliterate, albeit highly articulate. The spirit could be freed from the sandstone in any number of storied ways. Rattler told just such a story:

> The story deals with what we are talking about, turning the spirit free. It was back in the late 50s....I had a very good principal....If it was for the good of the child...he didn't mind breaking all the rules...and once a week we had this lady come in...and she was very, very good working with children; she didn't mind breaking a few rules...but we had this brother and sister.

As Rattler told it, this brother and sister as part of a travelling family had reached their junior high years without being able to read and write. The collaborative staff decision was to "forget about the books and texts and so on":

> The girl was a very very good artist....The other boy was a natural; he could do anything with his hands. He was absolutely fascinated with science, particularly electrical sciences.

Over the next few months, literacy took care of itself and naturally grew out of the high interest situational learning in both art and science. By the end of the year, thanks to a collaborative team more mindful of person than program, "they were reading very well and [were] very interested in their work." Then years later, and in the tradition of all good stories, Rattler and a friend were walking down a street in Calgary when suddenly,

> we looked and here was a beautiful Rolls Royce. (laughter)...Standing admiring this, we went around all sides, oh it was a gorgeous car....This young man came out of the building, and he looked at me. You could see he was going over to the Rolls Royce and he said, "Rattler?"

That young man, now a very successful chiropractor, was the same individual who could not read in Grade 8. It tickled our Rattler that such success could come from breaking the rules, that the spirits of two young people could be freed by a great love and a caring act:

> They were two that'd really succeeded with me....We always said, "Why can't we start a little school like that—just dealing with kids like that?"

As Rouse (1978) writes, "The hard part is to help people without entrapping them" (p. 36). This may be particularly true in the act of language instruction whereby an educator struggles to release and not restrict his/her youthful charges.

Literacy was but one way to free the spirit and but one way to align the individual with the group. In the Rattler sense, literacy was a kind of spiralling movement or journey; again, one that connected the internal and the external world, an unceasing attempt to bring the unconscious into a state of consciousness. Grandfather even referred to the symbol of the Crete spiral:

> It's in a spiral....You know that's a very common figure, the spiral, which starts small and works like this, outward....This one is done in a spiral, and it's actually been printed...in other words...it's been stamped, probably done by the first printing press, 4500 years ago, stamped in clay you see, then it's baked...but it's done in that spiral design, and no one knows whether you start reading it from the outside to the inside or from the inside to the outside.

The individual's and our elder's relationship to language and the relationship of the oral to the written was itself a kind of Cretan spiral. Although the symbol could stand alone, it still depended upon the existential situation, the context of the readership, for its meaning. And as the readership changed, then so did the meaning: the spiral continued. A living message, for example, could come from the symbols of the now dead, and the fixed print of the word could liberate or unfix matters of the spirit. Grandfather's fascination with the anecdotal history of Alberta was itself an exemplary labor of transubstantiation whereby the stories and conversations of the recently departed took on the protean shape of the literary:

> The nature of oral and written language and the interplay between them is ever shifting, and these changes both respond to and create shift in the individual and societal meanings of literacy. The information to be gained from any prolonged look at oral and written uses of language through literacy events may enable us to accept the protean shapes of oral and literate traditions and language, and move us away

from current tendencies to classify communities as being at one or another point along a hypothetical continuum which has no societal reality. (Heath, 1982, p. 115)

In the protean shape of the storyteller, Grandfather was delightfully awash in events both oral and literal and certainly free of "hypothetical continuums." His bristle brush celebrated communities rather than classifying them.

And in a manner similar to Rattler's, the northern storytellers seemed to take the conversation on literacy out of these unceasing continuities and into the protean shapes of living events:

> This is the great teaching of all the greatest teachers...not to disengage yourself from natural life and law, but at the same time, not to become bound to the world of sensory fact. (Campbell, 1989, p. 40)

To Mosum, storytelling and life itself was an unbound oral act, an act of memory:

> If you had a real long-term memory...they could remember what they had seen (laughter) cuz they didn't learn to write things down, they didn't write it down. Everything was up here. He said at times he went to see an elder in the evening, bringing him tobacco, and the real great ones could tell stories all night. They would remember the details of what they were talking about.

And when I asked Sabochees why this was, why people preferred the oral stories, he replied,

> They were never written down, no. I don't know why. I don't know why because people knew how to write in Cree syllabics. They used to know how a long time ago, but they never wrote it down....You just have to remember in your head....I've seen a few old people like that, who could go on and on. There was no way to stop them.

I have heard on several occasions both Mosum and Sabochees draw the connection from "being Cree" to "speaking Cree." To them, the articulation of the Cree language was essential to one's navigation within the culture. Writing Cree, however, was described more as an enhancement, as a gift that only some possessed. Pesimwastches said it this way:

You know, when I hear people say that they are able to read syllabics and able to write syllabics, when they really needed it desperately they used it. And these people, you know, not everybody wants to be able to write the language or read the language. Various people were chosen....My brother, he was chosen; it went straight to him. He didn't choose the language.

Perhaps a hunting lifestyle of movement and travelling about lent itself more to oral skills and matters of the internal rather than social acts that depended upon objectives. It may be also that oral memory more suitably facilitated the personal movement from sensory facts to matters of the spirit. "To be trained" did not mean "to be lettered." Rather, both recall and interpretation were a living narrative act:

I never saw a [mud fireplace], but I think I know what they looked like. I've heard. My Dad told me about it, what they looked like, not just my Dad, but some old people. They told me what it looked like. I know what it looks like, but I've never seen it.

Learning by story maintained familial and friendly connections, bringing generations together. And as a result, learning had much more to do with relationships and much less to do with literate acts. When I asked Sabochees, for example, what he looked for in a school teacher from his perspective as parent, grandparent, and veteran school board member, he replied,

If a teacher comes to us and wants to teach kids here, he has to believe what the people believe here. He has to believe in our culture. If he doesn't believe nothing, he doesn't know what to teach…he'll never be happy here.

The best teachers were those who would facilitate and maintain the relationships.

Although literacy in a second language was important and increasingly essential to small community survival, fluency in one's first language meant a place within one's own people. Thus, to my northern storytellers, their humanity was not defined by a literate act, in either English or Cree, nor did they normally measure others by their degrees of literacy. Again, to be learned, one need not be lettered. Speech was a gift from the Great Spirit, and no amount of written insight could replace that gift once lost. I am reminded again of Sabochees' teaching when he struggled to have me understand and fully appreciate what it meant to lose an elder. "It's just like you've lost a book, thick like that," he had said, slipping into the metaphor of the day. And the considerable energy that was going into the writing of the first language, that is, Cree syllabics, through classroom instruction and community curriculum development, was perhaps more in the celebration of a first language orality rather than in the facilitation of a transference into a second language literacy. Perhaps one could record the learned through letters, but it was unlikely that the learned could be created by letters. Interestingly, however, Pesimwastches, too, slipped into the metaphor of the book when he talked of stories:

> [The stories] are not in me all the time, but they're there. Like you know...when they store away a storybook...they're stored away. You put them on the side....Sometimes you take that storybook and you're in a situation, almost similar to that story, and you use that story to help you get out of that situation.

Thus, to both Sabochees and Pesimwastches, the metaphor of the book meant "something stored away," a kind of grouse's pouch filled with latent life. As a veteran of innumerable meetings, from the informality of tea fire get togethers to the formality of governmental symposiums, I have long been a student of communication and meeting performance. And on many occasions, I have witnessed my friends from an oral background, speakers and not writers of language, pick up a report or newspaper or government document and shake it passionately, persuasively, as they engaged themselves in the oral disputation. They shook their words and in doing so clutched the medicine of the metaphor. They shook their words and gave testimony to the power of things stored away, to the protean power of resemblance. Perhaps therein lies the dilemma, for there are those who look to the written word for cultural hope, for the preservation and celebration of all things oral. To just as many others, the very act of preservation itself threatens. It may externalize what rightfully belongs on the inside. I am forever reminded of the time Sabochees and I strolled about the Provincial Museum and of the moment when we happened upon the Native artifacts. After a good deal of silence, a good deal of looking, Sabochees turned to me and said, "They have lost their power here, on the wall." I know that same struggle resided in the soul of our elder. For as much as Sabochees wished to commit his culture to syllabic print and posterity, he worried about what that act might symbolize. It is one thing to celebrate with literacy, but it is quite another to "store away" and mothball one's culture, to commit one's ancestors to space rather than sound, to museulogize one's own people.

Most often in the oral North, I believe it is laughter that suggests a way out of a difficult situation. From the agony of the "hypothetical continuum," it is fitting that we paint an eyebrow with our words. A dear elder, years ago, told this story of literacy that it might be put into the children's schoolbooks:

> You see, there once was a mean old man, Kiseyino by name, who thought more highly of his dog than of his son, Oskineko. The old man refused to give any money to Oskineko, although the youth remained home and worked dutifully. Indeed Kiseyino preferred the company of his highly intelligent dog to that of his son. One sunny day, however, Oskineko thought of a way to deceive his father. First, he carefully wrote a letter to his father, then secretly delivered it to the post office. A few days later, it arrived. Kiseyino did not know how to read and so replied, "Son, tell me what the letter says. It must be important!"
>
> "Father, this letter was written by some Whitemen. Even though they live far away from here, they have heard of your dog Atim and how smart he is...they wish to give him further training, Father. They suggest that I bring him soon for this instruction," Oskineko explained.
>
> "I agree to it," Kiseyino quickly decided, "and you shall take Atim to these people as they suggest. Here, take this money for your travel expenses and here is some more for Atim's schooling."
>
> And so the young man and the dog travelled to the city. Then, a few days later, Kiseyino received a letter from his son requesting more money. When the friend read that the dog was beginning to talk, even speaking several languages, the old man happily obliged. Several such letters arrived over the next few weeks, each boasting of Atim's successes. And each time the old man sent more money. Finally, however, Oskineko grew weary of his travels and returned home...after his father sent the money, of course. But when Oskineko arrived, he was alone, no dog.
>
> "Where is my brilliant dog, you 'son-of-a-puskisikun'? What have you done to him?" the old man raged.
>
> "Dad," the young man carefully replied, "I'm so sorry, but I had to kill your dog. You see, not only did he learn to read and write, but to speak also. And once he learned to speak, he said he was going to tell on a certain old man, who although he had been married many years, still chased young women!"

"You did the right thing my boy," Kiseyino whispered, as he affectionately patted his son on the shoulder. (Nanooch, 1987, pp. 19–25)

Perhaps it was best that some things remain "stored away," our elder joked. This same sense of laughable unease was reiterated in a conversation that Pesimwastches had with an old timer, and not surprisingly, the subject of their talk was once again the spiritual lives of the young:

> My grandson, that little spruce tree over there, standing up...that's part of Mother Nature's dress, that's part of her dress....Look at all the bad things that have happened to mankind because they don't treat the tree right. Look at what you get out of trees...almost every product that is for sale and each product is in your hand...humans don't respect that tree. There is paper made out of trees, and when you have paper, you have pencils made of trees, and with pencil and paper, the laws are made. Things are written down, and you must follow all these things that are written down, and you must follow all these things that are written against human people....It's a way that Mother Nature is trying to tell people to respect her.

As much as literacy is touted as a liberatory tool by the many, there are those, like Grandfather, who find themselves the victim of that same literacy. Literacy told them who they were not. By their stories, they tell of an oral time more negotiable, more human. Pesimwastches, himself situated in both the metaphor of the book and the metaphor of the campfire, suggested that

> in the written word you're directly where you are. In the oral, you could be three places all the time.

It becomes almost inconceivable for the literate to imagine thought without writing, thought in and around speech only. As Raymond (1982) writes:

> Literacy, then, despite its advantages, is a human problem in much the same way that wealth is. It is, ironically, the condition which makes illiteracy possible, just as wealth makes poverty possible. (p. 12)

I have known too many adults, good people, important to the planet people, who have felt less than human because of their "illiteracy." Betty, in her work with children of special needs, has told me of too many children, important to the planet children, who felt themselves less, always less, because their gift was not of the written word. My northern storytellers have made their plea for a world that regards ability and proficiency as a spiritual gift rather than as a cause for separation. Their plea was for cultural celebration rather than for problem identification. Much of the world seems bent on brushing away the scar of "illiteracy" rather than celebrating the world's orality. Pesimwastches painfully remembered his own parents' decision to send him to the Mission school, again in the name of becoming literate and something more:

> It was a hard time....You're going to have to sit in a warm house 10 months of the year and enjoy yourself and put yourself into the books and no contact from us.

And in the cause of literacy, in the promise of the medium, our trickster teller was to live much of his later life haunted by the shadows of that experience:

> I thought my parents didn't care for me...that's why they sent me over here, with a bunch of people dressed in black with a white beak on them...coming at me all the time, constantly with a piece of leather...trying to fight me because of my language...kneel on my knees and say my prayers again....It used to haunt me, you know.

And that may be a central message of the northern storytellers: the extent to which a good intention can oppress. As John Davis said,

> What I can remember, I will say.
> What I cannot remember, I will not say.
> I cannot read and write.
> I can only remember. (Ridington, 1990, p. 204)

Their discourse was much more than mere paper, their stories much more than only remembering. The words and the stories shaped their reality, their auditory world, making it unique and their own. By their words, they were able to see in the round:

> To depict a whole object on a flat surface, literate man employs three-dimensional perspective: he shows only that surface visible from a single position at a single moment. He fails.

> In contrast, Native artists of British Columbia represented a bear, say, in full face and profile, from back, above and below, from within and without, all simultaneously. By an extraordinary mixture of convention

and realism, these butcher-draftsmen skinned and boned, even removed the entrails to construct a new being, on a flat surface, that retained every significant element of the whole creature. (Carpenter, 1972, p. 24)

Good storytellers participate in that gift as well. They enable the listener to "see in the round" and not merely from one fixed place at one fixed time. Their nonliterate words serve as celebration of the very "unfixedness" of our human condition: "It was Aristotle who said that the man who dreamed up Atlantis also made it disappear" (Rouse, 1978, p. 83).

As assuredly as our northern storytellers expressed a comfort in the oral medium, Sparrow expressed a comfort in both the literary medium and what the literary spawned, the electronic. Sparrow, like our Northerners, however, understood the literary to grow out of the oral with word of mouth as the originative media substance. For example, in her description of the practice of test questions:

> How would the people know if Henry Hudson died; how would the people know about him? Well, like, guys would tell their kids, and kids would get older and tell the other kids, and it would keep on going down the generations and generations and then finally get into an encyclopedia writer, and he'd write it in a book...and then Henry Hudson would be famous and everything.

Thus, at such a young age, our "littlest storyteller" naturally understood books to come from talk and from talk that marvelously connected to the ancestors. In a figurative sense, it was the metaphor of the book that not only shaped Sparrow's story of the past, but also allowed her to imagine the shape of the future:

> Not really books....They'll have this little computer thing to write down your notes...and when teacher writes on the board...you'd press a button, and there'd be a little thing on the end, and it'd be pointed toward the thing, and it'd write it down for you.

It was this metaphor of the book that situated our little friend on a "hypothetical continuum," somewhere between the old guys who talked a lot and the literary laser receptors. Sparrow's love for a book story, however, was no hypothetical thing. Nor was literacy simply an educational means to an economic or recreational end:

To be truly literate is not to demand the easy satisfaction that formula romance or thrillers provide, but rather to seek out books which initiate conversations on those subjects from which we most want to hide, but about which we most need to know. (Keefer, 1990, p. 119)

In that seeking out, Sparrow depended on her parents. They were her spirit guides. It was Mom, herself a school librarian, who first created that folkloral and magical world of the bedtime story:

We really sit on [my little sister's] bed, and each of us gets to choose a story: and she reads a story about that each of us want....Like [my little sister and brother] choose big storybooks....They want to choose the longest ones that stay up longer. (laughter)

And to a lesser extent perhaps, teacher also intimated a literary world of wonder, but one with an academic agenda attached:

Our teacher...like in L.A...she gets like stories out of the newspaper...like bedtime stories...and puts them on this thing and that you can see on the board, and we read it, and she asks questions about it.

This act of reading to a child, Sparrow in this context, was not simply an introduction to the nice language of books. As Meek (1991) points out, the "read story is the longest monologue of connected language that children hear" (p. 111). It provided also the symbol pattern and sequence of episodes that constitute a story. And beyond the rich experience of narrative language, bedtime stories

provide the listeners with an increasing imaginative repertoire of ways of coming to terms with their emotions, which unlike other aspects of their being, are full-sized from the day of their birth. (Meek, 1991, p. 113)

It was the bedtime story that began the episodic process by which Sparrow the child listener was to become Sparrow the adult reader:

Mom would stop the book and...she would say, "What do you think is going to happen? What do you think is going to happen?"

Thus, Sparrow slipped early into the metaphor and discovered how a book story could provide a way to "name the unnameable," to initiate a conversation on what she most needed to know. Although her early memories of school were seldom themselves literary acts, Sparrow's literary competence provided a way to story her young life:

> It was my show and tell, and I told like what I got. I was wearing my new pair of black spandex, and I was wearing them when I was talking....I had a book, like you write in your diary and you tell what you wrote for the day when you're special...and then I walked back, and I told about my spandex...walking so nice.

In the retelling, the story took the shape of the literary folkloral. For example, when Sparrow thought back to her kindergarten days:

> It was the second day or the third day of school, and there was this kid that I don't like anymore....He would pretend he was his dad, and I would pretend that I was his mom, and then we'd be like husband and wife and we'd play house....We'd put on an apron, like there were clothes in there that we'd change into, and we'd have kids. That's how I remember it...stupid....Now I don't like him.

Just as the little ones slipped into the clothing of adulthood, so they slipped into the story and traditions of a literary world. It was a world in which the story was frequently the best part of the human relationship. Gregory (1977) suggests that "it is living by fiction which makes the higher organism special" (Meek et al., p. 122). And Sparrow certainly lived in her love of literary fiction. It brought her to the unnameable, to the mystery. For example, why did the Titanic sink?

> One night they were sailing, I think it was like 1 a.m....1 o'clock at night and then this guy yells out that they hit an iceberg and then everyone, like rushing and screaming. First of all, they didn't really believe it...only the ladies and the babies were allowed to go off....They only had a couple of lifeboats....There's no such thing as an unsinkable ship.

Is there a "mysterious Bermuda Triangle that swallows the ships and planes," Sparrow wondered and wrote:

> There has been many investigations into this strange happening, many investigations, but no real answers.

Sparrow's world, although artfully fictionalized, was no less real, be it "neat or funny or scary." As Sparrow says of one story collection full of suspense, "you've got to be ready for lots of surprises!" Literary life for Sparrow was surprise and her extensive reading only sharpened a taste for it:

> Lots of people died in there, and it was true, and then someone grabbed her shoulder, and she uttered a last...she uttered a loud scream, and then it was another chapter, and so you're just waiting. Oh, who is that person that grabbed her shoulder?

Minutes later, and in the retelling, Sparrow told me of her own recent astonishment and accompanying scream. She and a friend had been caught unawares:

> It sounded like a cheetah scream, a cheetah scream, but oh that scared us, hey, I got so scared I boogied man....I was like fast, you should have saw, as soon as [my friend] said, "Run," I ran and I was at the house and she was way by the gate.

Indeed, life was a surprise for Sparrow and, like the metaphor of the book, chaptered by literary events. It struck with wonder. She proudly announced to me one day:

> Oh I read like a lot of stories. We have to do 10 book reports in our class, like for every month, 10 throughout the whole year...and I got already my 10 book reports done, and I already finished two more books [by December].

The assignment was a chapter completed, as was the entire school year. Even a literary life was episodic as each literary event brought Sparrow one step closer to the next surprise. And, yes, school, probably more than anything else in her life, imposed an order upon Sparrow's experience and sense of wonder. It was important that her literary expression take the show and tell format of the ritualized classroom:

> And we also write poetry for contests: like Remembrance Day contests and I forget, there's this other kind of poem, something about electricity, we had to write a poem on.

At a very early age that show and tell format took the shape of the literary examination. Sparrow remembered her Grade 1:

I was being really quiet and like there was a test and the teacher came up to me and said, "Are you feeling OK?" Like she was really serious...."Are you feeling OK, Sparrow?"...Like because I was quiet....I was laying down on my desk...and I was doing a test yes. I should of said, "Yes," and I would have missed it! (laughter)

Even Sparrow's great love of the theatrical was being shaped and considered in the light of a schooling context:

In acting, you have to pass courses....It's a contest to see who is going to be like Kevin Costner, and so you have to act out against all sorts of other people and so you can win, and then if I lose, I have to start from scratch.

Inevitably Sparrow's young life was being shaped by the container that held it, and that container was the literary event we call school. Learning to read and write, however, was only her most obvious accomplishment. She was also busily engaged becoming the kind of person whom the rest of the world could like and even praise. School for Sparrow, as for her schoolmates, was all about success and failure:

A hundred good deeds, environmental deeds...that you do, like not using scrap paper for your math and stuff. You write it down, and then when you get to the top, like this prize.

I have a loud voice, and I can memorize lines good...and I was Snow White, and I got the leading role again.

And like we were really good, and then I remember in Grade 4, I think it was, last year, we had another air guitar, and we won first.

Sometimes I like the first day of school because you get to show off your new clothes and shoes and everything.

Needless to say, Sparrow was fully engaged, and her many accomplishments in literacy stood as testimony to her involvement in the day. This engagement not only took the form and the metaphor of the book, that is, written literacy, but also the metaphor of the microchip. Sparrow would often begin her particular tale with the apology or clarification of the originating source. For example, as prelude to the folktales *Pinnochio* and *Snow White*:

Well, I read a book when I was a kid about it, and I watched a movie.

I learned the story of Snow White from a book, and then I guess the movie....We have it.

Thus, Sparrow seemed equally at home with stories both written (that is, the typographic) and electronic. Her electronic repertory of video folktales included such stories as *Fern Gully, Robin Hood, Pinnochio, Snow White, Cinderella,* and *Beauty and the Beast.* That the story originated for her in either print or tape did not seem particularly important. What was important was the story itself. For example, in our futuristic musings, Sparrow suddenly recollected an appropriate tale:

You have wallpaper....They have little fruits on it, and you'd lick it and taste the fruits. There's a really cool story...like then this kind of rhyme that makes you float up in the air. It's totally different stuff. That's really neat.

It was of little consequence to Sparrow that the video-movies and cartoons she so loved were all meticulously based on written scripts. Just so, it was of little consequence that much of the orality that Sparrow witnessed and engaged in each day was itself the secondary orality, the scripted orality of movie and television. Through the electronic medium, the "flat" characters of oral folklore were becoming increasingly rounded, and Sparrow eagerly participated in this reality of complex characterization, a reality sensitized to the fine nuances of the individual temperament (Ong, 1982, p. 152). Daily our pony-tailed storyteller engaged in the consciousness-raising activity of print, by virtue of her reading and writing. She became protagonist in the plotted stories of print that surrounded her. But Sparrow also became protagonist in the episodic and nonpyramidal tales of the impressionistic medium of television and its structure of "memories and echoes, suggestive of early primary oral narrative with its heavy reliance on the unconscious" (Ong, 1982, p. 151). Although Sparrow lived in a world and an orality quite unlike that of her great grandparents, it certainly held the shadows of the ancestral. In a fascinating way, her literacy connected the primary orality of the ancestors to the electronic orality of the everyday. Both oralities, the ancestral and the modern, promoted a sense of community in the present. Sparrow belonged, particularly when we spoke. Sparrow belonged to her stories in a way that her literacy struggled to express. For Sparrow was not only the protagonist, but the shadow also that held the pencil and eternity in her hand, able to live both in and out of the sentence. Her every story, be it spoken or penned or taped, gave new body for her soul to live in.

Like Sparrow, like the others, like the shadows, we are born and named and not necessarily in that literate order. Our first squealing sound is given a space, an identity, a naming word. For so many, the genesis and their birth is itself a literary event. And then for our brief tunnel of fantasy in this world, we wrap ourselves up in words and writings. We bundle up our babies in syllables, and as they step each through their Shakespearean seven stages, it is words that mark their passing and shining days. But in spite of both the poetic and the footnoted, we journey from the nameless to the nameless, with life but an interruption, a data blip in the silence. I believe that our glory may come in the power of the unnamed, the untold, the unwritten, the unfilmed. For that is where the little ones will inhabit. And when they as elders leave, they, too, will take along their storied words and writings and leave in their vacated spaces a perfect silence. It is this unnamed place that beckons out for the next child and the next, and so we name our little ones, then give them birth, brief sound into space. Their job is to lose that name and then find their Sparrow shadow in the unwritten silence and thus brush on the eyebrow, the transubstantiation of sound into space into silence: "And no one knows how many of the dolphins that leap in the waters of the Inmost Sea were men, once wise men, who forgot their wisdom and their name in the joy of the restless sea" (Le Guin, 1975, p. 141).

In the Chinese folktale of the marriage of Wu Fang to Chen Lien, the young couple were ceremonially and symbolically joined at the ankle by the red cord of marriage. Their coming together was itself an act of the Gods and their marriage an external expression of an internal joy and union. The red cord symbolized the new and enlarged identity, the constitutive identity.

This symbol of the red cord and the matter of personal identity appears also in the Jewish storytelling tradition. There are a great many humorous stories told of Chelem, the City of Fools, and of the Chelemites who were forever begging the question "Who Am I?":

> As the story goes, Herschel the baker was deeply concerned that he would be taken for another if not for the clothing which set him apart. And what was to happen to him when he entered the bath house and set aside his clothing? What if he were mistaken for Moshe the water carrier and obliged to carry the heavy skins of water for the rest of his days? What if he were mistaken for Yoshe the shoemaker and forced to make leather shoes for the rest of his days? Naturally, Herschel was deeply concerned but concentrated thought soon suggested a way. To mark who he was, our friend Herschel tied a red string around his ankle

when he entered the bath house. And for a time it worked...until one Friday afternoon...after the most wonderful of baths, Herschel emerged from the water only to find that the red string had fallen from his ankle. And to make everything worse, our friend noticed a red string on the ankle of a perfect stranger. What confusion!

"Friend," said the unhappy baker to the man with the red string on his leg, "I have never seen you before, but I know who you are. You are I, Herschel the baker and now that I have told you who you are, please be good enough to tell me who I am, so that I may know where to go and what to do!" (Serwer, 1970, pp. 68–73)

By metaphoric license, I would draw an analogy from Herschel's red string to an act of literacy. For just as the red string on the ankle helped Hershel answer the mystery of "Who Am I?" so by our acts of both orality and literacy do we gain a sense of identity.

Our Israeli storyteller, Dafna, found and continually rediscovered her narrative self through countless and historic acts of literacy: "You begin by using symbols and end by contemplating them" (Dillard, 1982a, p. 170). Dafna's own life was that unique blend of symbol and contemplation. Literacy very often connected the two. For example, as a small child, Dafna remembered the first joy of the ballpoint pen and the symbolic import it held in her growing life:

> When we were allowed to use the first pen...how excited we were, just sitting and pushing it in and out, pushing it in and out to see how it works....I just remember it today. It was Grade Four, and-uh the funny thing is, after we all used this thing...when you really wanted to give someone a nice gift, you would go and buy the old fashioned pen, the one with the nail at the end...if you really cherished someone and you wanted to buy them something nice, this was a very popular gift by the way, to buy for someone who became "bar mitzvah"...a Parker pen...with a gold nib. This would be the ultimate gift. You can trace the development of the culture by the presents that you bring to the people, to your relatives.

For Dafna, growing up had everything to do with literacy, and thus, its symbols and gifts helped mark her passage:

> At the time when the girl became 12 and the boy had his "bar mitzvah," the most popular gift would be either a pen or a book...a

book…we are called the "Nation of the Book!" I got for my "bar mitzvah" mostly books…really wonderful books which opened a whole world for me…uh, music, the first book on music that I got, I got when I was 12. One I had about the cities of the world…the seven wonders of the world.

The pen, golden nibbed; the treasured book, not just novels; the book bag with pen and pencil and notebook already enclosed; and from the closest family member, a first watch:

> My uncle gave me my first watch when I was 12.…I'm just choking when I think.…You are a different person now, you should keep track of time, too, I guess. (laughter) You don't have all the time in the world anymore.

Dafna not only attached a great import to the gifts of an emerging literacy and adulthood, but also to the dedications that they carried. These flyleaf consecrations ritualized the gifting occasion:

> On the first page of the book there was a dedication, of course, so I knew exactly who brought me what and at what occasion: because they are all for the occasion of "you know."

The inscription personalized the text, reaffirmed the relationship between the giver and the receiver. It formalized for all to see the relationship, the literate connection of one generation and one person to the next. And it was a point of real concern for Dafna that the gifting traditions were themselves changing:

> You do not put your personality on the book anymore, there is nothing of you…it is just a book from the store that may change hands.…I still give from time to time a book, but mostly you don't, commonly now money. Isn't that something? Money…and you can see a world in the change.

Our storyteller friend was deeply anxious over the increasing materialization of her culture. Her remembered youth was more of an affair of the book, which was itself a symbol of the spiritual. As a child she loved nothing more than the curl up around a good book. That special read in some ways was synonymous with childhood, the red cord that bound the ankle, the passion lifted from a page and transubstantiated into a young girl's heart. It was no wonder that Dafna sought out the written word for the very Hebrew and Israeli air she breathed was of a literary substance. As a girl of 8 or 9, Dafna remembered the young woman next door who one day invited her over to see the new baby. Now next door meant in the next condominium, just across the wall. And as it turned out, the young mother was married to a partner in a publishing firm, and they were themselves the proud owners of a fine library. Over the next 4 or 5 years, Dafna read every book in that living room library, every book, Somerset Maugham, O. Henry, all of it, from shelf to shelf, the complete wall.

Schoolbooks, library books, gift books, next door books, Dafna read with a passion that echoed the writers' own energies, French, American, English and Russian literature, Dafna read:

> This was my bedtime, and I really feel that mainly I have a very diverse cultural point of view....I feel that I have this with me. It's like my book, and I know this is my advantage.

Within a culture that held the written word in such high esteem, with a father who recited Russian poetry by the Mediterranean seashore and a mother who could teach her child to skip and freely laugh, Dafna quickly found her ankle marked by the red cord of literacy. Reading was a love for literature, the passion of Tolstoy and Hugo and Zola, Hemingway, Steinbeck, and Chekhov. Reading was relationship and situation. It placed the child Dafna into the passion of others. It revealed the species through both biography and autobiography:

> I was passionate about stories. I really loved them, and I read them and read them and read them, even at the time we were not supposed to read them anymore. (laughter) And I did...I really loved them all...and later I liked a lot of biographies and autobiographies...all sorts of people...mainly all sorts of creators, artists and authors, musicians....I always wanted to know what made them that way.

Perhaps the stories both provided a connection between the accomplishments of others and the aspirations of a growing child and suggested a dialogical and passionate template by which one might enter the conversation. It was and was not a matter of gender:

> In what you take in school, I would say that most of the writers are men...but we do have more and more female writers. Even when I grew up we still had some very good poets, women poets...among the best in Israel...and it is interesting that we had more poetry by women than books, you know....Most of the writers of stories and books were men.

Perhaps it was in the literary stars that Dafna ultimately chose a teaching vocation and felt free to do so, a profession in which she could share her deep passion for all things written. Thus, even though Dafna felt that her society applauded, even cherished womankind, both in prayers and deed, there was room to do more:

> We can do better than we do because if we look back at the beginning of the century, when I tell you that women did mostly what men did...dried out swamps, and they worked in the fields, and they rode the horses, and they did everything because that's what they wanted to do. They talked about equality so they wanted equality. They wanted to change society.

As a teacher and as a woman, Dafna brought the stories of her people, her heroes, to the young. She saw her role both as a collaborator and custodian of the oral and the written, in home and school. Thus, her literacy helped situate her person and gender into the context of a people:

> I see myself as part and parcel of my culture and religion...so I really feel that my thought is based on the tradition of hundreds of sages that came before me...and I really absorbed the knowledge, at least some of the knowledge, and I read a lot as a child....I was one of those behind the book.

By her literacy and her reading, particularly, Dafna participated in both the Hebrew past and the Israeli future. Her heart beat to the rhythm and writings of the great poets of her people, or as she said, "We just knew them by heart." But as much as our Dafna brought passion and found passion, rhythm, and life in the writings of her people, her species, she transubstantiated again that temporal passion into an eternal spirit by the act of writing. Reading came along with youth. They travelled together. Writing, however, was an act of vintage maturation. Reading came with the books, while writing came in their absence.

In reading, the participant was the informed even impassioned guest and the created space, while in writing, Dafna became the creator of space. Thus, when our Israeli friend wrote the dedication on a gift and book, she brought herself as participant to the very process that had been essential to the survival of her people, the transubstantiation of sound into space, the scribal act. It was the scribes who had "carried on":

All those prophets that you read of in the Bible, they were very passionate people....They carried on with whatever they were supposed to carry on, even when they were scolded, hit, jailed, everything you know.

For Dafna, there was a lasting and historic connection between the biblical and the scholarly, with the result that the act of writing was itself a spiritual act:

> When the Jews were in exile or wherever they were, education was to be a scholar in the Bible and scholarly....He was considered highly regarded really.

And so when Dafna brought herself to the scribal act, it was never done lightly but always as a carrying on, an act of conscience:

> Words that you say just go and come, you know. And I always had this notion that once I write something it is forever and cannot be undone...it can never be.

Even in the everyday of her profession, Dafna wrote with great sensitivity, mindful of the red cord that bound her hand to the scholarship of her ancestors:

> I was so careful everytime I wrote something, especially on children's books. I almost always wrote it on a piece of paper and just then put it on, to make sure it's fine, not grammatically, but so it would not offend the child and so it would not have double meaning...and when I used to take in larger pieces of work every year they had to do a personal project, I would write a whole page of comments, like a big page, and then I would write it many times for each child. I look at the stuff we have, especially in Judaism, it is so old and it was given from father to son, from father to son for so many generations....Everything that is written became sacred. You cannot change anything....You are not allowed to change even one letter in the Bible.

As Purves (1990) suggests, the act of writing enables our species to transform an idea into a spatial reality that exists somewhat independently of both time and space. The auditory has become the visible, the temporal now eternal. Thus, a piece of everyday Dafna text was able to not only travel from school to home, but also from childhood to adulthood. Dafna was able to devote a great amount of her life to that symbol of literacy, the school, both as a teacher and as a student. And in doing so, she had committed her considerable energies into the creation of fellow scribes. It, too, was a sacred undertaking:

> I could never tear a page from a book...never mind how old it was and how shabby it was, you know....Never in my life [could I throw a book away]...I could never....And it took me a long time to be able to write in a book, many, many years. They are very, very important....Even if it's a letter to someone, it stays forever.

I am reminded also of Dafna's description of the synagogue and our discussion about the images of God. Dafna, years before, had been surprised by some North American churches and their paintings and statues: "and the angels were hanging all over the place." She talked about the Jewish synagogue:

> Five books of the Bible, the first five books written in scrolls...they are kept in every synagogue, a set of scrolls, handwritten. They are supposed to be written only by hand. There is a master who does that. You are not supposed to do anything unholy with them....Special people do only this. I meant you cannot be writing those books and be a merchant at the same time.

When Dafna brought her own student pen to the graduate task of writing, it, too, was a holy textual act, done with great care and deliberation and as a lasting point of reference in a scholarly life:

> Text means tissue; but whereas hitherto we have always taken this tissue as a product, a ready-made verb, behind which lies, more or less hidden, meaning (truth), we are now emphasizing, in the tissue, the generative idea that the text is made, is worked out in a perpetual interweaving, lost in this tissue—this texture—the subject unmakes himself, like a spider dissolving in the constructive secretions of its web. (Barthes, 1973, p. 64)

In the holiness of the act, Dafna had become the text and part of the tissue of her people. Her writing had caused her to first appear then dissolve into the constructive secretion of its own web. The life of scholarship was all about meaning and the web that bound story sound to story space, child to elder, a people to itself in a folkloral way.

Dafna told with great feeling of Rabbi Akeevah and his pursuit of the scholarly:

For 40 years, he was a sheepherder....He was a sheepherder for a very rich Jewish rancher...about 2,000 years ago. And, uh, he fell in love with this rich person's daughter and she fell in love with him. Can you imagine?

And when the rich father heard of their love, he summarily dismissed it for Akeevah was "an ignorant" who could neither read nor write. The daughter, now disinherited, did wed the shepherd and on the promise that he would one day soon learn to read and write:

> They lived in a barn, and he would go and study with the 4- and 5-year-olds that would study from, how do you call those, slates, and you used to see a 40-year-old man with the 3- and 4-year-olds and learning how to write and read the letters.

The gifted Akeevah "carried on" and pursued his studies with "a conscience." He travelled alone to a distant city and studied with some renowned rabbis and became famous himself:

> About 10 years later, when he was very famous, and a whole entourage of people were always following behind him, he came back to the city where he had left his wife. And a big crowd was standing on the outskirts of the city...awaiting this famous Rabbi Akeevah who came back...and all this time a woman, between the crowd, was rushing and pushing everyone...trying to get closer. This was his wife, of course...and he saw her from afar, so he said, "You should all move 10 steps aside and let her go because it's only because of her that I am where I am now."...And he brought her as a gift "Jerusalem of gold," which is a bracelet with the shape of a Jerusalem Temple...and she kneeled when she came close to him, she kneeled on her knees, so he lifted her up, and he presented her to everyone, and he said, "Just because of her...and she deserves all the honor in the world."

In the act of literacy, both the Rabbi and his wife were "lifted up" and brought to the honor of their generative story, as was our teller Dafna. All were given a narrative part in the tissue that bound them together, in the Rabbi's words that urged each to "love thy friend, as yourself." The hand that held the stone held also the brush that healed with willow-shaped eyebrows.

As Le Guin (1975) writes, the word wizard was one who could forgive and create "a binding spell that gathers the mists together for a while in one place" (p. 20). Dafna's life in literacy was just such a binding spell. Her literacy fixed the stars into a constellation and afforded our friend narratable travel:

There is a Japanese tale told of a fish vendor who regularly travelled from the sea to the mountains and back in his profession. On one particular journey he came upon a net made of fine red cord which had been set along a lonely mountain trail. And in that net there was caught a copper pheasant that the vendor dearly wished for himself. There was, however, no one around to pay or bargain for the fine pheasant. Finally, the fish vendor took three fish from his basket, giltheads they say, and placed them in the net in exchange for the pheasant.

When the mountain villagers came along, they were greatly surprised to find three fish in a net that had been set for pheasants. They took the three giltheads as a sign from Heaven and built a little shrine in celebration of this divine visitation. It was called Kurodai Shansho Gongen. People came from great distances to worship. And by the time the fish vender came along again and explained his exchange, the shrine had become wonderfully prosperous. (Yanagita, 1972, p. 138)

 I like that, particularly in the bridge, the snare of metaphor. What if one were to have a dream of fishes only to awake and find scales on the table? I, too, have devoted much of my waking life to the gilthead of literacy, and I have languished with a profound joy in the scribal art. It has been my storytellers, however, who have taught me that the mountain snare of expression was once the copper pheasant of orality. And with or without the divine guiding hand, I still favor the shrine. It could remain a favorite place, a holy space where the exchange of pheasant and gilthead took place, symbol of the transubstantiation of form and substance. Sparrow, Rattler, Sabochees, Mosum, Pesimwastches and Dafna, they have all led me to this mountain shrine of the human soul, to the place where the copper pheasant of experience is transformed into the gilthead of story and story and story, where the scars are covered by the willow-shaped strokes of a bristle brush, and where the crowds open to honor each of us, everyone.

 Some words need a brush, others a gold-nibbed pen, and still others only gesture and intonation. The red strings of our word-nets and species seem to catch it all: syllables of story and gilthead and copper pheasant and everything. I wonder now how many of the word singers and heroes, the kitchen table poets of my youth, transubstantiated their own silences into the lady of verse and the tiger of memory.

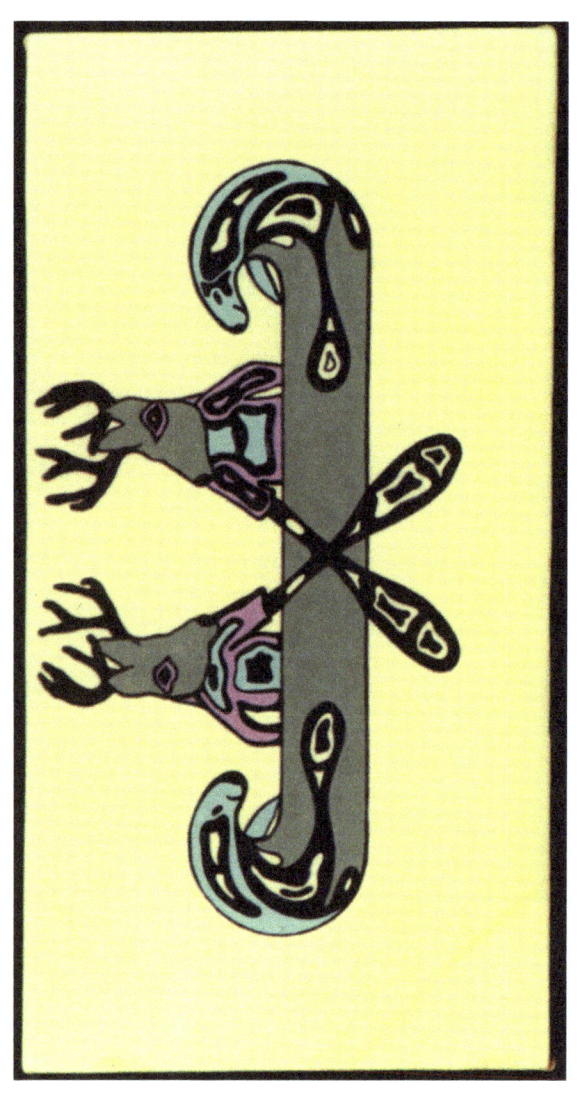

Deer Hide Painting:
The Medicine Canoe

Chapter 3
Metaphor

STORY IS A HOLY LAND

There are buffalo and sage
and holy trails that you and I are on...
grooved like 78 records,
our eyes and ears are in an Old Man River coulee rhythm,
going round and round like needle on vinyl...
and one moon a year
the Great Spirit allows the buffalo one-night-jig
in a secret and Holy Place,
like a good story
that you and I once heard,
with Pachelbel's Canon in our ears.

Story is a holy land. It is where we go for the medicine that will allow us to continue the one-night-jig. We do. We tell of the doing, and we tell of the telling. As with Scheherazade of *The Arabian Nights*, telling means living (Anonymous, 1946). We on the living side; we fill the narrative space around the thing with our presentations, our representations. We prefer the story and hurry through each day that we might tell of it. Our eyes are the exclamation marks of the storied air, our hand the designer of out-of-body telling space, our ears the catchers of dreams and souls. With the likeness of story comes the tribal memory and hope of a holy land, the narrative herb that will cure us each of oblivion. With the telling of story comes antidote to the consumptive maw of self. With story comes the holy land, the first star, the storyteller's night.

It is through the power of metaphor, the art of resemblance and likeness, that story is able to seek out and create these special places. In the New Guinean Tale of *The Fall* (1975), we are given a sense of holy land lost and the evening revisitation cycle:

> For all people once lived happily in the sky. And although the people could have visited earth by climbing down a long wooden rod, they much preferred their sky home and its happiness. The trickster Lizard, however, wished the sky to himself and so following a brief tour of earth, Lizard called everyone together. He spoke eloquently of the wonders of earth and encouraged the reluctant people to make a similar visit. Lizard talked of forests and ferns, crabs and fish, birds and snails and the people finally became curious. One day they began to climb down the long wooden pole to earth and soon no one was left in the sky home. Lizard was tour guide to the wonders of earth and everyone walked around this special place. Everyone picked fruit and ate it. Children played with puppies and men hunted pigs. All gathered flowers. Earth was indeed all that Lizard had described and promised. But one fateful day, something hairy with many legs bit a puppy and the puppy died. People noticed also that fruit on the ground was beginning to spoil and that the once beautiful flowers they had gathered were now ugly and withered. "What would happen to the people?", they asked one another. Everyone suddenly ran to the long wooden pole, wishing to return to their sky home and its happiness. Lizard, however, reached the rod first, climbed a long ways up and then began to chew through the pole. The people climbed quickly but just as they reached the Trickster, the rod was chewed through and the people tumbled back down to earth, their landing filled with tears and injury. Moments later, the top of the rod and Lizard and pole also fell tumbling to the ground. No one, no one lives in the sky anymore, no one. All must die...all. (Anonymous, 1975, p. 237)

In this life, however, among the forests and the ferns and the turtles, there is a continuing quest for the sky home, for this holy land. And in the place of the long wooden rod, we find story. Perhaps it enables us to reach for the other side of our experiences. Sparrow, our "littlest storyteller," her black ponytail punctuating the air, was one who so stretched. Her 10-year-old fingers traced the grains of the kitchen table as she told of her island:

> We used to call it "Our Island." We used to go there every week or weekend and Sundays normally, and we'd pack a lunch and, um, the island would be there....It was nice and warm like a lake, you'd swim in it, you could walk all the way across...all sand and mud and you'd run across it and everything...and we'd catch minnows there...and once we once brought friends there, and there was this big umbrella that we put inside the sand, and we'd hook up two sticks, and we'd put this big blanket over top....No one ever bothered to go there because they didn't know how hot the water was at the other end....We were the first ones to find it.

As Sparrow spoke, her silences seemed as important as her utterances. I felt in the presence of the holy, the important pauses, the important parts left unsaid. The place she called "Our Island" seemed familiar to her and a friend to her, a special place where the family walked round, a place visited and visited over and over again. The sand, the minnows, the sun all conspired to complete the ceremony of the place. But even this holy land required an alertness, a wariness:

> You'd swim there and everything, but you have to be careful of the current cuz if you swam the wrong way, it'd take you way out.

Sparrow then closed the story of her Athabascan holy land with one very brief and very telling phrase: "and then some people went there."

Human beings are so very hard on their medicine places. Youthful melancholy seemed to unite the tide of a little girl's heart to the sand and sun and river waves of "Our Island." As Langeveld (1983) suggests, "In the lifeworld of the child there exist hidden places which permit the child the possibility of experiencing in a normal manner access to strange and unfamiliar worlds around him" (p. 181). It is the metaphor of story that gave Sparrow both localized access and revisitation.

Sparrow's narrative of the holy land was at other times a more ritualized place, as when she shared this Biblical creation story:

> Hey God, he made two people, a man and a woman....Their name's Adam and Eve. And then He made every kind of tree in the world, every kind of plant in the world, and every kind of animal in the

world. And He, it was so beautiful and everything…and there was this one tree that He made by mistake.

In this sanctified place, a storyland she has heard of, beauty comes in composition, in the natural manifestations of a perfect world. But within the perfect world has again been sown and grown the possibility for the loss of that same world. God made a mistake. The creation of the apple tree, the tree of knowledge, would mean "a fall." Who could resist the narrative charms of Snake:

> I think it was Eve or was it Adam? I think it was Eve…."Eat an apple," he said, "it's really good. It's delicious!" And so she, she thought, "No, I shouldn't do," but then, then he said it was So juicy and Everything, and so she went…she tried it.

And in her turn, Eve plied a curious Adam with similar verbal charms:

> And then she told, "Oh, there's nothing wrong with, wrong with it. It's really good." So she told Adam to eat, to have a bite of it.

Sparrow's folkloral holy land was a place of synchronicity and surprises, where the apples must grow and the people must bite. The story could not be otherwise. Stories do cost, but even from such fate and such mistakes, Sparrow expressed hope:

> And then they had to make their own garden and everything. And they had to live their own life…and they had to start all over again.…Then they had kids, and the kids became and the kids, the kids, the kids…kept on going down and then some of them became explorers. That's like Christopher Columbus, how he discovered North America by telling the world it was round and not square.

Sparrow continued the story moment of holy places. She brought me back again and again to her own localized holy land, her island, with the person Sparrow as one of the first explorers. She drew me from the collective and public ownership of a Biblical story back to the personal internalization of a sacred Athabascan place. Like the visionary Black Elk of the Oglala Sioux who similarly spoke of a holy land at the centre of all things and at the centre of each localized being, Sparrow found her sacred place close to home (Neihardt, 1932).

At the centre of every holy land, Pirsig (1991) argues, is to be found the good, the noun good, not the adjective. Good in the telling we might argue, good in the quick climb back up the long wooden and oral rod, the narrative climb to God. And so the ritual of holy places is played out in the local nature of our time, the interplay whereby the ritual and colloquial simultaneously unravel in the kitchen table telling of our lives, turning squares into circles, forever new. As Sparrow would say:

And they had to live their own life...and they had to start all over again.

Langeveld (1983, p. 186) talks also of that secret place, the one Sparrow and I called the holy land, and describes how that place changes with age. The child, like Sparrow, will move her secret place from under the table to the attic perhaps, from folk fantasy to a life of personal adventure, and in a sense from the ritualized tales of childhood to the creativity of a localized self.

Dafna, her Israeli eyes aglow, spoke also of her personal holy land but this time from the vantage telling point of middle age. It, too, like Sparrow's "Our Island," was a special place of sun and sand and water and walking round:

We lived within a walking distance to the seashore so every Saturday morning....I really loved those days....Every Saturday morning my father would take me....I was 5 or 6 or 7 years old, every Saturday morning he would take me to a walk to the seashore...white sand and the water is very light blue....It's a sea, not an ocean, it's the Mediterranean Sea, and it's light blue....It's salty, but it is very light in color. And they also have not only the sand on the seashore, but we use to have, I don't know how you call it, this wandering sand, the sand that comes with the wind and it's beside the seashore. It's like hills, white hills....They were so smooth, you know, the wind would smooth them...like a child's face. You know nothing touched it.

Just as Sparrow's holy land was made perfect by the presence of family and those with whom she shared her geographic love, so Dafna, years and continents away, shared her holy land with the loving presence of her father:

And on the way he would, I don't remember him telling me stories in particular, but he used to cite, yes cite from Russian poetry, in Russian, which I didn't understand at all! Never mind, he went on reciting, and the sound of it, this beautiful language, especially in poetry...the sound of it was just....It stays with me to this very day, just unbelievable.

As Dafna shared her act of childhood listening, so I listened, and so I felt the sun, the sand, the Israeli land, words in hand, the spiritual nature of this storied place:

> We would stop there and sit down on the bench in the park, and he had wonderful long hair, nice hair, and he had a comb. I used to comb his hair. Isn't this wonderful?

Dafna spoke and her words shifted from past to present tense and her hands began to comb the narrative air, her eyes misted inward. It was a moment that even then, in the telling, took on treasured and recorded proportions:

> In Israel in the parks we have the picture-takers...men who used to come with their stands. Remember those cameras where you put your head inside and you had this black thing. (laughter) We had them, so from time to time, every so often, we used to take a picture of ourselves while on the way...sometimes.

Again it was a holy land of narrative conspiracy, one where the action, the characters, the setting were all in alignment, a medicine place, a sky home. And again it was lost or at the very least under the siege of aging and inevitable growth:

> And the sand is soft and white and wonderful...and then you'll meet your neighbors from next door because they also go to the beach, and you have the conversations, of course, and then when you grow up you don't go with your parents anymore.

The child Dafna had moved into her own space and into the perpetual and folkloral search back, what Langeveld (1983) calls the movement out of fantasy and into dreams. The beauty of the beach was all the more poignant for its disappearance:

> White sand and the water is very light blue...before it was...it's more polluted now...and we used to have lots and lots of dunes...but the more we build the country, the more they disappear....We build on them...and at the time we used to find lots of shells, but not anymore.

The secret place of the Israeli child then had shifted from the present to the represented, from the enacted to the recorded, from the cave shadow to the Platonic ideal. The memorable had become story and a story cast in the glow of a special sunlight. Dafna described this Israeli light as:

> When painters started to paint Israeli paintings at the beginning of the century, they called it...they painted with the Israeli light....It is almost always sunny, and the light is very strong, so it is almost always very, very bright, and it casts...this light is on everything.

By the metaphor of story, Dafna's childhood and her holy land were similarly cast in bright light. When she spoke, when her body spoke with its hand and shoulder shrugs and flashing eye punctuations, the listener, too, was bathed in the bright light of the narrative performance. The child has lived, the holy land has survived, for it was being narrated still. As Townsend (1987) restates, "We cannot look steadily at the sun or at death," and so we live as storytellers and listeners by the reflected light of a narrative moon (p. 139).

At home with the localized holy land of the beach was also Dafna's store of ritual story, one example being her teacher memory of the Israeli poem *The Golden Fish*:

> One day...a young fellow...tells his mother that he wants to go and look for the golden fish...and he builds a ship, and he takes it to the water....His eyes are sparkling and the sea, the day is bright and the sea is deep blue, light blue, and he goes on and goes there and one day and 2 days and 3 days and 4 days, and the sea becomes dark, very dark, and his eyes are shadowed and no golden fish...and the sun comes up and the sun goes down, and everybody goes on and on.

Where lived the holy seashore of her childhood, so lived also the sensation of the golden fish. The ritual and the local places, or as our elder Mosum would suggest, the seen and the heard, seemed to suffer no separation, no disconnection under the soft glow of retelling:

> And then one day Mother hears a knock on the window, and there is a seagull. And the seagull says something like, I don't remember the words, but the mother understands that he is never going to come back...of course it's not really a golden fish, but it is his truth, or his faith, or his whatever he was looking for life to give him...and, uh, it is actually something that you want out of life that you cannot get.

Both within and around the poetic folktale of *The Golden Fish* was Dafna's seashore. The narrator and the narrated verbally shared the same water, the same sand and the same bright light. Perhaps as teacher, Dafna had become spiritual guide to those who must also tell of their holy land. Dafna's students, for example, always asked why Mother didn't warn her young son of the impossible nature of his mission:

> We talk about that even if she would have told him, the young person needs to experience it for himself. We can never take someone else's truth and embrace it....You get the feeling of the sea, you know. It goes up and down, and you get the feeling of how the colors change from bright green and bright blue and white and the sun is shining, then everything becomes darker and darker.

Continuity and hope, as with Sparrow, come in the retelling. Dafna's holy land is a personal place, embraced and made real by the telling of its impossible nature. It is no wonder that breath has long been associated by the ancestors of all cultures as the centre of being, the centre of life. Is it any wonder that our most holy places, both the Mediterranean seashores and the Athabascan islands, are each reached through breath, silence and sound? Similarly, Carpenter (1972) shares this telling image of a Society Islander practice:

> When a sacred recorder (harepo), famous in life for ancient knowledge, is dying, his son and successor places his mouth over the mouth of the dying man to inhale the parting soul: in this way, lore is transmitted. (p. 128)

Albeit, the search for the golden fish and the holy land is a personal thing, its telling and breathing is made possible only by the silent listening of others, the same inhalations. When the folk fell from Lizard's chewed pole, it was not only the sound of injury and crying that was heard, the careful ear could also have heard the wakening and first sound of the first storyteller's first two syllables: "one time."

The storyteller Rattler was one similarly given to the enunciation of those two syllables, word weavings connected by great bouts of laughter, his bespectacled eyes upon his hazelnut and amaretto cream coffee then suddenly to my face and eyes. His word tales eased up on me like a prairie rattler, perhaps Le Guin's hoop snake, and when I was most relaxed, most at journey into the rattle of his words, he would strike. At the home and centre of his stories and story being was a sense of holy land as well. As listener, as fellow traveller, I have seen his special place, this place of walking around: it is the Red Deer "badlands" of Southern Alberta, hoo doo country, the remembered land of his childhood. Rattler's stories, wonderful concretions all, never strayed far from this special place. There was always a connection, be it a story of the Old Mexico Ranch, his grandfather the veterinarian, the trickster Shady Green, or a 9-year-old boy's willow airplane flight. There was always a tie back, like rawhide lariat from saddle horn to branding heel, always a tie back. Rattler once described his holy land this way:

> All that river land, particularly through the badlands....It's also the last of the short grass prairie in its natural state in the world, so it's a...not only do you have the traditions there, you have the, uh, environment as well. It's a peaceful spot. I often go and just sit there...and, uh, there's this one area where I still see a good many mule deer....They'll come jumping across the plains or coyote will come out and look at you, you know.

When Rattler did the narrative-time-slip-shuffle with his words, it was the "you know" that not only gave grammatical connection, but also determinacy to the listener's presence. As much as Rattler and I occupied chairs at the kitchen table and were thus situated in one geographic dimension, by the artistry of his narration, we knew no time bounds. Again, years, culture and experiences apart, Rattler joined with Sparrow and Dafna through the words of his holy land. It, too, was a place of water, river this time, and sun and uncluttered land. It, too, was clean of our human passing. The sounds were not necessarily quiet, but they were natural. No muffled motor hummed tastefully in the background. Similarly, the living and the telling took on the composition whereby the storyteller was first subject, part of the scene, and only later the metaphor, the verb, the teller:

> It's still wide open over there, occasionally even the cattle which roam there seem to have protective rights. I remember sitting there and I saw this great bull come out, and [he] gave a great beller, and I thought..."Is it time I should be leaving?"...But I sat there, and what it did, it called its flock in and away they went, follow the leader, about 150 cattle, and he took them to the farthest corner of the field, about 3 miles away...interloper!

Even the humor of the situation helped to give story to Rattler, to further locate and infuse one teller into his holy land. And when I asked Rattler of the ritual stories of a holy land, he recounted with wandering passion and little hesitation the creation story of Napi, Old Man. By way of introduction, Rattler first demonstrated his own relationship to the tale. Like all storytellers in all cultures, he first situated himself in time and place and person. This meant the acknowledgement of one's sources:

> He was an old, I suppose he'd been a storyteller in his 90s....I was talking to him a couple of times, you know. This was in the early 40s, so he would have been, he'd be telling stories that he'd remember from the, you know, almost 100 years before...and, uh, he was a Plains Cree, you see, and he was all through that Badlands Country. He always claimed that Indians from all over North America have a similar legend, and he thought it was in the valley....But they called it the Indian Eden, you see?

By these introductory remarks, Rattler not only situated the listener in relation to the emergent tale but placed himself in the same tradition of Old Man Creator and old man teller from Hobbema. And throughout the lengthy telling of this ritualized holy land, Rattler let the voices of his own education be heard:

> He was the son of God also, and he came down to earth and was wandering through that beautiful country, felt very lonely and restless, and he came to the hills just south of Stettler...and it was a big hill, a sort of butte, called the Gopher Head. It was shaped just like a gopher, and when Peter Fiddler came through 200 years ago last fall.

Every phrase within the story seemed to bring the storyteller home, seemed to more intricately weave letter into story, into listener, into everything:

> Napi decided to see if he could have a dream, a vision of how he was going to get over his loneliness. He lay down on the Gopher Head, and it is a very rocky hill....It's actually glacial till, you see, a glacial deposit.

The story moved on as did Old Man, and as Napi sought out a comfortable dreaming place, so Rattler moved his agile body about the kitchen table in empathetic search:

> He got up and lay down and put rocks all around where his body lay, you see, you can still see those rocks laying down there, the formation all laid out down there and you know his arms were out like this...his legs there splayed and strangely enough they have between his legs the figure of a turtle...creation.

And remarkably, as Napi walked around to the Red Deer, so we heard by Rattler's own search, his story within "the" story:

And, uh, just about the Tolman Bridge, there is a sacred site…this is very real. I found the pits there that the…from the Little People of the Plains…the pit houses the Little People of the Plains had lived in…I found last fall, no not last fall, spring. I found the tool they used for digging out these pits.

As the story of Napi was told, so Rattler relived the land, tracing the journey of the Creator to "the flat ledge," a flat butte overlooking what they call the "Indian Eden." Story pieced it all together, the ritualized creation and the private discovery, becoming finally more than the sum of its narrative parts. The story of Rattler's Eden, his ritual holy land, became a spell. I inhaled its sage and soul. While Old Man emerged in his search for the perfect creation place, so disappeared the individualized Rattler, the storyteller fading into his own words, making me heir to a similar creative impulse. And where I once sat, now waited the next storyteller. Words do not have to be in the holy places, but nevertheless, they often are. They are the way back to the holy land, and as we are so often instructed by our elders, we always do go back. Whatever the face, we always return, as Campbell (1949) so eloquently describes in the hero cycle. The return journey itself is a holy land.

Finally comfortable, Old Man is able to see the Red Deer flowing by, Buffalo Lake to the north, and is ultimately able to have the vision that must serve as precursor to an act of creation:

He was sleeping beautifully, and in it He had a vision that He would create a creature, uh, from the mud of the banks of the Red Deer and [so] in the morning.

Napis' created holy land stemmed from a state of comfort, of relaxation, much as Rattler's own creative tellings were situated in the comfort of the kitchen, its hazelnut coffee and tan cookies, the living room clock slowly ticking in its distance, poplar branches amusedly waving in the kitchen window. Old Man, Napi, and Rattler were brothers in this birthing act. Each creation depended upon another, the creation of man led directly to the creation of woman, to the creation of buffalo and all wrapped in the creation and narrative of a sacred tale.

As Rattler eased the tale to its completion, he returned to the landscape of the story and assured me that should I study and walk in his holy land I would find·it just as he had spoken. He could take me to the high hills where

Napi sought his comfort and Alberta Government Telephones put their tower; he could take me to Old Man's bed or to Buffalo Lake:

> The teaching was that that area was the Eden, the Old Man's bed was there, all those three spots where he had been uncomfortable, you see...the Buffalo Lake, which is in the shape of a buffalo, you can see it from the sky, from an airplane, but again this incredible ability of Indians to walk around something and know the exact shape of it.

It may be that a holy land is most recognized and remembered when one is no longer an inhabitant. As storyteller, Rattler, too, walked me around his holy land repeatedly through the visits and left me wonderfully free to determine the shape of that walk. I sensed a kindness that began with vision.

It is perhaps ironic that what one group of people called "the Badlands" another culture called "Eden." In his person, the storyteller Rattler seemed to bring these two very different worlds a bit closer together. By his words, he suggested that ultimately both groups would one day look inward to find this same holy land. Thus, Rattler expressed a need for the protection of the stony landscape:

> All that river land, particularly through the Badlands, will be government property, and they may lease some of it out to local farmers and so on, but you know, they'll have control of it. They are setting up the United Nations, I should say, tell you all that site of the holy ground is now part of the United Nations Heritage Trust.

In his stories, and particularly in some of the Rattler laughter, there was, however, a shadow, a melancholy like Sparrow's "other people" or Dafna's "disappearing dunes":

> [Napi] got up and He laid out the stones, which is still beautifully laid, you can still see the Turtle Formations, they are still in quite...except the head, when the cowboys first came, some Indian storytellers told them there was a fortune buried under the head of Napi, and of course they took it all out.

All three storytellers, all variations upon the holy land theme, took the narrative from celebration to protection. It was not enough to simply inform by story. Rattler through telling of his holy land, like all the storytellers, either found or put the mystery of God into the sun, into the sand, into the face of the water. And like Dafna, he became spiritual guide to others:

> I'll take you out and show you the creation country, you know, and show you the hills where all these traditions started from.

Or, when as a professional educator:

> I spent so much time in my last years of teaching taking them down in appreciation for the country cuz, you see, we're very fortunate in Alberta, there's still great paradises.

The student and listener can walk-round and know the shape of a holy land and through the telling of it be a part of the ceremony. For the northern Sabochees, the holy land was also the place of his birth. It was from where he had come. It was specific. It was also the place to which he periodically returned:

> Harper Creek, where I was born...sometimes I still stay almost a month, 2 weeks, 3 weeks there in in the summertime. Sometimes we stay in the wintertime, too. Like this winter, we stayed about 2 weeks....We came back just before Christmas.

Sabochees had accepted the storyteller's traditional gift of tobacco, but he did not smoke as he similarly journeyed inward and word painted his holy land, Harper Creek country. He had quit smoking for Lent and instead pushed the baby's ceiling swing as he chatted on:

> When you see it the first time, that place, everybody says it is beautiful country. It's good to look around, it's an open place, and it's good for everything.

Like Dafna, worlds away, his eyes misted inward, and his story hands began their accompaniment, their dance. The openness was told of with a right-hand sweeping gesture, long fingered and decisive, the back of his hand fire-burned in places:

> There are fish there in the creek, ducks, all kinds of different things that don't grow around here. They grow at Harper Creek. It's good for moose, too, especially in the wintertime, in February, they are starting to come back to the river. In February, that's when they come back.

The holy land is enough. It is where the people and the gifts of Mother Earth come together. It is a place intimately known by those ancestral:

Old people say, you know those red willows along the river, those red willows, that's what they [the moose] come for and the saskatoons. That's the time, that's what they say, too, in February sometime...it should be pretty soon now.

Again, the storyteller Sabochees extended the relationship from the holy land of his birth to his retelling and the revisiting of it. Just as the ducks that came to the sulphur creek were a gift from the Great Spirit, a gift to be respected, so the words from the Old Ones were such a gift, something to be treasured. And when the mustached and long black-haired Sabochees conversationally moved from the localized holy land of Harper Creek, the place he had seen, it was to a time when animals could speak and people could listen, to a metaphoric place of which he had heard. Sabochees then told the story of Mother Groundhog and her little ones:

A long time ago, kayas, kayas, our animal brothers, like the groundhog, used to talk. The Groundhog would spend its winter days under the ground, and in the spring it would come out. Mother Groundhog, too, spent her winter days under the ground with three babies. When she thought the cold days were at last over, she decided to go up and look. "Is it spring yet?" she wondered. She left the nest. When she returned she said, "No, spring has still not come, so you can't go out! Soon perhaps." Every few days, Mother Groundhog would go out and walk around the special place. When she returned, she always told her babies that spring was still far away. In truth, it was now summer, and Mother was lying to her babies. She was afraid that her children might get injured if they went outside.

Just as Sabochees's own children were to discover the gifts and medicine of Harper Creek, so the young ones in the story were to have their childhood, their special place of sun and sand and summer:

One summer day, Mother Groundhog went out and ate some green grass. "Still not spring, my children, but soon perhaps," she said upon her return. One of the baby groundhogs saw a piece of grass sticking to his mother's lip. It was spring outside! The next time Mother went out on a groundhog walk-round, the babies later followed. It was a beautiful day! The babies ran and jumped and danced in the soft green grass.

Sabochees's rhythmic voice went on; there were no pauses or wandering connectives, and when later he was asked why, he replied simply that he knew the story. There was a background wash of sled dog howl, then like Dafna and Sparrow and Rattler, the teller again and ominously faded into the ritual tale:

> Suddenly a marten crept up on the baby groundhogs! "I pulled a little groundhog in two," he sang as he killed the babies, one by one. The marten did not even eat the young but left them lying dead on the green grass. When Mother Groundhog returned home, she found her babies torn apart. "Noooo," she cried, "why did I hide spring from my children?" She could not bear to look upon the bodies of her loved ones, and so she walked tearfully to a nearby tree. Slowly she climbed halfway up the tree and stopped. "I shall stay here and grow to this tree and let all know of a mother's grief. The young must be given knowledge of the coming of spring." Even today you may find such trees, such growths, and such grief.

When the story stopped, the silence began. Sabochees then spoke of the usual response of his own children. "They cry," he said, "but that's o.k." The holy places, the stories, need retelling; for as Kroeber (1992) suggests, "Stories improve with retelling, are endlessly retold, and are told in order to be retold" (p. 1). Within repetition lies protection. The ritual, the groundhog story of spring in this context, existed in clear storyteller connection to the localized holy land. The groundhog nest may have been at Harper Creek. The witnessing of both came from the tellings. The holy places in Sabochees's life have everything to do with culture, as they do for Dafna and Rattler and Sparrow. They go to the centre of culture, but although they speak to the group, these holy places are told of by the individual:

> If somebody like an old man told you the story, then you could tell it yourself anytime. Anyone, it's yours, just like it is your own. That's the way they did it. When I get a story from some old people, my dad, my uncles, other old people...I've got those stories. They're mine now. That's the way it goes because I need a story. That old man gave me that story...I've got to use it for the young people.

Sun and sand and water mark the passings, storyteller to listener to storyteller, with the mythic needs of the group met by the spiritual powers of the individual. And again in the telling of these sacred places, Sabochees also struck that familiar and melancholy chord:

> If we don't go to school, like five families, if five families never go to school, just stay somewhere in the bush, that's where you're going to

find the stories. Out there, everything is good...the relationships of people...respect for the elders...respect anybody.

Stories need a holy land, but within the Sabochees pause of a "sky home lost," there is again hope in the telling:

> I know some young people like that, not all of them, but at least some of them....I know some young people that like to listen to stories right now. Some of them remember the stories. Sometimes they come to me and sometimes when we go somewhere in the bush, some young people will tell a story.

The storytellers walk-round with their words and briefly reveal a holy place and nature at the centre of their being, be it Sparrow and the Athabascan "Our Island," Dafna and the Mediterranean seashore, Rattler and the short grass "goodlands," or Sabochees and "out there" in Harper Creek Country. These medicine places are found both in the colloquial and the ritual, in the witnessed and the unwitnessed, in the seen and in the heard. They may be a place of birth, or rebirth certainly, and always with a connection to childhood. As for me, I, too, have a holy place. It is on a long sweeping river hill where the dark green and grey of bush meets the yellow grass of prairie. It is the canvas canoe that waits for me and the twisted sandbar river that carries me along. There I am a little boy still, with broken straw hat, cardboard six shooter and a belly full of washbasin jello. There I am freckled in the full joy of boyhood, blue jeans warmed by the hot chair of river hill, little boy fingers tickling first crocus. There I am the wind itself on back of bay Shetland pony. There I am part of the quicksand called holy:

> *And it seems*
> *that all the holy places*
> *in my firefly years*
> *have been eyebrowed by sage brush...*
> *the little river boy days*
> *of washbasin jello and black snake filled boots,*
> *the gopher and magpie hunts,*
> *the lady on a sweating bay mare*
> *and the Cree prayers*
> *of circulating berries, tobacco, and pain*
> *by the rock and sage steam...*
> *these days*
> *I carry a little dried sage in my hat band*

> that I can slip out and smell
> when I am in a tight corner
> wishing that I had laughed with Grandfather
> one last time
> and needing my Holy Land...

> "What will the young do
> when the hardship comes?"
> Grandfather used to say
> before he joined the chorus line of the Northern Lights
> and faded into the Holy Land and smell of sage.

That one river hill, specific and holy as it was, grew over the years and through the medicine of story into a more ritualized place. My holy land became and is today the "land of character." Our kitchen table was always a place of character, either real or just discussed. It is where I met the great brooding grandfather and had first glimpse of his tin snips, wide-eye listened to the cowfolk couple Jim and Georgie dressed in their American pointy boots and Bull Durham roll-your-own cigarettes, the Grade 1 school marm who square-danced river youngsters through their academic days, an 80-year-old Grandma who straight-back ice skated each Sunday to the band, long-johned Skinny who lovingly cut both ears off his river cows; my holy land became a storied place where the "characters" lived. They marked each landscape with the word spurs of their passing. And as Todorov (1977, p. 76) writes, in order for them to be fully alive, they had to narrate. The characters walked-round and became my Old Man of narrative, and they gave one prairie boy back to the soul of the place. The C.P.R. slough in the front field became the place where the horse Golden Nugget bogged down on rodeo day, Big Joe's smokey pool hall was where old Paul had his heart attack, and by the railroad tracks little boys found flare tips for their spear hunts. Story place brought the sun and the sand and the water into alignment. As Carpenter (1972, p. 128) writes, often to a child, the words are partly the thing. They characterized the landscape and made my ceremony of boyhood complete. I discovered myself in the stories of my holy land and came to prairie terms with what Townsend (1981) calls "the human predicament of being mortal" (p. 139).

Mollel, Tanzanian author and storyteller extraordinaire, shared this similar glimpse of his holy land, his boyhood:

> I guess my holy land would be my childhood because that's almost like storyland, like where many things happened...the place where my father

was teaching....It was away away from Arusha, and it was kind of like open country...and it seemed to me like everything was possible at that time, and there was a river that ran through this place all year round, which was unusual, a lot of rivers dried up in the dry season, but this one ran all year round...and the soil was really good, you could grow anything and-uh anytime of the year because you could irrigate....You could go anywhere, and-uh in the bush it was unconstricted.

It, too, was a place in and out of time. The storytellers all, Sparrow, Dafna, Rattler, and Sabochees, drew a similar parallel from the unconstricted character of their holy lands, external, to the childhood character of their holy lands, internal. Just as their thoughts separated them from the sun and the water into a later narrative memory or represented state, so their expressed thoughts also took them back into the land. That heroic act of separation and return was a holy undertaking. It happened because they, like all mythic characters, dared to walk-round and inhabit for a time the openness, all year-round. Their journeys tell me, as an educator, of the vital importance of the holy places and of the secret power of where we metaphorically live. In the telling of our embedded lives, story is indeed a holy landscape, and one that calls:

> Sometime, surely, for whether we hear it or not, we are continually hailed, continually being summoned. We need to make a silence for that summons. (Travers, 1989, p. 128)

Deer Hide Painting:
The Story Birds of Hope

Hope is a Rattlesnake on Your Bedroll

If individual heart cells are placed in a petri dish, each contracts with its own individual rhythm. When some critical number of cells is reached, however, all fall into a synchrony which is characteristic of the normal action of the heart. (Combs & Holland, 1990, p. 43)

Story is hope. In the particular metaphor, the bridge of narrative, is expressed and so found the elusive hope. Hope is a rattlesnake on a bedroll, a plantation worker who could fly, a saddle that chose haunthood over oblivion, a rice cake for the waiting tiger, the masquematuay or bag of rolling meat. Hope is all of this: it is the people, it is their stories and their flights:

At Jenner,
1955,
one room prairie school,
I must remember
the swing
and its license to sky heaven.
First, at first,
little boy legs down,
then pump, hip pump, hip, hip pump, pump and back glide...
And then at the end of recess
hand bell grade 8 boy ringing,
hip pump and back glide and let
go
go
go
full high
and wide
to the sky...
airborne, born of ai...
freckled boy to the cloud freckled sky...
down only much later...
if if ever, if ever...

Hope is a swing at rest,
feet in toe-grooved earth,
still and possible.
Hip pump and back glide and sometime release,
that in a metaphor

is the joy and hope of story.

You choose,
swing and hope at rest
or board and rope swing into little boy sky.

Through the fragile narrative weave of metaphor, the individual becomes part of the story fabric of her community and so learns hope. If living is art, and not simply behavior, then any elaboration of that art, any elaboration upon hope would engage our most human and expressive faculties. In metaphor, through metaphor, we are able to both capture and enhance. Our expressive interpretation is itself story, and thus, by celebrating the storied hope of others, we give hope. As Shor and Freire (1987) suggest, to the extent that knowing is unveiling an object, the unveiling gives the object "life," calls it into "life," even gives it new "life" (p. 118).

And I would add that this unveiling gives hope. Our metaphors allow us to travel beyond our systems and, as Bruner (1990) writes, "explore connections that were before unsuspected" (p. 20). By metaphor we are able, you and I, to fly, to fly if only we know the opening magic words: born of air and sometimes release.

Hamilton (1985) retold a most incredible story of how her people could fly. It is a story of hope:

> You know, long ago, people in Africa knew magic and knew the way of walking up into the air. When folks were taken for slavery, they shed their wings because of the crowded conditions on the slave ships. They shed their wings but they kept their power. It was a secret in this new land of slavery and struggle. One such old man, Toby, worried over the young mother Sarah. She was "worked and scorned." One day the baby on her hoeing and chopping back began to cry and cry. The hard as coal driver cracked his whip and the mother and child fell to the earth. Toby came to her side and she whispered "I must go soon." Driver kept whipping and cursing and mother and child bled into the earth. "Now Father," she cried out at last to Toby. The old man said the magic words, words as soft as whispers, and the mother and child flew up into the air. The magic, "the African mystery," carried her up right over the trees. No one spoke of it, and although Overseer rode cursing after Sarah, she was soon gone from the eye. The next day several fell from the heat and each time Toby said the words over them and each time they flew away, over the fields and the creeks. "Grab that old man that is saying those magic words" screamed the Overseer. Toby just

laughed out…"we're the ones who fly." And all those who could fly, straightened up, joined hands and rose up into the sky. They flew away to freedom, they did. Some stayed behind, not knowing how to fly, waiting instead for the chance to run. Driver and Master said it was "a trick of the light."

And those who couldn't fly, told their children of it when they were free. "When they sat close before the fire in the free land, they told it. They did so love firelight and Free-dom and tellin." (p. 166)

Hope is all about shedding the wings but keeping the power. Hope is someone knowing the right words at the right time. Hope is about flying (and about telling). Hope is about one's people. And so with my own storytellers, all about the foundation stone of their own particular kitchen tables came the unveiling of hope. With Sparrow, her young fingers curled about the glass of Pepsi™, talk was story. And although Sparrow was only 10 years of age, the talk would inevitably turn to the cloud over planet earth, literally:

The ozone layer…can't go outside like in the summertime, it'd burn your skin, like for more than half an hour say, a little, if it's really hot out, sort of, like don't wear muscle shirts anymore…that's what they say.

So young to lose the holy land, the sky was falling for Sparrow and, even more poignant, her separation from the environment and her perceived loss of the trees. How does a little girl climb like a trickster to Heaven without trees:

They pollute the earth, and they kill trees, but then they plant them again, and they still kill them and plant them and kill them…so what's the use of them planting trees….If they plant them, they are still going to kill them again…and they, like they use a lot of machinery and that still pollutes yet. It kills animals and pollutes the rivers and lakes…lots of stuff.

Those charms that most characterized a little storyteller's sense of the holy, the sun and the soil and the water, seemed to be the most threatened by the pernicious "they": they the doom speakers, they the rechopper of trees. And yet in that same conversation, and in the same breath, our Sparrow turned from the once unimaginable scenario of planetary suicide to talk of a different kind of tree and a different kind of imagining, one filled with hope:

The best time is Christmas time when you set up the tree and you're watching the news and only the tree lights are on, like it makes me feel so comfortable....Even at school we have a Christmas tree in our classroom, and it makes me feel so comfortable....Christmas Eve is like the best day...you're waiting and waiting...the night's funner yet, like you're just waiting, you can't wait until the morning and you go to sleep, don't worry, it's not going to last, last, it's not going to last long, you can't even tell when you're sleeping.

And what could be more deliciously hopeful than a child on a gift-giving eve? Most important for Sparrow, the next day always brought her family, her people, and in that relationship there was a hope secured:

Mom made a rule last year. You cannot wake up more than over 8:30 in the morning....[One sister] would go into [another sister's] bed, and they'd talk and they'd wonder what they'd get, and then I and my brother would read until 8:30...and then we'd go to Grannie and Grandpa's and open the presents...and show other people and like maybe phone your friends and ask what they got...and every year we make a place like where'll we go...all sorts of kids running around the house, and there's this big table of desserts because there's lots of people in our family.

Sparrow was able to balance and discover the generalized story of universal dilemma within the localized tales of her own people. Again ceremony was protection. She looked to the elders to perform and protect her sense of ceremony. The way it was last time is the way it will be and should be next time. As all middle-aged storytellers soon learn, one does not tinker with a child's sense of proper story. Richly steeped in story as she was, Sparrow had developed a keen sense of the possible and what the impossible sometimes required of one. According to Tolkien, within the folkloral story, the youngster is able to experience "escape, recovery, and consolation" (Baker, 1981, p. 15). Thus, through the folkloral act, through the storying of her experience, Sparrow was able to ritualize hope in both escape and recovery, as the listener discovered in Sparrow's telling of *David and Goliath*. Story enabled frustration to become understanding:

Then there was this really strong man, and there was David, and David was not very strong and everything. He was a shepherd....Goliath had long black hair, and he looks strong, and he just had like a sort of like a small top and small shorts and sort like wearing the fur and really strong and drool coming out of his mouth and everything....He looks really mean and scary....David, I think, has curly blonde hair or reddish or a little light red hair, and I think he has curly hair, and he wears whites like with his things and strap and just sort of like a little dress thing.

Hope was given a ritual body by the storyteller and wore "whites with his things":

I don't know why he had to fight with him...something about his religion probably....He started with a fight, and he was weak and everything, but then he got praised like in blessed...like he only had a slingshot. The other guy had whips and everything, and David did get hurt a little, but then he he shot his slingshot and just shot it right here...and the guy just about died, I think he did.

When Sparrow completed the traditional tale, she considered again the upset, the win against all odds, and added:

I betcha [David] got blessed by God and he got, he was allowed...he...if he just shot him, even if he just touched him a Little Bit, he'd probably fall down.

It was not important that David only fight, anyone can do that. It was important, however, that he have curly hair and be blessed by God. Both David and God needed one another. Together, in relationship, they were the narrative instrument of hope, and together they provided one small storyteller with the Jungian archetype she needed in a world that could imagine global annihilation. Story facilitated the kind of interiority that allowed a child to travel from escape to recovery to consolation. Sparrow turned round to her kitchen window and pointed to last night's new calf, a 90-pound metaphor, one that would keep us all from dissolving into the window pane. We go our separate ways in story, but as Sparrow consistently demonstrated, in the telling we are all one. In the telling we are consoled. As the wordsmith Le Guin (1980/1981) writes, "Take the tale in your teeth, then, and bite 'til the blood runs, hoping it's not poison" (p. 195).

In his delightful meandering way, Rattler, too, bit the tale. Words were either his current story or the conversation that joined stories together. Softly spoken, intimating, feint and verbal thrust, Grandfather Rattler taught the listener of the metaphoric relationship of talk to tale. The tale was third person island in the river; it had a beginning and an end, sort of, and was at arm's length from the storyteller. Story talk, on the other hand, was the other side of Grimm's mirror. It was the conversational sheath that held the folkloral sword, the intimacy of the first person vernacular, the windbreak of the storyteller's life.

It was this interplay of conversation and story, Rattler tale and Rattler talk, that signaled such hope to me. It was hope, be it battered and bloodied at times, that endured and suggested and flew with me to the end of the tale and through the Alberta night. And if metaphorically the tales were islands, the talk and the river water body, then it was hope that gave current to the life called river. Annie Dillard (1991) urges the penholder to "write as if you are dying" (p. xii). Good storytellers, like our Rattler, did that also. They told as if they were dying. There was no abbreviation, and by that urgency or care or story, they gave hope to me. The air around them became an electric hopeful place as when our Grandfather told of the rattlesnake on his bedroll. It began, as always, with his sideways winding into the story:

> I can now connect with more real history than I could in the past because this was history that was lost in an Anglican church in Ottawa....The first mission work was done by Father Lacombe, then by an Anglican missionary, but it was a pocket of history there that was completely lost until he dug it out of this old mission in Ottawa.

It was this interest and connection with the historical that led Rattler to the task of indexing a provincial history series and to the Blackfoot Reserve for an interview. As it turned out, Rattler had gone to school with the Chief's sister, years before, another connection:

> I got reacquainted with [the Chief], and I knew he knew a lot of traditional Indian sites...in the back country where no one ever got on to, you see....It was almost sacred land, you see, he had to somehow pick the person he took on to it, at any rate, he took his camper and we went down.

I sensed that it was no flip of the coin that took Rattler to his awaiting fate, just as it was no act of mere chance that brought me to Grandfather's kitchen table. Rather, a thousand early morning spider webs tied the thing together. Did the story begin with Father Lacombe or Rattler's school-day acquaintance, or did the story begin at all? Was it always on the way, in hibernation, waiting for the verbal intimations and trails of a syllable spring:

You used to go out with miles and miles with nothing but miles and miles of trails, and he was heading out, and all of a sudden, we turned a left turn, another trail, right turn and another trail.

Grandfather had me, the listener; he knew it, and I knew it. Each detail of the trip to fate was added on lovingly, not in an informational way, but in the sheer joy of the episodic telling, the event. And as I, the listener, bounced across the miles of Blackfoot prairie, I heard of the "Little People of the Plains," of the eastern Blackfoot, of Crowfoot and more. Finally, Rattler and I arrived with the Chief at a particular knoll:

"You know," he said, "Indians always camped on a knoll in evenings because winds keep mosquitoes away," which makes sense, you see.

The storyteller Rattler slipped in and out of the various personae: now Chief and guide, now historian and tourist, now storyteller in reflection. It was with delightful jocularity that I heard through the supper, to the evening, with the Chief retiring to his truck camper, "whiteman style," and Rattler retiring to his bedroll by the campfire, "Indian style." And then it happened, as we knew it must:

I woke up, I suppose probably around 4 and no sign of sunshine yet, but there was a slight glimmering in the east that you know you could see that the sun would be coming up shortly...and I had a feeling that on the back, the bottom side of my sleeping bag, I wasn't alone. (laughter) Just a pressure there; I felt a pressure....I felt a pressure. (laughter) Isn't that funny? So I had my flashlight under the thing just in case something did come up or I heard some sounds around and I could spot something, so I got the flashlight up and I peered up and I turned it on and I saw undoubtedly the biggest rattlesnake in Western Canada....He was all curled up, you know, in a nice roll, fast asleep....I guess it was a cold night.

Rattler had reached that precious moment in the story when time becomes something else, the place when Toby's words caused Sarah to fly, the place when Sparrow gazed upon the Christmas Eve tree. Like Scheherazade from *The Arabian Nights*, who told her tales to live and awaited each separate dawn, I waited with the teller for the sun to come up:

It was the longest night of my life, I can tell you that. (laughter)...I didn't stir a muscle, I just lay there, and finally dawn slowly rose, and hours and hours and hours later, the sun started taking off a bit…and the mists were rising and it was probably a very beautiful morning. (laughter)…The sun was heating things up, and I felt a slight movement.

There was a relationship between the slow rising of the sun and the storyteller's words. Both were full of promise and hope, but most of all, both were full of suspense. How would it end? And at this point of the story, I felt a weight on my own legs:

> It gradually, inch by inch, uncoiled, you see (laughter)…but it seemed to take 2 or 3 hours. (laughter)…I could just see this forked tongue shooting out…and gradually saw the thing roll out and slide into the grass and took off…to my great sigh of relief!

The relief belonged not only to the campfire Rattler, but also again to the storyteller and, perhaps most of all, to the listener. We all "bit the tale until the blood ran" and found it was not poison. In the spirit of Tolkien, we escaped and recovered. Our consolation came with the denouement, the final unraveling. I, the listener, learned of Rattler's eventual rising and early morning slingshot hunt for partridges. And with the now awakened Chief's mention of the penalties for poaching on Blackfoot land, a humbled Rattler confessed to his night adventure:

> "You know," the Chief said, "practically everyone that sleeps out has a similar experience to that around here….I think our rattlesnakes are spoiled!"

In Le Guin's (1980/1981) words of magic, "We all come to the end together, and even to the beginning: living, as we do, in the middle" (p. 195). Rattler gave us hope in the middle, the kind of hope that would comfort us in the celebration of our beginnings and comfort us in the contemplation of our ends. Like both Hamilton and Sparrow, we learn to fly in the magic of the words, and, as Pesimwastches also confirmed, in the exchange of power that always takes place between teller and listener. Rosen (1986) describes this exchange as a kind of seduction:

> Seduction is the means by which the storyteller acquires the right to narrate, displaying a capacity to occupy the conversational space of others without possessing it. (p. 236)

Rattler received the listener's traditional gift of "conversational space" and in his turn gave hope. His laughter, his escape was my own. For the medicine of personal hope, however, Rattler turned in his story talk to the example of his elders:

> Hail storms, epidemics...when you mentioned tragedies there was always eternal hope there, you know. They looked upon the tragedy itself as a challenge, you know...there was something more than a tragedy...."Well there was a tragedy, let's leave and go somewhere else." No, just accept it...death was part of living.

Rattler, again with tale, recounted a time in 1936 when two of his closest friends were drowned on a school night:

> I was supposed to go swimming with them that night, too....My mother wouldn't let me go.

It was the acceptance of this reality, be it tragic or comic, that gave Grandfather hope:

> I remember the next day, the teacher came in, you know. It was a one-room rural school, and we talked for about half an hour about what wonderful two brothers, boys, these were....Then she just sent us home, just dismissed the school....She said, "We'll just keep this in mind." I don't remember anyone having great trauma over it. They accepted this, you know....I think children today...I sometimes wonder if they live in a very unreal world.

Rattler lived and told of a world that cherished and celebrated its own "realism." He suggested that reality was hope and that only an unconfined spirit could clearly perceive this same reality. Through his brief anecdote of the Blackfoot spirit stones, Grandfather gave narrative structure to his meaning and allowed the listener to again witness hope:

> Everything lived...and the rocks were the home of the spirit, you see, the spirits...and the Indians had these special spirit stones which had to be specially blessed and remember I told you that I removed that one, a year or two ago, and it was going back to its niche...because they always kept a niche about the rock. Whenever I found one of these rock walls with holes in it, I'd climb up and feel up to it, just reach where what seems to be a natural reaching spot, and invariably,

there was a little pocket in there, and that is where it would be. It was left for the next person who would come and want to use it. And they drilled holes in the rock, and that was part of the ceremony of letting the spirit free. Once the buffalo spirit was out, then it meant it was safe to go hunting. The buffalo spirit would let them kill safely.

By drilling a hole in the face of the buffalo jump, the spirit of the buffalo was freed. As in Sparrow's story, it was the task of the older ones to perform this ceremony, just as it was the task of the youngsters to witness. Both ages gave the other hope. It was within the power of the one to liberate the other. Rattler spoke of the young:

> There's a period in which they [the young] have got to get confidence in themselves, enough to really want to....Once they get their confidence, you let their spirit free.

In story we are able to witness the little prairie boy swinging to the sky, Sarah disappearing like an eagle, Rattler praying to the night sky for the dawn, and buffalo spirit waiting for the stone:

> We are here to witness. There is nothing else to do with those mute materials we do not need. Until Larry teaches his stone to talk, until God changes his mind, or until the pagan gods slip back to their hilltop groves, all we can do with the whole inhuman array is watch it. (Dillard, 1982b, p. 24)

And we are here in optative witness, I think, that the sun will come up and that the rattler will flick his tongue then slip off to other prairies. Similarly, Dafna's very presence was hopeful and hope giving, filled as it was with animation and quick release. In her profound expression of Hebrew past and Israeli future, the listener felt an optimism for the human species, albeit a sometimes painful optimism. Again, both conversation and story, talk and tale, the colloquial and the ritual collaborated in the storytelling of her life. The result, as Clandinin and Connelly (1991) describe, is a life of narrative, unified, "seamless" in the retelling (p. 5).

It was a retelling by which Dafna the person was fastened to Dafna the people by a thousand narrative stitches. I felt at times that the noun hope was poetically synonymous with the noun people, the body social:

Everything we did as a child and as a school student, we always did it together as a class. We were a community and a class....We went on trips together, we did bonfire together, we went to movies together.

And at a later point in her narrative journey, Dafna told it this way:

> I do not look upon myself as an isolated island. I see myself as part and parcel of my culture and religion....I really felt that my thought is based on the tradition of hundreds of sages that came before me.

The storyteller Dafna was always in context, and hope emerged in that wonderful interplay of tradition and change, proud of the past and excited by the prospects of the future. At the centre of her context, at the centre of her person, was family, the story of her own ancestral line:

> My parents and the aunts were just like, you couldn't believe how close they were. So we celebrated all the holidays together, a wonderful feeling of closeness and trust and love that we shared.

Like Sparrow, that sense of family was confirmed for Dafna by her participation and subsequent retelling of the ceremony that bound all together:

> When I got married, I took over the place of my mother...so all the family gatherings, not even large, first we were smaller but then my sister and her family and my mother-in-law, father-in-law, and sometimes my husband's sister and her family, we would celebrate together....So the best memories of meals I have and I can still envision is among the people.

Be it at bonfire or be it at family table, there are times when existence, the stark fact of existence is cause for consolation and hope. Those kinds of stories are again in the folkloral tradition of escape and recovery:

> The best meals that we have are always with the larger family....This is still a tradition with me. That's how I grew up....See, most of my family perished in the Holocaust...most of my mother's brothers and sisters and my father's brothers and sisters.

In Dafna's stories, then, hope had everything to do with survival. As they say we narrate to live, and a good story, a story around the table or campfire is the sometime pinch we need to remind us that we have indeed survived and even healed. Or as Baker (1981) suggests, our tales demonstrate that "experience is really a form of faith" (Introduction). I believe that we listen for the stories that we need. Perhaps survival is that very interplay between experience and story.

On one particular occasion, Dafna sat at her kitchen table, the olives and cheeses and sambusak before us, her dark eyes aglow, and she talked of faith and hope:

> I don't remember which English philosopher said that "a man is a wolf, man to man, homino, hominus lupus, a man treats a man as a wolf." I'm not sure. Even if you had this point of view, still the survival part of it, maybe not out of love, but maybe you just want to survive...and I still have a little hope that we'll do it out of love, not just survival. I have hope. I have hope in the spirit of man.

Echoes here of Rattler's spirit stones and the sense that the transmission of hope is itself an unconfining and liberative act, for a people who could also fly:

> I have hope....It was strengthened from my experiences teaching because for many years I taught in very underprivileged neighborhoods....Even as a soldier, what I've seen as an Israeli and I know that if you gave them hope...they did well....I still have some hope.

Hope was sometimes the little act, the shared kindness:

> Let's say as a teacher you see someone who forgot his [lunch]...you automatically say who can share his so and so, and they will share...and they always come to you and offer "my mother baked these cookies, try one."..."I know you love strawberries, and [my father] just brought fresh ones."

Rosen (1985) reminds us that "we are disposed to arrange around people and things a meaningful sequence of events," with narrative as a way of the mind (p. 7). If human disposition promotes survival, then it is indeed hope that gives meaning to the sequence of events. It is hope and kindness that winds up the chronology of narrative happenings, and it is hope that connects our dispositions to our metaphors. It is hope that enables us to learn the big lessons in life while standing on one foot:

> There is a story that tells of one Gentile person, a non-Jewish person, who came to Rabbi Shamahi and asked him to teach him the Jewish

religion while he is standing on one foot....Not literally, of course, but in a hurry. So [Rabbi Shamahi] used to walk with a cane, so he just kicked [the Gentile] with the cane, and he said, "Go away from me. How do you expect me to teach you the Jewish religion on one foot?" So off [the Gentile] went to see the Rabbi Hillel, and the Gentile said the same thing, "Could you please teach me the Jewish faith while I am standing on one foot?" So Rabbi Hillel said, "Love thy neighbor like yourself, and the rest go and learn yourself. That's all you need to know."

It is within these stories of her people that Dafna both received and extended hope. Stories became much more than the sequence of events or well-performed utterances. They expressed the right reason for survival, and most stories, not all perhaps, but most could be heard while the ordinary listener stood on one foot. Just as Rattler's 1936 teacher said, "We'll just keep this in mind," so Dafna's many tales, both public and personal, have that aftertaste about them. I was able to take hope and heart and, in the magic and mystery of words, take later flight.

In the retelling of her childhood, just as Rattler had prayed for the emergence of sun, Dafna expressed that artful blend of suspense and hope in this story of Israeli train travel:

For many years I was an only child, and many times since, we only had a one day of weekend, just Saturday....My parents would go....We lived in Tel Aviv, and my mother's sister lived in Haifa....It is only about 100 kilometers...nothing, but in those days when you don't have a car, many times we used to take the train. Now we would go many times on holidays...and in the morning or afternoon, we would leave and go until it was over, the day back. This was the peak season, of course. Everyone was taking the train, so many times when we would want to go back, we would come to the station with our suitcases and there were thousands of people trying to get in! So my dad, and this is when the most frightening thing would happen...he used to pick me up, through the window, and put me inside and say, "Take the seats," and throw the suitcases after me! And I always had this awful fear that the train would take off and they would [stay behind] and I would go by myself! Oh I can't imagine this experience! It was an awful experience, and it kept on like that for many, many years! They would push me through the window.

Dafna paused after the telling, brief laughter, then assured me that her parents always did manage to get on the train. This same 1950 train journeyed throughout her stories, pulling the narrative coaches of suspense and hope and laughter and family and everything. It became one child's task to mind the suitcases and one storyteller's later pleasure to mind the stories, to further the conversation, to herself give hope:

> You feel that people have gone so many places before you…and there is something to get comfort from…sharing helps a lot…and especially those stories which touch upon simple people's lives because that's what you are….I come from a long, long family…not a long family, it's a long tradition, and it's one that never stops….I feel that I have something to give to my children, too, and they will probably carry it on to their children.

The train always moved on. The only child, with one eye on the suitcases and one for her approaching family in the crowd, learned to endure the times of "what if." The narrative seat was later held by an older Dafna, the train did move on, and the "what ifs" that did not go completely away became livable in the telling. The people, too, survived to tell of it, 30 years in the struggle and recall, 3000 years in the struggle and recall. They survived. Hope was alive. In the words of Davidson, "Understanding a metaphor is as much a creative endeavor as making a metaphor, and as little guided by the rules" (Sacks, 1978, p. 29). Hope was a train with all aboard. Hope was a people who survived to become their own metaphor.

Grandfather Mosum spoke lovingly, as well, of hope for his people, and in doing so, he continually returned to a faith in the Great Spirit. It was, however, a belief saddened by the current state of affairs on this, the living side:

> People don't understand each other, different countries, different cultures, different races, but they can't understand each other, and the other thing, one of the things that is placed above everything is, in many cases, the money, and that causes the division. The welfare of the people is placed back, and so a lot of people think more of the money than of their own, the young people. And the other thing is that people don't, because they think of the money so much, they don't think of leaving their life in this world…they don't think about God. What gives me hope is prayer and thoughts of God. God and prayers give me hope, to keep on going. God is the Only One that can change everything that has happened today.

Grandfather spoke softly in Cree, and as he did so, the grandchildren played in the next room. Hope was near at hand. There were echoes here of the African mystery, of special powers with the wings left behind when I offered Ni-Mosum the traditional gift of storyteller tobacco. Grandfather had responded with "and do you want a story of what I've seen or a story of what I've heard?" Hope must come that way to the elder as well, hope in the alignment of the seen and the heard. As deeply as our Grandfather did despair, in his faithful presence, in his calm, and especially in his laughter, I, the listener, did take hope. His admitted separation from the living world gave authority and hope and presence to the other side. A northern friend expressed this elder benefice this way:

> Nine times out of 10 the elder doesn't understand TV or radio, and if you're to translate what happened or what's happening on the other side of the world...the elder doesn't get excited for one thing....He sits there, thinks about it and has a way with words that makes you feel good....Just the words that he used or that she would use makes everything seem that it's going to turn out right, it's going to turn out all right, for whatever's happening out there...it's not, you know, don't lose hope, that you've got to have faith for one thing....From an elder, there's always hope....I always feel good after listening to one speak.

Again, there are those magic words, invocation to Sarah's flight, invocation to a Christmas tree, invocation to a rattlesnake dawn, invocation to a waiting train and now invocation to a northern elder. The words of the elder most often take the form of story for within story is the room to maneuver in the sound and silence, the gift of conversational space. "Living things act as they do because they are so organized as to take actions that prevent their dissolution into their surroundings," Young suggests (Mitchell, 1980, p. 193). Grandfather was one who with story helped the people stand out from their surroundings. Grandfather was story, and the continuance of his person, his continued telling was itself hope. Pesimwastches spoke of this relationship of aging to hope:

> That's my hope, that the stories will continue....When I see with my eyes that that person is putting on the emotions, the actual happenings of the story, the actual what is around, you know, then I know if I'm going to be able to tell that story. I have a head and I'll pass it on to a young person when I grow, when I'm old, when I talk to kids....You can feel the person's eye with the story...that person will never forget the story....I have the hope that storytelling will continue.

And although story is everything about the seen and the heard, like Dafna's narrative time slip from 30 to 3000 years ago, it is the stories of the elders that carry in their bones the spirit of prophecy. There must exist a fragile relationship between the verb prophecy and the noun hope:

> Everything God put on this earth has a spirit, and the language has a spirit itself...and if we believe in that spirit, it'll help you. It'll give you the powers to live. When you believe in powers like that, some powers will help you be able to predict the future through these, just by understanding.

For Pesimwastches, the spirit of God lived in the spirit of language and story. And the surprise is not that story could foretell the future but rather that anyone could be so spiritless as to have no prophecy, no future:

> Stories have a spirit in themselves, same thing with songs, songs that we sing; they have, each one of them has some sort of a spirit, something to tell the soul.

Hope came in this message to the soul, this prophecy. Another respected northern elder, Sakastenohk, gave his prophetic antecedents this way:

> What I hear from my Grandfather, the one I was working with, you know, they were telling me what I'm going to see, how the world is going to be changed, the things I'm going to see.

Prophecy was a cloud ladder to God, a way back to the sky home. That some would have such a gift was itself hope, albeit at times a painful vision:

> And the God is going to change this earth. There's not going to be water. There's not going to be fire. But it's going to be starvation....Everything is going to be polluted, the grain is not going to grow....There's going to be a sickness, there won't be no cure, but the sickness is at the doctor's side....The people they're not going to respect their own lives. They are not going to respect the next person's life. That's what they used to tell me. I seen that too already.

With Sakastenohk and Mosum, the recognition of self within culture meant the possibility of liberation from fate. There was a telling relationship between material affluence and spiritual poverty. To listen to the old people and the old stories was to release the spirit from the quicksand of materialism. There was a need for the listener to hear the story, for the individual to step out of his/her social context long enough to learn respect:

My wish is they can have that respect and understanding...respect what they're doing here in a daily basis...try to learn our children, you know, what the respect is and understanding. I think that's the only protection.

Fox (1991) writes that our habitations, as awesome as they are, are "also earth, earth recycled by humans who themselves are earth standing on two legs with movable thumbs and immense imaginations" (p. 7). Elders remind us with prophecy and story that when most in the midst of our creations and cupidity we stand most as the created. Story causes upward gazing eyes to occasionally glance down and learn respect. Elders remind us also that although we hurriedly recycle and retell from one new thing to the other we are in desperate need of the pause and unhurried silence that story gives. And finally, elders are themselves the remembrancers, those through whom our stories and lives are not acts of mere happenstance or random occurrence. They give us what Combs and Holland (1990) call "agency that operates behind the scenes" (p. xi). They help us believe that all of this has both witness and purpose.

From the northern kitchen table of our elder Sabochees came this folkloral embodiment of hope, the story of *Masquematuay*. As he told it, with pause but no swerving, Sabochees left his muskeg tea untouched:

> Many winters ago a family, living in a teepee in a northern bush, experienced great hardships. There was no food at all, and the people grew weak, the children cried from their hunger. The hunters tried each day but met with no success. Eventually the parents could no longer stand. Then one bitterly cold morning, a bag full of meats, a "masquematuay," came rolling into the teepee. It instructed a little boy with bow and arrow to shoot it. He did so, and the life-giving meat tumbled out as the masquematuay circled the fire. Moments later, meat still spilling out, the bag rolled out of the lodge and from sight. The child shook his mother awake and shared with her the meat and its story. Soon everyone was able to move again, and they then followed the trail of the masquematuay. It led to a cache of meat, previously buried under the snow. This meat gave life, and soon the hunters were killing moose again. Masquematuay and one child's arrow had saved the people.

In that story, the listener was given agency and hope. The people were worthy of spiritual intervention. The people were also worthy of a story that would provide succor to countless others. Masquematuay indeed saved one family unit, but the story *Masquematuay* gave narrative embodiment to the agency of hope: "We are all a plurality of other stories, including our own"

(Rosen, 1986, p. 236). It is that narrative plurality and its celebration that give protection, the first function of hope.

There were echoes of these northern storytellers in other parts of the globe as well. Tololwa Mollel, with illustrations from his children's books framed on the wall behind him, also spoke of this expectation of good. Once again hope was in the recounting. Hope was from where he came:

> What is it that gives me hope....Maybe it's where I come from, my background...the fact that we didn't drop from the sky, that-ah you know, we descended from somebody. I have another place where I can take the kids...that really gives me hope that I've got all these stories that I can pass on to them, like where I grew up in a different place, my Grandfather was this, and we had a coffee farm, and-uh, there were certain values, and there was a certain order to a life....I don't think about it a lot of the times, but whenever I do...I think back on where I came from.

There is that sense of an earthly origin but always in light of a destiny that looks heavenward and with expectancy. The storyteller was able to give "a certain order to life," just as the northern storyteller found order in prophecy. Both take the situation, the experience, and breathe it full of possibility, a sort of counter-reductionism. Thus, from the stories of hope, the children have gained not only the traditional tales, but also the means to trust, the manner by which the young speak the magic words and attempt their own flights into the horizon. The past then becomes embedded in the future. As the people prophecy they recreate a past, and out of the silence, out of the foreground, will emerge their words of hope.

My own life has been a hope in pursuit of itself, often the hope given by movement, by my family's travel to small northern communities. The first of these communities was Chipewyan Prairies, and for me, Chipewyan Prairies was Jonathan! Betty and I, a teaching couple, green-as-the-grass, had just flown in by Cessna 185: new community, new language and culture, new jobs! Betty had Grades 1 and 2, and I was to offer Grades 6, 7, 8 and 9 to about 24 young people in an old leaky single-wide trailer. And there was Jonathan that first morning, my first student to arrive at the aluminum door, pants pulled up high, old baseball cap and runners, and a grin bigger than a Chipewyan sunrise:

> "Are you my teacher?" eyes jigging, he asked.
> "If you'll be my student," I joked, and so the northern dance began.

In looking back, or ahead, Jonathan was my teacher and my hope. He taught me about oatmeal duck soup, catching pickerel in the Christina River, hooking up dogs to a birch and canvas toboggan, the important things of the heart. Jonathan taught me that teaching passion did not always work, but that it was enough.

"I have a complaint," the Chief, Jonathan's father, said to me one day at Harry's Trading Post. "Jonathan doesn't want to stay home anymore and make fire....He always wants to go to school. Oh well, nobody's perfect," he chuckled.

The seasons passed, and Betty and I eventually moved further north, family growing, homesteading the summer months, lives filled with laughter, mint tea fires, teaching passions. And there was always Jonathan, either dropping by or dropping in. To his community's honor, Jonathan completed his Grade 12 Matriculation at Fort Smith and then went on to work in the gas industry, a cherished employee, hard working, considerate, kind, and a face full of laughter.

"I'm calling Ian to say that you've lost your student," Jonathan's dad whispered over the early morning telephone, "...cancer."

By the end of his illness's journey, our young Jonathan had become an elder. This wonderful young man had given me a place to come from, and in his heart, he had given me a people. And I have asked myself each, each day since his passing: "As an elementary teacher and friend, did I do anything at all to comfort or hearten him in the last battle? What about our stories of Shaka, was there anything?" Each, each day, as I engage in this educational act, I first ask, "Is there something of Jonathan in this thing we do; is there hope?"

And it is to the elder Thoreau and Bellamy and Skinner
And More and lived senior of every smoke
who have ever sat by the tamarack fire
who have ever called for Utopia
And mercy for the greening young...
 that I call
 that I call...
One More fire old friends
One More time over mint tea
And wordy hand-punctuated ceremony,
One More leather eldered whispering
For the perfect moose wind
To send our hope-kites and darings up
And perfect dreams of childhood
Into the sweet sage of an Onotchito Moon...
Perhaps our love and dream spiders

Will turn loose a kindness, a hope, a Jonathan,
Old friends
And we full children again...hai, hai.

Jonathan gave first friendship, then story. In its unravelling and telling, I found agency and a purpose in the continuing, a mythology of friendship that came without prediction. He taught me that there is someone listening: "We imagine that it is through a felt moment of awareness with the way we are making sense of our world, of how we are living and telling our stories, that lead us to what we call here awakening" (Clandinin & Connelly, 1991, p. 7). It is the stories of the heart, friendships, that gave me metaphoric shift, the awakening and, in the new realization, hope. I became able to live with stories that have no beginning and a mythology that has no end. I became equal to the metaphor.

A writing committed to "story is hope" could only close on a folkloral note, and so we turn to the South Korean tale of Grandmother and her rice cakes. According to Je-Nee, there was an old old woman so bent over from either hard work or poor posture that she used a cane. Her greatest pleasure came in preparing Korean rice cakes for her daughter. On one particular day, having nicely cooked the cakes, Grandmother set out through the mountainous countryside to visit her loved one:

> As soon as she climbed the first mountain, the tiger was waiting for her, and Tiger said, "If you give me that one rice cake, I will not eat you so you can go to see your daughter." So the Grandmother gave a rice cake to the tiger, and she climbed another mountain. The tiger was waiting for her again, (laughter) so the tiger said the same thing, so she gave another rice cake to the tiger.

And so Je-Nee's story continued in the rhythm of climb then tiger then rice cake until at last there were no rice cakes left in Grandmother's sack:

> And finally, Tiger ate the Grandmother....It was a very popular story....Sometimes the story is ended, yeah Tiger didn't eat Grandmother and Grandmother went to see her daughter, but I don't remember that story.

One can only hope for a life where the rice cakes are tasty and many, the mountains appropriate and few, and the tigers inattentive. As the stories of Sparrow, Dafna, Rattler, Mosum, Pesimwastches and Sakastenohk all suggest, one can only hope. There is, at the very least, a good story in that.

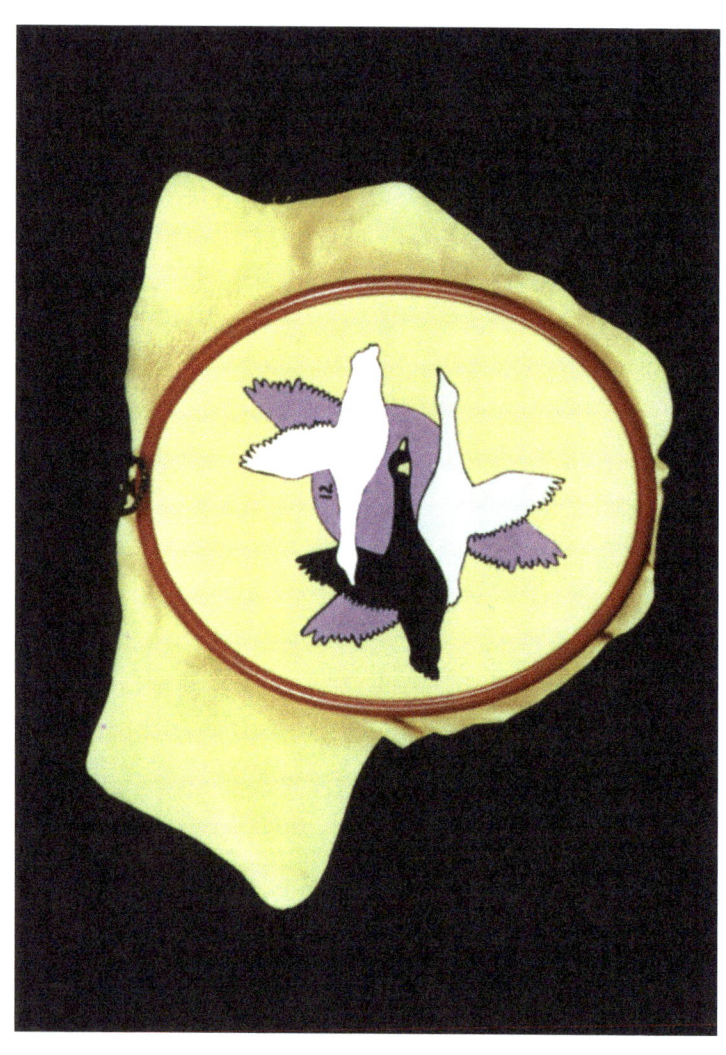

Deer Hide Painting:
Goose Wings of Fidelity

STORY AS HIGH FIDELITY

> Some say that we shall never know and that to the gods we are like the flies that the boys kill on a summer day, and some say, on the contrary, that the very sparrows do not lose a feather that has not been brushed away by the finger of God. (Wilder, 1955, p. 23)

Brother Juniper sought, throughout his life, the truth of the accident that a later novelist would call *The Bridge of San Luis Rey*. And yet for all of his cataloguing of testimonies and trivialities, did he or the novelist Wilder find truth, find the "central passion" of the characters' lives? Is it enough that each in his way sought and struggled with fidelity?

The plaited world of the storyteller is all about fidelity. It lives and dies on notions of true and untrue, both in the stories and in their telling. When I on occasion spin a tale to a group of youngsters, they invariably ask, "Is it true, is it really true?" They want to know if I have spoken with faith and intention, if I have adhered to truth, if our moments together have been of high fidelity. As I sit writing, here on the green Dunvegan banks of the Peace, I similarly reach out my hand for the Great Spirit, wishing to write with fidelity of my storytellers, wishing to intimate the central truth that is their lives. And to attempt that pursuit, I must begin naturally with a story of truth, the story of the white crane:

> I think the first person I met was Nabew, having just moved to the northern and woodland community of Spirit Rock. He was hunched by the edge of the river, shooting his .22 rifle at little pieces of driftwood that floated by on the Peace River. And not just shooting, but hitting! The man could shoot. No one could touch him. There was not a better hunter in the village, I soon learned. That colored fall Nabew killed 14 moose and with his wife distributed the meat to the community, the old way. His immediate family kept only the bullet-shot pieces. Even the hides were fairly distributed for tanning.
>
> That next spring, Nabew was out with his partner trapping muskrats and beavers. And early one morning, while kneeling to sip from a freshly thawed creek, Nabew's tobacco pouch slipped from his shirt pocket into the muskeg water. But just as he reached down to retrieve the pouch, Nabew noticed the reflection of a magnificent white crane on the surface of the water. He quickly wheeled about to catch a glimpse of this rare creature, but not quick enough. The Great White Crane had already disappeared into the northern sky.

Nabew meant to continue his spring hunt, but just the thought of that incredible creature filled his every moccasined step. "You take my dogs, traps, flour and tea, partner. I must find that Great White Crane. It's something I have to do."

Nabew, the hunter, returned to the village of Spirit Rock and began to approach the elders, one by one. "Grandfather, have you seen the Great White Crane?" he would ask after the gift of tobacco. Unfortunately, no one in the community could help our brother. Nabew consequently left home and family and began his search with visits to the neighboring villages.

"Have you seen the Great White Crane?" he would inevitably ask. "No," was the usual reply, "but come in and have a cup of mint tea and a smoke. Give us the news of your people."

"I would like to, Grandmother, but I must continue my search. Forgive me my hurry," he always replied.

Nabew's walking about and search for the Great White Crane went on and on. The days became moons and the circle of the moons became years. Nabew had become an old man.

And early one fall day, during the time when the moose were running, Nabew arrived at yet another village, this time Middle Prairie. "Kayas Kokum," he nodded to Grandmother, "have you seen the Great White Crane?"

"Why yes, as a matter of fact I have...when I was just a little girl we would travel through the Caribou Mountains in our hunt for caribou, "atikiwak." I remember one day my brother and I were setting snares when suddenly we saw the Great White Crane fly by. My grandparents said they saw it seven times in the old days, once for each generation."

"Of course," Nabew cried out excitedly, "I should have known it would be in the Caribous....All this time I have been travelling in their shadow...all this time."

And having thanked the old lady, Nabew quickly left the village, striding like a young man again, his face no longer lined with frustration.

Nabew, the hunter, walked straight for the highest peak in the Caribous', knowing in his old heart that the Great White Crane would live nowhere else. And as the old man began to climb, an early snow fell upon his aged bones, his worn out clothing offering little protection. He continued to climb, heedless...and at last reached the final ledge before the summit. There, just beyond his reach, sat the Great White Crane!

The sinew in his old arms stretched and in that final reaching moment...the Great White Crane flew off into the northern distance. And in that same moment, our Grandfather's heart stopped—a single white feather clutched in his dying grasp.

The people say that the old man died well for the Great White Crane was not a bird at all. It was Truth. And our Grandfather was fortunate enough to live his life in pursuit of It. So they say. (My northern retelling of an old African story)

I felt in Sparrow's words this same sense of the reaching out for truth, stretching her syllables in grasp of the single white feather. Fidelity may come in the reaching and not the grasp. In her excited and repeated telling of the folkloral *Cinderella*, for example, Sparrow brought the listener to the metaphor, to the mystery and "finger of God." Sparrow introduced the traditional tale this way:

The first fairy tale that always comes to my mind is Cinderella, the first one that comes to my mind. It's about this girl that, or this kid, she started off as a kid...and her Mom died, and then her Dad married a new stepmother, and then the stepmother was really mean, and then soon her father died, and then she had to stay with her stepsisters, two stepsisters and one stepmother.

In her additive way, Sparrow framed the injustice, setting the stage for the fairy godmother and the traditional unravelling of the tale:

And-uh she left a glass slipper behind and so-uh the prince...like the prince really liked her and wanted to whether whoever fits the shoe...was going to marry him, and so they went to every person in the house...but Cinderella was locked in her bedroom and the mice uh-opened the door for her, turned the key somehow...and then she makes it just in time before they leave...and then they marry each other and live happily ever after.

Sparrow's storytelling could have stopped here in the silence of narrative completed, but she did not. Our littlest teller only paused then queried with:

> I just have one question....why, you know the glass slipper, if she turned back into regular clothes and in her old shoes...then why was her slipper still glass? Wasn't it supposed to change back into that old brown slipper of hers that she wore? Wasn't it supposed to, like everything else? Her hair became messy again and the pumpkin became a pumpkin again.

"Why was the slipper still glass?" Sparrow asked me. I felt all the world in her question. My little friend wanted truth, the place in the 20th Century where science meets myth, where culture meets religion, and where the Great White Crane lands. Why was the slipper still glass?

For my part, I detoured with a diatribe on the origin of the tale and why, with its preoccupation with little feet, some scholars felt it to be Chinese in origin. Then I could not resist; I asked Sparrow if it was true. Sparrow thought a moment and replied with uncertainty:

> No [the story is not true]....Well, it's a fairy tale cuz a pumpkin can turn into a big carriage, mice can talk and stuff like that...but it could be t-t-true.

Sparrow's voice lingered off, with perhaps the heart of childhood exiting at the door of adult reason. She then told me, her grey-whiskered listener, that truth was when "mice run on four feet, not two." That was truth. It sounded settled, but on several later occasions, Sparrow returned to her tale of *Cinderella* and her lingering question: Why was the slipper still glass? And perhaps appropriately enough, it may be this same single story of *The Little Glass Slipper*, first, although formally, recorded by Charles Perrault in the 17th Century, that most appeared in countless oral forms throughout the ancestral storytelling world. As Hallett and Karasek (1991) write, Cinderella is itself a "fragment of psychic history," a wonderful testimony, I believe, to the pursuit of fidelity in childhood (p. 3). *Cinderella*, in its many versions and with its many counterparts, gives ample evidence about how the folkloral takes the listener (and the historian) to the inside of things, to worlds in which the spirit is able to come out of the ashes and into beauty, a world in which lizards become footmen, and the literal and the figurative are as one in the retelling.

For Sparrow, truth was bound up in this human dynamic of speech, of telling. If the slipper was glass, and in the story it inevitably was, then in part, it was told that way. The fidelity of a story was to be found in the fidelity of its telling:

> Truth is something you tell. Some people just have to tell the truth when they go to court cuz they swear that they'll tell the truth...like they already swore to God that they'd tell the truth... and like I have to tell the truth...like when someone gets hurt you can't say, "No, I didn't do it, no, I didn't do it," so maybe they think "Who did it then," and they're never going to believe you or anything if you don't tell the truth.

To Sparrow, it was telling that most implicated intention. What came out on the breath testified to what lay hidden within.

Sparrow came haltingly at times to the plasticity that is ideas and principles and adulthood. At times, our little friend lived on "the ladder of thin slats swung out over the gorge" of her years (Wilder, 1955, p. 3). Although she lived in a world animated by "testimonies and trivialities," a world where mice walk on four legs, Sparrow also lived in the world of *Pinocchio* and *Snow White* and Anne of Prince Edward Island. Story brought her to the confluence of these two traditions, the scientific and the mythic. As Noddings (1986) suggests, fidelity is a quality of the relationships between people. It may be as well that fidelity is a quality of relationship that the teller has to his/her stories and that the stories have to each other. How is it that the stories live together, sometimes on four legs and sometimes on two legs?

On a later visit Sparrow told of a school field trip to West Edmonton Mall and the Fantasyland therein. It was a place where beauty could rise from the ashes of the everyday, for the right price. It was a place where the ordinary life of a little girl from Northern Alberta faded into wonder at all things imagined:

> We went on this, we went on this...it was really scary, man we went on this one that was called the Zipper, and it goes upside down, and it stopped when we were upside down, and boy that scared us people! We were so scared that our hands were sweating on these bars...but we were buckled up, and there's these big bars and there was like a cage around us, and we still freaked out! Boy that was fun!

I went on this Lazer Zone, it's called...three people go in, and they put this big, big vest on, and it has lights on it and a gun. It's big and it's windy inside there. You shoot the person and everything, and you get 10 minutes in there, and you have a little clock on your gun, and they give you 10 minutes....You have to push with all your might and jump out. You had to pay 3 dollars to go in, but that was worth it!

They bought this bird for 700 dollars...that's a lot....It's yellow and has hair, and it even talks. It was for a birthday present...stupid, but they're rich enough.

They have lots of good stores....They have all sorts of make-up and chap sticks, and they have bath soaps, full of bath soaps and everything!

Indeed, for Sparrow, the entire mall was a fantasy land, full of Zipper rides, Lazer Zones, yellow birds that talked, and bath soaps—a mythic journey into appearance and technological sensation. Our "littlest storyteller's" negotiation within this world demanded both inner resource and, in the finest heroic tradition of truth seeking, a spiritual guide:

I memorized Fantasyland in the back of my head now....It's so easy....It's just a little circle, and I know where everything is.

I was the second youngest people that were there, and we had this person that whenever we left the Fantasyland she would come with us.

Sparrow explained how a parent conducted her along for reasons of child safety during the shopping and store browsing. I found it fascinating, this apparent flip. For in our tales of the ancestral and mythic, the young heroines or heroes invariably depended upon their spiritual guides while within the fantasy. With Sparrow, however, assistance was necessary only when she re-entered reality. In other words, for Sparrow, reality may have been a more dangerous place than fantasy. Forsooth, she would seek out her truth of the glass slipper in a world where fantasy was technologically induced, for a price. Fantasy could be told about and thus understood. And at its best, fantasy remained a mystery. The reality of the 20th Century, however, for our Sparrow, held more ambiguity and less mystery. Why did the world continue to chop down its trees? Why did children find themselves in hospital cancer wards? Why was the slipper still glass? Was anyone listening out there? Perhaps for Sparrow, *Cinderella* was the easy part of the pursuit of the white feather. The inner world of myth and the outer world of science wrestled and overlapped in our little friend's storied soul. Novalis (1798) writes that "the seat of the soul is where the inner world and outer world meet. Where they overlap, it is in every point of the overlap" (Combs & Holland, 1990, p. xix). In the overlap and in the telling, Sparrow was herself in training as spiritual guide.

Just as Sparrow underlined this relationship of truth to telling, so Dafna also storied the points of overlap. In doing so, Dafna brought the polarities together, be they the metaphoric and literal or the scientific and the mythic:

> I think I just live with [the polarities]. Sometimes I'm more scientific, and sometimes I'm more with the myth, the stories, that's all...because I don't want to begin to resolve it. I cannot even begin to resolve it, no need, no way, and I don't think I want to be bothered with it....Maybe I am just running away from it, I don't know. Sometimes I lean on this part, and sometimes I lean on the other part. I live with them both. I live with them both really.

Again for Dafna, life and truth were found in the confluence, in the places where the points overlapped. And so for our Israeli storyteller whose childhood was filled with the imaginings of a host of literary masters, from Tolstoy to Grimm, truth lay in both traditions. Her sympathy, however, went to the stories and the world of sentience they conjured up:

> The stories lived for thousands and thousands of years, and you know, the way science has developed is quite recent. The story will go on forever, we know that. I don't know about science. Maybe it will destroy the world, I don't know. I'm not sure. It is interesting how children just love to hear stories, again and again and again. Why is that do you think?

The survival and continuance of her people brought Dafna to the larger macrocosmic truths. That general story of cultural struggle and perseverance exposed the human dilemma and brought it to dialogical light. It was a story in pursuit, however, of the daily and the ordinary. Truth was to be found in the small triumphs, in the microcosmic stories closest to home, in the telling between friends. One Alberta winter day, while Dafna beautified the kitchen table with hummus, spicy chickpea balls, and pita bread filled with savory barbecued lamb, she shared this amazing tale of truth:

> I'll tell you something that you'll see is truth in life. We have two very good friends in Israel....The one is a survivor of the Holocaust. He was a child when the Holocaust...he was really a baby, 2 years or so,

when it happened. Now he was an only child. His father, at the village where they lived, his father was the head of the Jewish community, and he didn't feel that he could leave and run....He was the head of the Jewish community, and he wanted to take care of his people. But his wife had a single sister, so he said to her, "Take my son and go with him and leave because I know we won't survive...now take him and go!" And she did, and for 6 years, I still shiver when I tell this story, she took care of him, and they went from village to village, and they hid. And they were just at the mercy of good people, and all this time, many times they had no food, day after day. And what she did all the time, she used to tell him stories, all this time. When he was hungry...she used to tell him story after story. That is, if he remembers anything from this war, it is the stories she told him all the time....She sustained him with her stories.

Dafna shivered in the telling, and I shivered in the listening. As Keillor (1985) writes, everything she said "went in one ear and right down my spine" (p. 273). She had taken me through the fidelity of her retelling to a place of truth and caring. Truth was to be found where the intellect overlapped the emotion. And as Noddings (1986) writes, the spirit of fidelity came from "the maintenance of community, the growth of individuals, and the enhancement of subjective aspects of our relationships" (p. 510). Story, for Dafna, was not simply the means to truth. It was truth, the Great White Crane, and each separate mythic tale a single white feather. As process, story allowed both Dafna and Sparrow to situate the details and data of an informational age into the stories and mythic traditions of their people. Their stories, once told and then retold, became part of that myth, part of the world's dreams and part of the world's pursuit of truth. Campbell writes that "the myth tells me about (the human problems), how to respond to certain crises of disappointment or delight or failure or success. The myths tell me where I am" (Cooper, 1990, p. 307). Thus, stories also gave a relationship to truth. To the young survivor of Dafna's tale, stories were sustenance, and that was the retold truth of it all. The story of Holocaust survival spoke of a truth that a mall fantasy land could not imagine. It was a truth founded on relationship and the ownership of experience. It was far more than a matter of digitalized sensation whereby the clock ran down on the gun. Fidelity seemed to be a place where the actors celebrated and storied experience rather than falling victim to it. They came onto the stage from a personal intention.

Dafna told this international story. It was the tale of a family that had two children, both of whom were in search of the elusive bluebird:

They got very curious, and they wanted to hear this special bluebird. So they decided to leave the house and go look for the bluebird. They went, off they went, and while they went they had all sorts of adventures....But then they met someone who told them that "you know, the bluebird is in the back of your house."...They went back, and funny enough, they found the bluebird! While they were looking for truth all over the place, it was deep in their house and hearts. That is the main thing. The truth is within you, around you.

Just as Sparrow returned from Fantasyland to tell the truth of it at the kitchen table, Dafna also slipped into the ancestral metaphor of the folkloral to bring the conversation back home. The bluebird of fidelity was all the more elusive for being so close to hand. Truth was the place where the vital most often fell prey to the incidental.

Rattler's cauldron of story was perhaps more filled than most as he delightfully enwebbed the listener time and time again in this separation of the vital and the incidental. With Rattler, too, the pursuit of the metaphor of truth, bluebird and white crane, was a telling affair. Truth seemed to come in the narrative journey around a thing and seldom directly to it. I am reminded of Rattler's earlier years and his Metis friend and guide who could walk around a large lake and then know its shape:

> You could take him around a lake that he had never been around before and ask him to draw it, and he'd draw it...a natural sense.

Rattler's stories worked in that metaphoric way. They went round and gave shape to the thing. The arrival at small truths, the separation of the incidental from the vital, became a natural inevitability. Truth or fidelity was unhurried. For example, in another and following conversation, Rattler told me of his great love for rocks and of his experience as a photographer. It was in that capacity that our Grandfather happened upon ancestral hand symbols:

> I've seen them on winter counts, and they're very common on rocks. They simply put it up and chalked around it, you see, and sometimes they would engrave around where they chalked.

These rock hand symbols launched Rattler into a consideration of social change in the aboriginal world. What did the outlined hand suggest? Was it a visual warning to intruders of a sacred world within, a no trespassing sign? In his wondering for truth, Grandfather went round again, story into story, the pursuit in the telling. Integral to the oral journey was again the fidelity of the performance and the interrelationship of the stories. As Dafna might say, our storyteller had the intention, that is, the passion with just the right flexure of truth. And in a wonderful way, truth could go beyond itself, take liberties in the name of exuberance:

> The old Indian elders, they were marvelous. They had this wisdom, and you could always tell when they were starting to exaggerate because their eyes would start sparkling. (laughter) You knew exactly when the story was going to go a bit beyond the truth, you know, cuz those eyes would start sparkling. (laughter)...But only the Indians seemed to recognize this. (laughter) You know, I'm sure that half of the histories of Western Canada are full of tall tales (laughter) that were told by these Indian elders. (laughter)

For Grandfather Rattler, truth was not a hard taskmaster but an old friend and one who knew that the shortest distance between two points was seldom a straight line. The telling of *Big Mike and the Ghost Camp* was one fine example. From a general conversation of elderhood, across both culture and gender, Rattler circled in with Dafna's sense of the specific to one elder and one story. First, as always, he elaborated upon his oral copyright:

> There was one elder...over 100 when I met him...from the Buffalo Lake Reserve...spoke mostly Cree...my mother had a wonderful story.

"There is only, as Professor Tolkien observed, the cauldron of story, which is available to all of us through the unconscious, and from which we all draw" (Cooper, 1990, p. 314). By an act of verbal artistry, Grandfather had pulled from Tolkien's cauldron but slowly and in the next few telling minutes gave narrative flesh to an intellectual skeleton:

> This happened when Prohibition was on, must have been about 1918....Prohibition came in '17 in Alberta and went out in '22....It was sometime between '17 and '22....The Badlands, you see, was marvelous country for bootleggers, for stills. My mother, in fact, stumbled upon...she was out riding in the hills and all of a sudden her horse started going straight down.

We listeners were brought with careful detail to the main character, Big Mike, a "Mountie" in Drumheller at the time. In doing so, Rattler abbreviated the years from 1917 to '17 for example. It was as if the year had been softened and worn down with the retelling. It may have been also that the storyteller was so completely situated in his generation that only a brief cue, a rock hand signal was needed.

Rattler then and similarly situated his character into a foreshadowed action:

> He had a motorboat patrol which he patrolled up and down the Red Deer River, you see, with a spotlight at night….He'd go up the river then sort of slip down with a paddle, you see, watching for lights in the river, you see.

Lovingly, Rattler brought the person of Big Mike to the pivotal situation, to a Conrad-like heart of darkness:

> On this particular occasion, he got up as far as my Grandfather's….There was a storm coming….I guess had coffee with him. He was going up as far as Trochu and then he was going to come down you see…."I know there's people down here, but I can smell it, the fumes." (laughter)…At any rate, a storm did hit, a terrible storm, sometime in the middle of the night, and they said that at about 3 in the morning they heard this banging at the door.

Big Mike was at Rattler's grandfather's door, pasty-faced and stammering. They filled him with medicinal brandy and soon coaxed an incredible story from him, the story within the story:

> The waves were getting pretty high, the river was getting pretty rough, so he pulled up and tied his boat to a cottonwood…crawling on this flat, you see…appeared to hear some noises, peered through the bushes…in the middle of this rain field there was an Indian encampment…a campfire…flaring…and they were all sitting around in the middle of this rain…an old elder I guess with his pipe, passing the peace pipe around in the middle of this rain…dogs running around.

Big Mike's vision came to a sudden end when he stood up and shouted. Lightning had struck the cottonwood behind him, and he was knocked unconscious. He awoke hours later, a dog licking his face, no sign of a camp, the teepees gone. Big Mike, still shaking, told his story, but he was jokingly dismissed as a lawman who must have been sampling the evidence. Rattler's mother, however, continued to tell the story.

And Rattler, that curious blend of the artistic and the scientific, would not let it go. Years later, he returned to both the site and the story. His quest was again of the white feather of truth, a story within the story within the story:

Shortly after the war, I went up to the Tolman Crossing. There was a ferry there...walked down and I found a flat where there was three Indian teepee rings...very, very old, you see, they were deep...three Indian teepee rings, and there was still...a campfire ring. There is a big old cottonwood, you see....I could see where you could easily pull in a boat and he'd come in, and the story all fit....It bothered me.

Again Grandfather could not let it go—the fidelity of the story was at stake. Truth seemed to be the story which came after the story, and so:

I wonder if anyone, if there were still any Indians living that would remember this time....I knew some of the old McDougalls...the friend of my Grandfather was still living, and so I contacted his daughter who lived in Edmonton. She phoned him, and-uh he said, "Why yes, there is, there's a man in Hobbema who's about 106, 107, a really old elder."

The story or stories had become a corroborative act. I sensed that the Rattler was about to strike. Each new part gave strength to the body and pulled the listener closer and closer to the ledge on Caribou Mountain. And so came the fourth and final narrative round:

He was very old, and this was in about '45 or '46. I guess I just started teaching. He said there is still an old man who...would remember back to the '30s and '40s and '50s [i.e., 1800s]. I went to see him, and between my very poor Cree and what little smattering of English he had...I finally got him talking. I brought him a bunch of tobacco and things he wanted, and he was very happy, and he finally started talking.

The ritual observances had been made as something was given for the gift of the story. Again Rattler had carefully demonstrated his oral copyright. In the telling, "it all fit" for the elder Cree indeed remembered Rattler's mother's story of a camp of three teepees along the valley:

And one of the children was sick....They had camped with their horses and their dogs....Only one had survived the illness. A smallpox epidemic had struck, and only one survived, and-uh, that was a friend of his mother's as he told the story...and I thought this fits perfectly. He'd travelled through, he'd camped in that country on the river....I said, "Well I bet that was the spot." It was a death camp. There was still, when my mother came, there was still an old death lodge, they called it the Death Lodge Valley, just up the river from the camp...and my mother used to say that when you walked back in there.

But that was another story, and so it goes tricksterish-on without end. Truth, as so wonderfully demonstrated by our Grandfather, was in the corroborative fit of the narrative. I am reminded of the African tale of the honey gatherer and how it took an act of caring, or not, to piece the old man back together each time. What most characterized our Rattler was the length to which he would go to find those pieces, all in the name of fidelity. He did not stop at telling the question; rather, his story life only then became committed to the glass slipper. Like Sparrow, Grandfather did not for a moment question the existence of the slipper but only its divine nature. The ordinary years and places held extraordinary truths. From the earliest of the Upanishads, the *Great Forest Book* (Brihadaranyaka) of about the eighth century B.C., Campbell (1972) writes this about divinity:

> And he himself is all the gods....He is entered in the universe even to our finger-tips, like a razor in a razor-case, or fire in firewood. Him those people see not, for as seen he is incomplete. When breathing, he becomes "breath" by name; when speaking "voice;" when seeing, "the eye;" when hearing, "the ear;" when thinking, "mind:" these are but the names of his acts. Whosoever worships one or another of these— knows not, for he is incomplete as one or another of these. (p. 259)

And so, too, did the storyteller Rattler enter the universe up to his finger-tips.

Just as self "is the footprint of that all," Rattler taught me that story fidelity was found in the narrative composite, All. Truth was not limited to the single act, to just the voice, for example. The varying traditions of inquiry, diverse as the minds that imagined them, drew closer in story, even as they attempted to live and tell apart. In ritual I became corroborative listener, as when a dear friend told me this following tale:

> In the folkloral tradition of tales and truth, there is a story told of a young and intelligent person who decided, like our friend Nabew, to go out in pursuit of truth. It was indeed a somewhat strange and heavy undertaking, but one which was heartily sanctioned by both her family and employer...to their credit. And so, as the story goes, this young woman, Iskweow, began her journey. She travelled by small fuel-efficient car, sometimes by Greyhound bus with the washroom in the back, sometimes just walking and walking like trickster, and on rare occasions by dreams. The days became weeks became months, and at

last, one evening about sunset, she came to a home near a wooded valley. Iskweow knocked on the door and was immediately welcomed in and set to the kitchen table. Over the repast of perch and long-grain rice, all became friends, and inevitably Iskweow was asked what she was about.

"Strange as it may sound, I am out in search of Truth," she replied hesitantly.

"Well are you in luck," the nontraditional family replied, "that old lady Truth lives just 20 minutes from here, in a small log cabin down in the valley. You can't miss it."

And so, after a good sleep and a breakfast of individually packaged porridge, Iskweow hurried along the valley path and within 20 minutes came to the described cabin. She knocked with the first knuckles of her left hand, and who should come to the door but Truth! Well, that old lady Truth wasn't much to look at. Her teeth were more remarkable for their absence than their presence. Her eyes were red and rheumy and studied the world by individual orbit. Her hair, well it was wispy and knotty and the color of old lumberjack socks. But looks aside, Iskweow and Truth hit if off right away. Their friendship grew, and again, the days became weeks became months. Finally, after a fine year together, Iskweow decided that it was time she returned to her understanding family and equally understanding employer.

"When I get back," Iskweow said, "they're going to ask about you Truth. What should I tell them?"

The old lady paused a moment and then replied, "Tell them that I'm young and beautiful!"

And they laughed.

In their laughter, I heard the holiness of their journey, their friendship, and the humanity of their attempt. As an elder teacher said to me of children, those little bundles of truth signified, "you've just got to love them." My storytellers, and particularly Pesimwastches, the trickster teller, confirmed that also. He suggested that you have just got to love the reach regardless of the finished grasp. You have just got to love the pursuit, with the passion of a Dafna, the detours and details of a Rattler and the uncluttered clarity of a Sparrow. Pesimwastches also had a trickster way, a "tell them I'm young and beautiful" way, of dealing with the glass slipper:

> If the kids ask me "is this true?" I usually say to the kids...I wouldn't tell you this story if it wasn't. Would it be nice for me to go through what I went through...try to copy a wolf...the way they act...do you think I would be doing that if it wasn't true?"

This was Rattler's truth with a twinkle. Again the questions of glass slippers, rock hand symbols and the whereabouts of the old lady Truth were all within the story. Grandfather Pesimwastches, in his quest of fidelity in story, spoke of the need for the story to move with the generation. Traditionally, in the Woodland Cree storytelling world, the old and special stories often began with the expression "Kayas, Kayas." Translated and in this sense, "Kayas" meant long ago, and each repetition of the word seemed to situate the story further back. Our storyteller Pesimwastches felt, however, that in the name of story fidelity a different opening would be sometimes more appropriate. This was particularly important if the story was to have power and allow the listener to pursue the truth of it:

> My father said, "I'm not a storyteller," he said. "I'm not a storyteller, my son, but everything that I saw and everything I've done and everywhere I've been is a story. I don't have to say "Kayas" or "mekwach" [i.e., presently].

The argument is for the power of story, independent of the deftness of performance. By contrast:

> He says, "wapahta"...look..."wapahta"..."mamitone," "yihta"... think...look and think....You have to have that story to be able to move along with each generation....You'd say a broad prospect of a story...let's look at it....You know there's a beginning, but there's sort of a never ending thing.

Thus, in his pursuit of the white feather, Grandfather underlined the importance of the fit of the generation to the story. And that fit was accomplished in the careful detailing of the story, that Rattler sense of corroborating detail:

> Grandmother used to pinpoint everything that she told me in a story, every single detail, you know, everything. She explained the day and she would explain...well the pines....They were moving in the trees,

that one tree was swinging this way more than this one...and that's how it is everyday with us. Everything we do is a story...whatever you saw on the way.

I believe that the contextualized truth of the Pesimwastches narrative was irrevocably situated in pre-understanding. The sense of truth found at the northern kitchen table went hand in hand with a consideration of the elders, and these elders symbolized, more than anything else, pre-understanding. As Gadamer writes, it was their bent or predisposition that gave "positive possibility" to their interpretations (Hekman, 1984, p. 339). As a consequence of this interpretation, truth was seen to build upon self-understanding. Therefore, when Pesimwastches cited his father's narrative technique of look and think, he was calling upon the unique experience of his father's interpretation. Like Gadamer, too, Pesimwastches was more deeply interested in continuing the "conversation of mankind" than revealing some objective and eternal truth (Hekman, 1984, p. 349). If anything, for Pesimwastches, truth was again found in the fidelity of relationships and in the wonderfully secret places of his elders and culture:

> As a young person, if I was growing up now, regrowing...I would be closely tied to the elders more than even when I was growing up....Everything that they say, that they saw in the past, has come to pass today, and it will continue.

Truth here seemed to have very little to do with the polarity between "positivist and interpretative positions." Instead, a consideration of truth very often appealed to a foundation story for grounding. I think, for example, of our elder Plato and his ironic use of the metallurgical birth story in the *Republic* (Edman, 1928). Creation stories, necessarily told or written long after the fact of creation, give truth to consequence, truth in the retelling and truth that, as Pesimwastches expressed, moved with the generation. The kind of utopia or republic Grandfather called for depended upon a particular kind of foundation myth. As Rattler would say, for truth to occur, the stories had to fit. In her telling, our Korean friend Je-Nee similarly shared this truth, this foundation story of her people:

> We, we had a pride, we have a pride that our people is very strong, internally....And the spirit [is] the foundation of our country, you understand? It makes us strong...and the spirit of our country is a foundation...is our story. About the story, you always tell that story to our children....There are two animals, the bear and the tiger, and both

of them wanted to be a man, so they went to cave with garlic, only garlic, some garlic....So they should stay in the cave for 100 days to be a man. But tiger couldn't, couldn't stay there, so tiger ran out from the cave, but the bear stayed there for 100 days, only with garlic, garlic. I don't remember exactly but it's very small food...I don't remember exactly garlic, but anyway it means very small food. She, the bear, became the woman, not a man. So she got married to a person from Heaven, the sky, and they have children...they had a child. He was the person who founded my country. So from this story, our characteristic, the people is patience. Do you understand? Tolerance...he is the person who established my country, Dan gwangh.

The story gave understanding, and in a reciprocal way, the corroborative nature of storytelling depended upon just such pre-understanding. From a more universal perspective, truth came from "a" story, not "the" story: stories of a white feather, a bluebird in the garden, a glass slipper that remained glass, a death lodge in the river valley, a bear in the cave for 100 days. In each narrative instance, the story shaped the truth every bit as much as the truth determined the story. Now back to Rattler's Metis friend and his natural sense of the shape of things. The corroborative shape fit and that was truth, somewhere in the narrative countryside, beyond the twin peaks of the strictly metaphoric and the strictly literal, "between the angels' word and the analytical processes that follow" (Roszak, 1986, p. 212).

Years ago now this spring, my teenage son, the one with long feet, arrived at the University to cheer his student father up. Between tours of the city and its special hamburger places, I remember saying something like "I'm going to work on my thesis for a few minutes, kid. Why don't you go for a bike ride along the river? There are some beautiful trails down there." The student minutes became an hour and suddenly my son burst back into the apartment! "Dad! I think someone just killed themself!" he blurted out in his cracking teenage voice.

After a quick call to the city police, Longfoot and I jumped into the old blue station wagon and raced down to the river. My son filled in the details on the way:

> I was riding along the east bank of the river when I came to the end of the bike trail and began to turn around and then further up the trail I saw something...something white flash through the willows along the shore. I biked to the spot. A small dog, like a little terrier, was running up and down the bank barking at...an older woman with a white coat on, out in the river, maybe 20 feet out, just past the beaver dam.

She was heavy, wet curly hair, maybe 50. Why would she be in the river? When I got there, I asked her if she was OK. She said, "Yes," then she kept calling her dog. "Sugar! Here Sugar!" I asked her again and she seemed real calm. Then I rode away, but when I got to the bicycle bridge...I just had to go back. It wasn't right. It didn't matter what she said. Something was wrong. But when I got there Dad, she was gone, and Sugar was still barking along the shore. That's when I came for help.

The constable and I found the leash, neatly curled up on a rock just where my son had said it would be. We did not find the woman nor did the divers who searched all that week. I sent Longfoot back north, back home, promising to let him know the outcome. The city police, to their credit, had treated my son with real sensitivity.

A few weeks later the poor woman's body was found under a beaver dam. She was identified as someone known to the police for unbalanced behavior. The sergeant cryptically suggested that my son was indeed fortunate not to have been found with her. I felt a cloud pass over. Now, what to tell my son? I knocked on the door of an elder professor and dear friend: "Sir, should I tell him a story or should I tell him the truth...my son is so young. I could have her walk out on the opposite shore...the river was shallow," I asked him and myself. "Tell him the truth, Ian," my Deweyesque and bespectacled elder replied, "tell him the truth. It is no less of a story for being true. I know he is young, but if he gets the truth now, he will be able to recognize it next time. You can't pick these times, Ian. Tell him the truth, and the truth is he did go back."

Longfoot and I talked. Four years later, last summer, a coworker shot himself. My son helped the victim's family through the tragedy. Longfoot is OK, with truth. Sugar, however, still barks along the east bank of the river, her leash curled neatly on a stone by the finger of God. Perhaps she barks for that "old woman Truth."

Deer Hide Painting
Sled Dogs Pulling Laughter From the Void

Chapter 4
Laughter

STORY AS A LAUGHING MATTER

Say you just lost a loved one,
someone visits you
someone tells a funny story
and you get into it
and you laugh...
Well, at that moment when you're laughing,
you sort of have a feeling in your heart
that life is still going on.

Have I told you the story of the "fish and game of it?" A few years back, the hunting law had it that one hunter was only allowed to shoot one mule deer per season in and around Alberta. Well one day, as the story goes, a man went into the northern bush and saw another fellow come walking out with a fine mule deer. He stopped him and said, "My goodness, that's a beauty. Do they grow many around here as fine as that?" "Why sure," replied the successful hunter, "It is a fine one all right, but you should see the one I got last week over at Dunvegan!" The man stared at him. "Do you realize who I am? No? Well, I'm the Fish and Game Officer in this area." "Well," came the hunter's quick reply, "Do you realize who I am? I'm the biggest storyteller in Dunvegan!" (Creighton, cited in Anderson, Aubrey, & McDiarmid, 1979)

Creation itself is often born of laughter. Some would even argue that no One, not even the Great Creative Spirit, is perfect. As educators, it may be more important to be fast than right. Sparrow pointed this out in her story of Genesis:

And there was this one tree that He made by mistake. It was an apple tree.

It may be that in lieu of perfection we on the living side have been given the gift of laughter. By laughter we create and recreate ourselves, together. By laughter the relationships of humans to deity to animals to good and evil are established. Laughter keeps us in our relationships. Our oracy is filled with laughter. It connects the silences, the pauses, the expressed syllables in an immediate way. It can be found in beginnings and endings, in both the moments of umbrage and those that are lighthearted. As Pesimwastches suggested, it is laughter that so often restores balance to the universe and dissipates the overshadows. Both story and laughter are born of breath, and both suggest a way beyond mere opposites and intellectualism.

And yet, in spite of the world's propensity for laughter, there have been great traditions of sullen austerity. It would be appropriate to first shake out these concepts and circle in on this laughing matter. What better place to begin than with the elder Plato? Laughter to him was certainly no cause for a solfeggio of chuckles.

In the begetting of Platonic thought, there was confirmed a tradition of the unfunny. Our Republican elder surely thought-launched a thousand thousand philosophical ships, a thousand thousand allegories of the cave. In the ritual of our grandfather's thought, however, was the metaphor of separation. Animals became separate from humans. This was a far cry, for example, from the aboriginal creation stories in which earthbuilding was such a collaborative act. Rather, Plato's epistemological reality consisted of "those who thought," and the best of these were dubbed philosopher kings and "those who were thought upon" the rest of us. These cognitive courtesans knew too much to laugh. Rather than gaining control and a Navajo sense of balance through laughter, the Platonic suggested that rational control was lost in mirth. Thus, Plato (Plato, 1945) often regarded laughter as uncharitable scorn, an unworthy act, a denigration of art, science, religion and politics. Aristotle (*Poetics*, 1967) joined in this view of laughter as an expression of false superiority. The glue that had probably held narrative together then, that is, our gift of ancestral laughter, became philosophically suspect.

The reason for our western laughter or lack of it may be found in our art and religion. With Christianity came sounds of urgency, quite unlike the laughter that rolled about the rocks and Gods of Mount Olympus. If God cannot be surprised, can She fully appreciate the psychological shift that is found in humor? Does the comic exist for One Who Knows All? To the faithful, humor often connoted the temporal, the absence of absolute, a distancing from objectivity. Jesus is celebrated for a host of reasons but seldom for his humor: "Woe unto you that laugh now! For ye shall mourn and weep later!" (Luke 6:26). This tradition of the unfunny then, this view of humor as a derisive act, had its learned proponents throughout the ages. Within Classical Greek and Indian cultures, for example, this negative attitude was fully expressed (Morreall, 1983, p. 86). In the 18th century, Voltaire eloquently expressed his contempt for the "ha-ha." Puritans closed the theatres (Morreall, 1983). The 19th Century Baudelaire described laughter as an offspring of the devil (Morreall, 1983). Laughter came from "the fall," Sparrow's apple tree by mistake, and in this tradition, it was a manifestation of all that was ugly in the human phenomenon: "The passion of laughter is nothing else but some sudden glory arising from sudden conception of some eminence in ourselves, by comparison with the infirmity of others, or with our own formerly" (Hobbes, cited in Lefcourt and Martin, 1986, p. 87). Other 19th Century scholars also warned that laughter was medically harmful, causing unwarranted stress to the diaphragm. Thus, the tradition of the unfunny marched morosely into the 20th Century in Rousseau-like fashion, with full expression about the undesirability of laughter. This motif was later picked up in Chinese Communism, Nazi joke courts, the former Soviet Union and certain Canadian classrooms, indeed wherever the musical peals of child laughter threatened the order and urgency of the business at hand.

The tradition of the unfunny, however, was itself uproariously countered by the funny in western thought and ceremony. For every proponent of the mindfully sober, there was a proponent of the light and joyful. For every individual spiritually driven by urgency, there was another individual who found meaning through amusement. Thus we have echoings, in the Navajo sense, of balance, neutrality. The Koran suggested that "he deserves Paradise who makes his companions laugh" (Long & Knight, 1979, p. 13). The Persian prophet Zoroaster was said to have been born laughing. Elizabethans from Britain felt that the justification of humor was that it enabled the weak to avoid vice. Others recommended laughter as an important aid to digestion: a good meal, good companionship, good laughter, good life. Eastman (1936, 1972) and Mindess (1971) were further examples of those who not only condoned but called for laughter as humanity's greatest gift and the liberation of our species. Cousins (1981) credits his recovery from a serious disease to equal doses of laughter and vitamin C. Thus, it would appear that every culture has placed laughter somewhere within the cultural paradigm. And all cultures have recognized laughter to be much more than a "baring of the teeth, a facial grimacing, a guttural sounding," much more than a "shock to the respiration, the heart rate and endocrine," much more than a "head bobbing, arm waving, and body jerking," much more (Lefcourt & Martin, 1986, p. 19). In all cultures, laughter appears fully fundamental to the human experience, both in the traditions of the funny and the unfunny. Morreall (1983), a thought trickster himself, defines laughter as "an expression of pleasure at a psychological shift" (p. 58). It is vital, he adds, that the change, whether cognitive or affective, be sudden and the shift be pleasant. The conceptual system has been tinkered within laughter. Satisfying loops and hoops become possible whereby laughter begets pleasant feelings that beget more laughter:

> I've heard the elders say you have to laugh, everybody has to laugh....That's where your feelings come from....You make people happy, feel good....That's a gift that everybody has to have.

And just as story lives in breath, so laughter lives in story. Of all my storytellers, it was Rattler whose stories most depended upon a generous sprinkling of laughter and pure joy. As I listened and imagined and listened more to wonderful tale after tale, my 17 facial muscles were on the constant ready for at any moment our laughter could burst out, like a pheasant from an Alberta ditch bank. We laughed together, Rattler and I, never alone or solo. One would release the whirling thing, the middle English "giggle," and the other immediately joined in. I believe my laughing helped tell his stories. Like the hazelnut coffee, amaretto cream, and chocolate chip cookies, it was another part of the experience to share in the whirling and oral chorus line of story.

Rattler's laughter was present in all the tales and all the talks, but there were those specific stories which most echoed with mirth, stories like *Willow Flight*, *The Carbon Ghost*, and *Spirit River Peyote*. From each of these stories, I have chosen one brief scene or interlude to provide insight into our Grandfather's way with laughter. Just as story lives in breath, so laughter lives in story. And when Rattler retold the adventures and misadventures of his childhood, I became party to it as listener and laugher. I learned that Rattler and his older brother once dreamt of flight, and as youngsters of the

1930s, both imagined themselves pilots, both listened to Jimmy Allan and Speed Robinson on the radio, both entered balsam and paper airplane making contests sponsored by the B.A. gas station. The brothers eventually chose real flight and so decided to make a willow airplane by "prairie patch up and pray." Building materials included the wood "Salax insular," basket willows for body and struts, flour sacks from the Rosebud Mill as fabric, flour paste as a tightening agent, stove skis made from old oaken barrels, and all powered by a cream separator motor from the town dump. Once completed, an early snowfall in November that year provided the perfect day for the boys' date with aviation destiny. Now appreciate that our Rattler has come to this telling point in an incredibly circuitous way, even wandering, but always back to main narrative channel, always back:

> To the top of the hill, braced it well, and there was a problem, you see. My brother had to work both things [i.e., steering and cream separator]....I was going to stand behind it and point it in the right direction because if it went straight down, with lots of speed, but if it kept on going in that direction it would land in the creek. (laughter) It was all rocks at that point, so I had to give it a quick twist, you see, (laughter) and point it right so it would go over the flat part of the hill. Anyway, in the process of my getting lift off, kick off, I was pushing behind, you see, getting this start. He had it all worked out, and it was braced. He would pull this lever to break this brace, and it would take off, you see. (laughter) Anyway, the point is I was going to give it this twist, turn it in the right direction....I fell! (laughter) He went zooming over the hill and there was a thunderous crash...snow came up...the whole line of hill and through this mass of smoke, I saw my brother's face (laughter) and he was Angry! You've probably heard of Roger Bannister breaking the 4-minute mile, 1953. Well I'm sure that I beat it! I saw that face and I was out of there to the house, upstairs, locked the bedroom door. (laughter) I can still hear my brother's swearing....So that ended our aircraft experiments. (laughter) And I remember my mother asking sweetly, "Whatever happened to your airplane?"

The story of *Willow Flight* brought round upon round of laughter to our kitchen table that day. What had been a climax and denouement of nervous terror for one younger brother brought side-aching laughter in the oldster retelling. The elder Rattler and I equally viewed humankind as in a struggle with itself. Two prairie lads, raised on "patch up and pray," tried the almost impossible task of little boy flight. And although the willow biplane did crash, if anything, the story was better for it. As we hear so often, a private loss is very often balanced by a narrative gain. In the telling, the struggle was won and so the laughter. Rapp, in *The Origin of Wit and Humor*, describes laughter as a "vocalization of 'triumph,' with its origins to be found in hostile physical gestures" (Morreall, 1983, p. 89). With the baring of our teeth, the elder and I gave control back to a situation that had been completely out of control. The laughable telling gave balance to the unlaughable doing. In teasing himself, his earlier self, Rattler also brought justice to the occasion. It is perhaps no wonder that traditionally Greenlanders exercised contests of ridicule to secure justice. But as well as bringing justice to an act, laughter celebrates. A childhood was not something to be merely survived but to be relished. In Rattler's laughter, the little boy lived on and ran Bannister's mile over and over again. As the story words trotted out, there was a wonderful synchronization between event and enunciation. It was as if the God of the Kitchen Table stood conducting carefully what came out as narrative abandon:

> Everything would start happening at once, and you've heard of synchronization, because I fell. (laughter)...I was thinking of the twist and push (laughter)...the one human element.

The humanity that imagined a process of "twist and push" was the very humanity that "fell" and that later rose in the retelling and laughter.

A few prairie years later, Grandfather was inextricably involved in the *Carbon Ghost* adventure. In his tricksterish fashion, the Rattler began his story with a story. A Drumheller Valley coal miner of European extraction was noted for carrying his savings in a money belt. Late one night, after his midnight shift and on his way back home, the coal miner was struck on the skull with an axe. The tragic victim, murdered and robbed, became a ghostly figure, they said, visible and lingering on moonlit nights. Rattler and several young friends, all on special release from their boarding school, mounted an expedition in quest of the Carbon Ghost. Weeks in the preparation and several minutes in the telling, Rattler brought us meandering to the heart of the story just after their first sighting of the ghost:

> It seemed to be coming up the hill directly towards us, so this time we thought maybe it was an appropriate time to get back to the car with the girls, too (laughter)...and I said, "I remember seeing those two barbed wire fences going, but I didn't remember seeing them coming back!" (laughter)...I leaped over them, you know. (laughter)...Anyway, I knew there were footsteps right behind me, but all of a sudden, I heard this horrible scream, (laughter) which sped me up even

faster...and by the time I had got to the car, of course, the girls had locked themselves in and were hiding under the seats (laughter)...and boy did it ever take convincing that I wasn't one of the ghosts (laughter)...and Bill was back, but there was no Matt! So, what do we do? (laughter) Where was Matt? (laughter)

Lovingly, Rattler set the details of the story, taking a twist when the listener most expected a turn. Again, when the adventure was most out of control, the telling was most punctuated by excited laughter. The incongruity of things fed the storytelling moment. One seldom heard what one expected to hear and so laughed. I laughed through the adventure of the *Carbon Ghost*, my expectations puffing into nothing as the tale unravelled. Only much later in recalling the narrative details did I realize that my laughter was born of the telling, the Rattler performance of body and sound. The words were a secondary reality and disappeared as quickly as they emerged. The presence of Rattler, however, lingered and laughed on and does still. His laughter was the incongruity between a concept and the thing itself, the mismatch between conceptualization and perception. In both *Willow Flight* and *The Carbon Ghost,* the storyteller Rattler expressed a mastery of this mismatch. Things were never what they seemed to be. What I perceived as listener and was skillfully made to perceive by the teller was delightfully at odds with the concept. Thus, the end of the story was to come in yet another story, this time in a tale of Halloween and adolescent mischief and phosphorescent poplar punk that shone in the night. Tense expectation became at last a nothingness, a ghost, the stuff of incongruity:

> Do you know what the ghost was? Uh, we went down to where this old dead tree was, a great big old balsam tree, a balsam poplar tree. I remember Jim reached in and took out, it was just punk, this dust...he had his flashlight. It was getting dusk. I guess when he came and he went to a dark part and he dropped it in and it just glowed with phosphorescence, you see. The winds had caught it, and of course, the way the moonlight struck it...it looked to be a ghost, moving across the opening you see. (laughter)...Maybe that was the ghost.

More years later, Grandfather found himself homesteading in the Spirit River country of Northern Alberta. One particular memory and story came from the visit Rattler and his partner paid to an old French Canadian neighbor, Ernie. Yes, Ernie's life had been one of real hardship. He had no money, but in spite of that he was so glad to see you. (laughter)...He'd just add a little more water to the stew. (laughter) That was the first time I ever smoked peyote, he called it. (laughter) It was Quebec tobacco. I remember we were pipe smokers then, and he'd say, "Oh yeah, try my peyote." (laughter) He'd give us a leaf, and we'd crumple it all up and stuff it in, and it was so mild, and I remember Jim getting up and trying to find the doorway. (laughter) He was going like this across the room, and we just roared, and when I got up, I couldn't find him or the doorway. (laughter)

Here again we find the incongruity of homesteading and independent adults caught in a helpless moment: the result—laughter. And again, as listeners, we stand witness to that endearing human quality that allows us to laugh in the face of weakness and danger. It is interesting that traditionally the Bambuti of Africa sported no chiefs or political leadership. Instead, we are told that society depended upon camp clowns. Laughter certainly has a way of implicating our very human natures, a way of framing the laughing matter at hand. Following the joyful tale of the strong tobacco, Grandfather made this shrewd observation:

But he sure laughed, boy he laughed...had a sense of humor, but they were very mixed...McDougalls and Ukrainians and Indians...not considerers of race. It never came up. They were friends you could say, just people.

Laughter, according to Rattler, brought out the "just people" in people. It provided the experience that provided the bridge between peoples. And in that vein it provided within the single person the bridge between the disparate parts, commonality in the face of dissimilarity. An afternoon spent listening to the tales of Rattler was the therapy of laughter. I always felt like I had emerged from a traditional "sweat," reborn a bit, like Sabochees might say, "feeling good from the inside out." What an extraordinary gift Grandfather had, through only the telling of his person to be able to bring a listener to such averment, such averment.

But as much as Grandfather's giggles and guffaws came in the layers and the circling in, like a spring mallard to water, the laughter of Sparrow was staccato. It would suddenly appear, then just as suddenly puff away into the words of the next observation. Very often it was a big grin and then giggle, from the Icelandic "geiga," denoting a taking off in the wrong direction. Sparrow's laughter most often came from her delicious sense of the "weird," and "weird" usually meant laughable, for example, when our "littlest storyteller" imagined the future, and particularly the dress of the future:

> Well, they'll dress totally different, well I don't know, there's nothing else to think of to dress cuz already people are wearing their pants backwards and everything. (laughter) There's nothing else to think of for clothes.

Or again when Sparrow described the unusual in her family's herd of cattle:

> And we used to have this cow that be really, really fat...and one end and the other really fat...really, really fat. I mean it, like it was really fat (laughter)...and we used to have this cow that had a really, really big, you know, bag or that, she was really big, like touch the ground. I'm not kidding. Big! Poor calf...really hard [time sucking].

As young as she was, Sparrow had a keen sense for deviations from the expected, delighting in these tangents and expressions of the weird. For example again, there was that memorable time when Sparrow and two other Grade 1 friends participated in a school-wide air guitar concert:

> There was just two in the band, and they got third. They were, like Jason and Chris, oh my God! (laughter) They were so funny you could have laughed your brains out. They were really funny....It was weird music with a really funny beat to it...and they danced to it, (laughter) and they danced so stupid. It was so funny. And like one, Jason, he was my boyfriend in kindergarten and Grade 1, and then he gave me his speaker, the microphone he sang with.

Sparrow's joy in the "weird" expressed her own unique cultural orientation. The unusual found its definition and place through laughter. The funny dressers, the fat cow, the weird dancers, they all spoke as much to the norm as to the unusual.

But also running throughout Sparrow's stories was the laughter of oneself, the laughter this time directed inward. It, too, was a way of reconciling oneself to others, in humankind's struggle with itself. Phaedeus in *Fables* suggests that "the bow that's always bent will quickly break, but if unstrung will serve you at your need" (Widdows, 1992). Perhaps by the laugh at self, our Sparrow found her unstrung state:

> I got kicked out of class for talking too much. Yes. (laughter) I kept on talking and talking and talking, and she finally said, "Go on out of the classroom" and "no, no please" and "go out of the classroom" and "okay." (laughter) I got kicked out for talking too much.

Sparrow appreciated the full irony of the situation, and her laughter reflected that:

> I only talked, at least I wasn't bad, I just talked too much.

On another public occasion that same facility would be regarded as an admirable strength. In describing the upcoming 4H speech competition, Sparrow reminded herself:

> We also have to give an impromptu. They give you 1 minute to talk, and you have to talk about that subject the whole time...and it's going to be so easy for me, talk for 1 minute straight, and they have to listen. (laughter)

To Sparrow, speech gave life. They were inseparable. Indeed, life was performance, and one's ability to bring others to laughter was the acid test of that performance. Sparrow took particular pride in loosening the tensions on other's minds. In Drama Club,

> we had to sit on a chair, and they had to try and perform...like make us laugh, like I sat on a chair, and all sorts of people would try to make me laugh, and I just sat there. This is part of being an actress, you know....So I sat there, not a smile on my face during the whole entire thing, like even there was really funny things, people were like picking their nose and all sorts of stuff. (laughter)...I made every single person laugh.

There was great joy to be taken in the laughter release of others, in what Dewey (1934) describes as the "relaxation of strain." Through the sound of laughter, the trickster part of Sparrow's human cortex was recharged, and each laugh, regardless of its style or print or origin, bound our "littlest storyteller" to her species. She laughed best when she laughed with others, and I suspect very seldom alone:

I want to be an actress, a singer, and a lawyer cuz my mom thought I would be good as a lawyer cuz I always argue until I get it right. (laughter)

And perhaps of all the crafted stories that tickled Sparrow's funny bone, her choice of all the foolery and folkloral was *Fern Gully*. Sparrow had happily committed large parts of this cartoon-movie to her long-term memory:

> It is so funny from the bat, oh my God...like it's about the rain forest, and this human gets shrunk by a fairy, and then there's this bat, Batty, and he sings a song like "Hi, my name is Batty and my logic is eratty, potatoes and a jack of toys in the attic, bbb, bhh booo soh," and he sings all sorts of rap songs, and then he hates humans cuz humans fried his brain....(laughter)

It is again full irony that a movie committed to the preservation of the rain forest, a biting comment on the industrial maw, could bring such joy to young people:

> Robin Williams is the bat and...he sounds so funny, and he goes "tastes like a chick or it tastes like a chicken."...Oh my God it's so funny! It's a cartoon, but it's not really for kids because it has to do with the rain forest, and its sort of, like you have to get into it to see what's happening.

In a world of disappearing landscapes and penetrating sunshine rays, a child found both resolution and relief in the funny folkloral. Sparrow's laughter brought the inside spirit out. The elders would suggest that if there is time for this laughter then there is time for resolution. In laughter, the children, like Sparrow, join the world, with all its problems, but gain a pixie-ish distance that allows them to endure the human condition:

> I'm getting really, really, really tired and I'm getting sick because I'm so tired of school....I'm just waiting 'til I get sick....Once my little sister was sick....I put the thermometer that she put in her mouth, I put it in my mouth. I didn't get sick. (laughter)...Mom said, "You're going to get sick." I didn't.

Perhaps, as Lessing (1988) writes, our education "prepares us above all for the long littleness of life" (p. 382).

In Sparrow's laughter, I sensed that the traditions of the funny and the unfunny, the ordered and the disordered, the real and the reflected lived together. Laughter allowed Sparrow the means to go into things and see what was happening. And just as story lives in breath, so laughter lives in story.

Dafna's laughter was a wonderfully varied and passionate thing, ranging "from Rabelaisian laughter at a spicy joke to the rarified smile of courtesy" (Koestler, 1964, p. 30). Each time I heard it, I was reminded that the actual sound of laughter is a kind of laugh print, unique and in the specific image of its maker, unique both in origin and in manifestation. And so for Dafna, both culturally and individually, laughter emerged from matchless passions:

> I think the Jewish people are very passionate. You should see Israelis sit when they are together, visiting one another...the passion in the talking....I mean the roof can come down and everyone is so passionate about what he thinks and what he feels and how he interprets things. (laughter)

Dafna described her life as one of high energy and passion, not simply at the circle of the dining room table, but in her profession as well. The day called upon all of her:

> It is a very consuming job [teaching], and I do it...I work with all my body. (laughter)

Laughter was not only part of that passion, it made the rest of it possible. Perhaps Dafna came by this approach to life through the remarkable presence of her mother:

> My mother was the most laughable person. You could hear her 5 blocks from the house. This is one memory of her, her laughter....So if she was laughing, I did the same. (laughter) I take after her.

Dafna indeed laughed at times with great relish and abandon, her black hair thrown back, her eyes a twinkle with inner joy, like her spirited mentor:

> And this woman that was raised in Europe in a very traditional way came to me one day when I was 5. "It is time for you to learn to jump rope" because I was quite a chubby child and I didn't have too much exercise. In the middle of our living room, we lived only in one room,

she took out a rope and she taught me how to jump it. (laughter) Can you imagine? She had spirit really. She still does.

Like the elder Rattler, Dafna gave insight into the manner by which laughter allowed the retelling. Laughter was aswim in memory, softened the edges of experiences and enabled the remarkable to emerge from the everyday. Dafna's mother, in the retelling, was her own person and possessed her own laugh. It was a sound from the heart and the belly, not a mere political gesture from the throat.

For Dafna then, laughter often meant a nearness or propinquity to the everyday. One morning, for example, at the kitchen table, Dafna turned to her husband and made a remark on the recent winners of the Nobel Prize in literature. She had been surprised at their relative obscurity, anonymity:

And he said, "I'm surprised that you should ask it. Why did you ask it right now?" Because he thought of exactly the same question! (laughter)…And we just sat there you know (laughter)…and there was no news on, just music…and this was just so amazing, so we told our daughter last night, and she said, "You are becoming one, you see." (laughter)

There is a laughter shared by those on the inside, be it the inside of a people or a relationship. As the proverb goes, we laugh together but cry alone. Just as Rattler roared with laughter at the moments of *Willow Flight, Carbon Ghost*, both high passion, so Dafna found great laughter in the retelling of the moments terror-filled. There was that first day of teaching, for example:

All their parents came in with them, so here I am a 20-year-old, with 40 kids and 40 parents. (laughter) I'm here to teach the kids! What are they doing here? (laughter) I said, "Well, I'm sure you are grown enough to stay here with me and have your parents go and wait for you at home."…I don't know where I got the courage to say it. I just wanted to get rid of them! (laughter)…It was my first day in school. (laughter)…Life is unexpected!

The terror of the moment, 40 concerned parents who accompanied their 40 concerned youngsters into the hands of one concerned and beginning teacher, terror of the moment but great joy in the retelling. The unexpected, Schopenhauer's incongruity between a concept and the thing itself, led to later laughter. The retelling, the narrative, carried within it both the tension of the telling event and the relief of the laughter. Laughter allowed Dafna to relive that first day over and over again, without terror. Laughter enabled telling enabled laughter and so forever on with the complex art of story.

Like Sparrow and her treasured *Fern Gully*, Dafna's laughter lived also in the traditional stories, the formally folkloral. Just as story lives in the breath of both tale and talk, so laughter lives in story. For Dafna, there was a huge body of stories around the characters in the Bible that served as both religious and cultural connectives. I have chosen excerpts from two of Dafna's favorite tales, *Moulon's Robe* and *The Gift of the Bee*. Dafna's story of the bee was a retelling of the biblical. In the story, we are situated into the time of the Kings and Solomon, specifically. One day, while taking a nap, Solomon was stung on the nose by a bee:

> And there is a beautiful description how his nose gets redder and redder, bigger and bigger, and puffier and puffier.

Dafna recounted Solomon's discomfiture at the mischievous and unnecessary bee. Later, during a pleasurable visit from the Queen of Sheba, Solomon was asked if he could tell the difference between the real and the artificial for within several clusters of artificial flowers was secreted one real bunch. Solomon, somewhat flabbergasted by the question, suddenly heard a buzzing at the window. He instructed one of the servants to open it, and

> up comes the little tiny bee and, of course, sits on the real flower, what else would she look for, and he says, "This is the real flower."...Sheba replies, "You truly are wise, the smartest man alive!" (laughter)

Dafna was touched not only by the story line, but by its aesthetic presentation, the performance:

> I just love the story. It's a beautiful story written by our national poet, the writer Bialik...and the language he uses, the humor, and the language he uses is wonderful and so full of humor! On one hand they show you this almighty king, stung by a bee, and he can do nothing about it, you know, and there comes this little tiny bee and saves his dignity. (laughter)

With her own humor, Dafna told of the almighty and their attempts at dignity. From the story of Solomon and the tiny bee we are given the metaphor of scale. Dignity was found in the small places, not only on thrones. And to shape the metaphor, laughter itself is a kind of bee. If both stings and restores. It can give the Navajo balance to things and make a life of thought endurable. Not only does it connect a people to their cultures and religions, to themselves, but it also bridges chaos and perfection, tradition and change, hope and despair. The bee of laughter indeed gives stature to the humanly elusive:

> I especially like the way they [the stories] portray the Kings. As you know, maybe they are almighty, but they are human like the rest.

A second folktale, *Moulon's Robe*, similarly spoke to Dafna's way with story laughter. Somewhere in an Arab village, a rich man once invited people to dinner and then seated them hierarchally according to the way they were dressed. Moulon, with his plain dress, was seated at the foot of the table and received only leftovers. Thus, the next time Moulon was invited to a meal he dressed up in a most impressive gown. Consequently, he was seated at the head of the table and treated with great respect:

> When the soup arrived, the first course, he was given the soup first. And when everyone was ready to eat, to the amazement of everyone, he took the…hem and dipped it into the soup. (laughter) Everyone was shrieking and saying, "What is he doing?" So he said, "Since [I] was invited to this important seat at the table because of [my] clothes, let the clothes eat!" (laughter)

In Dafna's storied laughter we are softened and brought face to face with our dispositions, our robes and our reality. Her laughter keeps us at the Israeli bonfire with our stories, and it mediates our tellings. As Schulz suggests, "If I were given the opportunity to present a gift to the next generation, it would be the ability for each individual to learn to laugh at himself…it is one of God's greatest blessings" (Baughman, 1979, p. 30). It is no small blessing that laughter so artfully connects all that narrative sound to the silence.

In all of Dafna's story moments, whether jumping rope, addressing 40 parents, chatting at breakfast with a loved one or sharing a folkloral tradition of Kings and hungry robes, the river of laughter ran through them. At times the laughter stung, at times it eased, but always it returned to lift the listener up, like the sight of a Canadian goose in spring. As Dafna would say, when you pull the storyteller tongue for words, who knows what blessings are to follow.

Sri Ramakrishna once wrote "do not seek illumination unless you seek it as a man whose hair is on fire seeks a pond" (Campbell, 1989, p. 202). What a glorious image of passion, and one that lends itself to nations and people of laughter. Pesimwastches, elder in training and woodland trickster, was similarly one who sought out and gave laughter "as a man whose hair is on fire seeks a pond." Pesimwastches, ponytailed and portly, lived in the shadow of the Kitchen God of Laughter. Like Buddha, he was rounded in feature, his knees a wonderful nesting place for little ones. And when our big brother laughed, the seven gods laughed with him, full body, hand slapping kitchen table, base introduction tapering off into a sopranoish coyote yip. Like Grandfather Rattler, Pesimwastches was a medicine man of mirth. When people first saw him, be his entrance by Elan ski-doo or Honda quad, they smiled, knowing their smile would soon give way to the widening ripples of good belly laughter.

In the Lakota culture, an elder has instructed me that there is a tradition of the funny fulfilled by the person of the "contrary." The task of the "contrary" was to maintain a backwards life, a posture of reverse. The "contrary" would walk backwards, dress in a backwards fashion, ride his horse while sitting backwards. This "contrary" enabled laughter to take place, even in the face of sorrow. Contraries embodied silliness and in doing so lightened hearts. Their contrariness made it possible for people to move beyond "heavy" thoughts.

I think Pesimwastches, in deed and story, artfully embodied that notion of the "contrary." He often introduced silliness into the talk and so lightened hearts. Perhaps his presence became somewhat ritualized into this role of laughter. As Nitotem, a northern friend, said,

> I can't imagine how a community would be without laughter, any community in the world....You've gotta have one person that always has a way of making people laugh....If you're 100% serious and no laughter in your life, then you're missing something, you're missing something big.

Pesimwastches believed that the Great Spirit gave something to each human being, some gift that was to be shared and enjoyed by others. He also believed that his particular gift was laughter and to withhold that joy was to deny the wishes of the Great Spirit:

> All I know is that I tell my stories and I am able to bring a smile on a person's face. Then when I do see that smile, I know I'm doing something.

For Pesimwastches, as for all storytellers, laughter lived in both the private and the public places, in story talk and story tale. In the narration of his youth, for example, Pesimwastches told of the *Groundhog for Grandma*. It seems that Pesimwastches and his two little brothers, Darryl and Douglas, were out for a walk and a rabbit snare when they suddenly came upon two little groundhogs. The brothers decided to kill the creatures for Grandma, as young groundhogs were a tasty delicacy for the elder. A humorous battle ensued but finally the little brothers proved victorious. Proud as punch, the brothers returned home, and Pesimwastches quickly skinned the groundhogs and popped them into the cooking pot. The meal was being impatiently prepared when the moment of story truth suddenly arrived:

> I was putting the groundhogs in the bowl....While I was doing that...Darryl was up in the cupboard...trying to pick up his pepper up there, you know....It was kind of hard to reach it....I turned my back, took the pot and put it on top of the stove, full of water. I came back, and you know what? Darryl put a whole can full of peppers (laughter) in this bowl, this bowl of groundhog Grandma was going to eat.

Although Pesimwastches carefully washed and rewashed the now tender meat, it was with great anticipation that the little ones waited for Grandma's first bite:

> We walked to Grandma's, and the kids jumped up on the bed to watch Grandma take a big bite of the groundhog, you know. She said, "I love groundhog. I've been wanting to eat groundhog for quite a while." She said, "It's going to be nice to eat." And-uh-Grandma was about to put it into her mouth...kids looked at her...she started talking again. Three times, Grandma put it up to her mouth to eat it.

The tension of the event and the tension of its relating were both relieved by great bursts of listener laughter:

> The last time, she took a bite and my Mom just walked in, and "BUUHH!" (laughter) My Grandma almost threw up, and the kids just laughed! Especially Darryl, boy he had fun (laughter)...And Grandma was still coughing away. Oh God that's a funny one! Yeah. Grandma's eyes turned red! (laughter) Boy it was funny, funny sight to see, and those guys sitting over there and having a banana each and laughing away. (laughter) Oh I laughed! Everytime I tell the story Darryl says, "It didn't happen that way...you're lying...this is how it happened." He's got his own version of how it happened....Two little

kids and Grandma got her fill of groundhog! (laughter) The next time we took Grandma some groundhog...she cooked it herself! (laughter) She called me "Moocheyenew," it means "crazy person." (laughter)

The silliness of the story situation brought tears to the crinkling eyes of our storyteller grandfather. My passive listening had been suddenly transformed into the active participation of laughter. The voice of Pesimwastches, once rhythmic in its story delivery, became similarly lost in the peals of mirth. The storyteller, through body language and voice, had gained the respect and trust and attention of the listener. It was essential if listener–teller were to suddenly join in that cortex charge of laughter (Doggett, 1986). We laughed about our humanity, and we laughed about our laughter. An elder and a loved one had been brought to a ridiculously helpless state in the story, as had we by our own laughter. Just as story lives in breath, so laughter lives in story.

For Pesimwastches, the colloquial lived in and with the folkloral. Just as his *Groundhog for Grandma* had reached folkloral proportion, so the stories and laughter of others fed the storytelling moment. In the story of *Beaver Leg*, for example, Pesimwastches told in great detail about a trapper on the spring hunt. What made the trapper and the story unique, however, was the trapper's wooden leg. And early one April evening our trapper friend visited a remote pond in search of beaver and muskrat. He stood waiting on the beaver dam, waiting in clear sight of the lodge, hoping the beaver would swim over in his direction, when suddenly,

> he was standing there trying to figure out how he could get the beaver to come his direction....He was starting to hear this "ththththththth."

The beaver gnawing and the telling continued teasingly, until the storyteller, Pesimwastches, released the tension with:

> It's here somewhere! The beaver's here somewhere. And he looked around his body...around him...the other direction...and there was a little beaver chewing away on his wooden leg, right there by God! (laughter) That's a funny one because you know what happened to little beaver? (laughter) His wooden leg was half chewed.

As in the tales of Rattler and Dafna and Sparrow, the laughter tumbled out as "an expression of pleasure at a psychological shift" (Morreall, 1983, p. 58). The hunter, for all his wiles, became the hunted and the chewed upon. And again there was a sympathetic relationship between the character in the story and the listener at the kitchen table. Both had their legs pulled a bit. The ensuing laughter animated the told universe and helped to bond the oral narrative together and to the table of the telling. In our guffaws and titters and snickers and chuckles, we gained access to the soundscape of the tale. By our laughter we became part of it all, even part of the next elaborated telling:

> I've often heard it said by Iroquois friends that it is good to sit in a circle because on the circle everyone is the same height. Humor can be used to remind people—who because of their achievement might be feeling a little too proud or important—that they are no more important than anyone else in the circle of life. (Bruchac, 1987, p. 26)

The stories of not only Pesimwastches, but Mosum and Sabochees as well, were all filled with the laughter that kept listeners in the circle. At times, the story laughter was risque and at other times, just as suddenly, sacred. But whatever its character, this woodland humor always underlined "the importance of humility and the affirmation that laughter leads to learning and survival" (Bruchac, 1987, p. 29). And just as story lives in breath, so laughter lives in story.

In conversation with the Arusha Masai storyteller, Tololwa Mollel, I learned again of the kind of laughter that gave life in the face of death, laughter as contrariety, moving in opposition to the situation:

> My people, who still observe their traditions...like funerals, time for organized sadness, but there's a lot of laughter, too....Like a lot of stories, you know, about the person who died, and there's a lot of making jokes, too, like-uh, because in some communities they have a relationship, a joking relationship between communities where somebody can make a joke about anything and you don't get mad....So they make jokes about the dead person. You're not supposed to get mad. (laughter) It's that way, too, laughter is the other side.

In the Masai stories of his childhood as well, Tololwa talked of that same contrariety in the person of Hare. The trickster rabbit was cunning and acted as a foil to hyena who was

> everything awkward, clumsy, and and greedy and selfish (laughter) and and the villain, you know.

Within the stories, both colloquial and ritual, were the two sides, and it was often laughter that provided the hemispheric bridge, like a corpus collusum of sound. Tololwa's grandmother, for example, told of two Dorobo gathering honey:

> So one of them would climb a tree and the other one would be following and-uh he will see a…the one in front…a real python coiled up on the tree, and then he'd turn to the other one and say, "Oh, there's a lot of honey here, why don't you go forward?" (laughter)…And the other one would say, "Ah…where is the head of the honey pointed?" (laughter)

As Tololwa suggested, laughter is relationship, the relationship of an Arusha Masai grandchild to a grandmother, a Spirit River homesteader to a lonely neighbor, an Israeli daughter to her strong voiced mother, a Cree "contrary" to his buddy, and a pony-tailed little girl to an air guitar friend. Laughter is relationship. And when we laugh, really laugh, we set it loose, this sound, on a hero's journey of 1000 faces. In a sense, the laughter undergoes the heroic cycle of separation, initiation and return (Campbell, 1989). In this our laughter and person are mythological. It separates from us, enjoins the moments of others, returns in kind and celebration. We become that which we have created and, as Pearson (1986) suggests, the kind of person who not only can move mountains, but know mountains, "fully oneself, and seeing, without denial, what is, and being open to learning the lessons life offers us" (p. 10). We become the laughter, the metaphor. Thus, laughter's mythological journey is primarily a synaptic one, continually separating and rejoining in peals, "I" to the people, grease to the conversational wheel of humanity.

Just as Plato had his lips smeared with honey as a child so as to give him the power of oratory, or so the folktale goes, my own childhood lips burbled with sweet laughter. My early joy was to joke and tease, and I was continually drawn to those under the spell of exuberance. I suppose I have chosen my professional places as well for their medicine of laughter, their moments of pure joy. For example, as Supervisor of Curriculum and Instruction, I remember unofficially arriving at school by Elan ski-doo and birch toboggan and canvas carry-all one cold January morning. I had been 35 miles on the winter trail and was in immediate need of warmth and laughter. Thus, I unbuttoned and quickly slipped from the empty staff room to a friend's class of preschoolers. After greetings, we all listened to Teacher's warm-up story, his eyes and grin dancing about the very air, when suddenly Doyle, a little one sitting beside me, whispered, "Someone farted, Mr. Sewall!" I already knew, and in my best "English As A Second Language" whisper I replied, "We don't say farted, Doyle, when we're in school. We say 'someone cut the cheese.'" A few minutes passed and then suddenly yet another gaseous cloud descended upon our early morning group. "Mr. Sewall," Doyle whispered loudly, "there's cheese all around us!"

I laughed then, later I laughed in the many retellings, and I am laughing still. And just as story lives in breath, so laughter lives in story. When I recall the many fine people who have touched my life, conjure them up in tranquility, it is their laughing faces and stories that I most remember. Surely, there have been friendship times of quiet contemplation, even shared grief, but it is the laughing faces that first emerge from the river mist of narrative recall. The emergence of their faces and stories makes them present again, and I am made ever better for it.

Laughter has also helped me to understand change in others and myself. My partner's laughter has changed, I believe. It was, for many years, an appropriate laugh, nurturing, punctuating, and on side with her situation. Recently, Betty's laughter has moved from her throat to her belly. There is an abandon about it now. It goes out on her breath, like Dafna's, to the clouds. I think it is the laughter of those past child-bearing and of one who is greatly loved. And I, now I look for ways to make her laugh. It is a kind of bingo for me. If my silliness and contrariety works, I will be rewarded by this belly sound, this sudden umbilical cutting to the clouds. That is my bingo moment, my belief in good luck secured. Her laughter charges my cerebral cortex, enshrines the trickster moments, and orders my soul's disorder. It sings harmony to my lone coyote howls, and it gives me life:

All my life
I have looked to the sky...

The clouds for the suggestive faces
Of my grandparent's parent's grandparents,
The sky wind for the lappings
And whisperings of my love's ear,
The blue for a canvas wash
And pause for cerebration,
The rain for facial baptism...

All my life
I have looked to the sky
But most of all for the lightning of laughter

Its white fusing from the other world
Its missile of Thunderbird pleasure
To my heart...

And now I am told that "almost is not eaten"
That the lightning of laughter strikes up
That the lightning of laughter strikes up...
And that I have been on my head
This while
That immortality is what we do here
That chaos is where we go
And that the lightning of laughter strikes up...

You tell the Thunderbird,
I canknot.

Deer Hide Painting:
Sleight-of-Mouth

THE STORYTELLER AS SHAPESHIFTER: ARCHETYPES WE STORY AND LAUGH BY

Well, just as a Heyoka, a sometimes clown figure, he (Black Elk) liked to make people laugh; he felt happy when people were laughing. When there were any little children around he would always be doing funny things with them or telling them funny stories, to make them laugh. I think he understood that there is no access to a deeper spiritual reality if there is not the opening force of laughter present there. It tends to open the heart for receiving a greater value than that of this world. (Brown, 1979, p. 63)

I like that, I like that very much, the sense of laughter opening the way for truth. All of my storytellers liked to make me laugh. They accomplished it by their shapeshifting. Like an Iktomi, Badger, Coyote, or Anansi, they shifted throughout the talk and tales, shifted by oral word, by person, by gesture, and by surprise. Linguistically, somatically, they shifted and in doing so revealed to me those archetypes and shapes that we story and laugh by. They eased me, gracefully and painlessly, from laughter to insight. It was so smooth I hardly felt the shift "within" as I concentrated on the shift "without."

Norman (1990), a scholar and elder who I believe has done a wonderful service to the storytelling tradition on this continent, retold a Montagnais tale of *The Cranberry Partners*. In my own retelling words:

> It seems the high-bush and low-bush Cranberries were good friends, more than friends, partners.
>
> They lived in adjoining villages, their houses side by side facing the lake. Often they would sit together and watch for moose swimming across the waters. And they say it was impossible to embarrass the Cranberry partners in the spring or summer or winter. In the fall, however, the friends grew fat and juicy and lazy. And one autumn day, they were just laying around, soaking up the good feeling, when they suddenly heard a moose going by. The Cranberry partners jumped up, grabbed their bows and arrows, and raced for the door. But being so fat and juicy...thhup...they both got jammed in the door, unable to go either in or out. The moose, well he just nonchalantly walked on by and out of sight.

And that my friend is the story of how the moose embarrassed the Cranberry partners in the fall. There were probably other ways to embarrass them too. (Norman, 1990, p. 7)

When I first heard this cranberry story, I laughed, and then after the laughter, I thought of the partners and their fall shape change. The story for me was in the shapeshifting, and similarly, the storyteller Norman shifted from scholar to traditional clown in the telling. The traditional storyteller is a shapeshifter, a transformer, one who so often uses laughter to access a profound and narrative way of knowing. That after-laughter-insight naturally takes its shape from its origin, the creative personae. Within this tradition of transformer, the laughter continues. It does not really matter if the Japanese fox gets the child or the child gets the fox, if Anansi outwits Wulbari the Creator or Wulbari outwits Anansi, if the moose embarrasses the Cranberry partners or the Cranberry partners embarrass the moose. It can and does work both ways. What is important is the shifting of shapes, the laughter. Within the stories and the tellings from my own storytellers, I have come to better appreciate these archetypes we story and laugh by.

Sabochees, over the continuing life of one particular story, *Misisikak*, demonstrated this. The elder and I were January travelling to a nearby community. Once across the flagged ice bridge, the winter road turned and twisted its way through the black poplar along the riverbank and then wound more northerly across small meadows that would be hayed for and grazed by horses in the summertime. The road was like a white twisted piece of diamond willow. We shifted and smoked and storied our way along. And I remember Sabochees, himself a trickster, a Wesakychak at times, remarking on the quietude of the winter bush. He said it reminded him of a story that his father once told, a story of the Giant Skunk, Misisikak. Sabochees cleared his throat, pulled at his long black moustache, carefully lit a roll-your-own and then began:

> Kayas, kayas, long ago, our Big Brother Wesakychak was out walking, just walking, when he noticed that everything in the bush was quiet, so quiet. No sound at all from the creatures of the forest. Suddenly Wesakychak spied a weasel hiding under an old log. "Hey little brother, Sekos! Why the silence? Why is everyone hiding?" he asked. "We are afraid of Misisikak, the Giant Skunk!" Sekos replied. On hearing of the great fear of his little brother, Wesakychak decided to help, and so he called a meeting of all the animals of the bush. Then Wesakychak asked again of the group what had brought them to such a state of silence and fear. "Misisikak," they all replied. Our Big

Brother thought for a time and then announced that he had a plan. It would, however, depend upon everyone's help, and more specifically, one particularly courageous volunteer was needed. Again there was silence...until at last the voice of Wolverine, Kehkawhakes, was raised, "I'm the one." And with that the plan was made.

Later that night, Misisikak came sauntering down a trail on his way to the lake for a little evening sip of water. Suddenly Wolverine jumped from the bush, embedding its needle-like teeth right on the ass-hole of the Giant Skunk. And although Misisikak screamed and tore and clawed the very skies, our little brother maintained his deadly hold. Without his spray weapon, Misisikak was powerless. In the next few moments, all the other animals of the bush shot out of their hiding places and proceeded to jump on and trample the Giant Skunk. And in but a few moments the battle was over, Misisikak was pounded and dead.

However, there was still one problem; for although lifeless, the Giant Skunk was yet filled with terrible spray, and our little brother Kehkawhakes still held fast to those Gates of Hell! ("How do I get away from this asshole?" he must have wondered. Well, there are times in life when you've got to hang on for all you're worth and other times when you've just got to let go....) Wolverine let go. But in the doing so, a final burst of Misisikak's spray struck him. It left a white spot on Wolverine's throat, and you can see it there yet, even today, on his grandchildren.

I hardly remember that winter road, but I recall that Sabochees-telling like it was yesterday. We laughed and laughed and laughed. My elder was willing to leave it at that and simply moved on to the next story. But for a few magical minutes, Sabochees had taken the archetypal shape of his own trickster Wesakychak and brought a wonderful comic relief to our day. Like Hermes, he was both messenger and trickster. As Leeming (1990) writes about the archetype of the trickster, "He is profoundly inventive, creative by nature, and in some ways a helper to humanity" (p. 163). Sabochees had become a kind of Sioux "heyoka," turning the silence of the winter travelled landscape into the pure joy of laughter. Yet within the laughter, the door had been opened to the spirituality and insight within.

And so not many winter travels later, and not even realizing that Sabochees had committed his story to my bones, I retold this Misiskak tale. This first time, however, I told it for reasons of battle. A large group of concerned citizens were involved in a lengthy protest with a multinational conglomerate that proposed to clear cut much of the Northern Alberta boreal forest. They all laughed, these environmental warriors, as did I. But in our laughter, we looked one to the other, those who were hanging on still and those who had already let go. In that telling and in that laughter, I, the storyteller, had taken the archetypal shape of warrior and opposer. We all had.

Not many days later I was quietly approached by one member of the protest group. She thanked me deeply for the gift of the story, just as I had thanked my elder Sabochees. She told me then that on hearing the story she had returned home that night and retold it to her own four children. It seems they had lost their father and her beloved husband but a few weeks before in a logging accident. She said the story made them all laugh, that they had "a damn good laugh." When I awkwardly expressed my sympathy, she thanked me again and said that she and the children "would hang on." In her own retelling, our sister had undergone a shapeshifting. She had become the archetypal healer or shaman and in doing so had begun the healing with a "laughter."

The story does not stop there. It never does. For in this most recent and literary retelling, I, too, have shapeshifted. I have taken the archetypal part of ancestor or soothsayer and begun it with a laughter. I can only imagine, only imagine what shapes it will take in you, the reader's future. Thus, within the gift of the Giant Skunk tale, the teller(s) have shapeshifted from the storyteller archetypes of trickster and comic to warrior and "contrary" to healer and shaman to soothsayer and ancestor. And as Black Elk said, it was laughter that opened the heart for other things.

Thus, only one story, but one can only suspect the number of shapeshifts in the telling. Sabochees, master shapeshifter, could not imagine a world without laughter, nor could he imagine a people who did not go beyond laughter to other things. For Sabochees, laughter was very often both the beginning and the end of things.

The comic archetype of trickster storyteller grows out of the tradition of "once there was and once there was not." Estés (1992) writes that "this paradoxical phrase is meant to alert the soul of the listener that this story takes place in the world between worlds where nothing is as it first seems" (p. 75). It was Grandfather Rattler who, for me, most personified the archetype of the comic storyteller. He was a willing inhabitant of the storyland situated between "was" and "was not." Without exception, each elderly insight began with a laughter. And much of that laughter was generated by his story characters who themselves were much more than what they first or even later seemed to be. They, too, took delight in the paradoxical and were tricksters at heart, but as Norman (1990) writes, their "presence demands, cries out for, compassion and generosity toward existence itself. Trickster is a celebration of life, because by rallying against him, a community discovers its own resilience and protective skills" (p. 102). Rattler's characters were idiosyncratic and wonderfully unique, yet they possessed in common that spirit of the comic. Through our elder's eyes and words, they were able to make me laugh, and then having laughed, I was open to other truths. Grampa, Shady Green, Happy Jack, Jerry Potts, and Lord De Laval were but a few of these embodiments of "Raven" spirit, and to some extent, all of them were in the trickster image of their teller. They certainly lent themselves more to laughter than to classification, more to truth than knowledge.

One February mid-morning and at the island of the kitchen table, Rattler told this story of *Grandma's Copper Kettle* to me. He was told the story, in his turn, as a small child and on the occasion of some long forgotten misbehavior. As the story goes, a very young Rattler was standing in the kitchen corner while his grandfather supervised in a tender sort of way:

> "You know I was always in trouble when I was a child myself," he says. "You know when I was about 14," he says, "don't tell your mother this, when I was about 14...I was a big boy for my age...my mother used to take me for a walk, you see. She admired a beautiful copper kettle, you know. She was from wealth, she could have easily afforded it, but I guess it was kind of a moral issue, so she said, 'You know what, wouldn't it be wonderful if my children, two sons and a daughter, could get me that for a special present, sometime.'"

Rattler began the tale with a spinning inward. Thus, Rattler's story consisted of his grandfather's story which in turn consisted of his mother's story, a four generation narrative journey. And in traditional Wesakychakian fashion, it all began with a walking and then a wondering:

> And he thought, "Ah Gee"...he was the youngest child you see, "How am I going to get some extra money?" And he said, "It just happened that one day I was wandering downtown...the prize fights were on...and I think 2 pounds if you can beat the challenger. (laughter) Two pounds was the price of the kettle" (laughter)...so he said, "I'm pretty fast!" (laughter)

Grandfather, at 6'2" or 6'3", slim but very tall, 14 or 15 years of age, was not what he appeared to be. Indeed, Rattler's story has taken us to a world between, a world in which grandfathers become young and strapping. It was in the finest shapeshifting tradition:

So he said, "I had a motivation." (laughter) "Never fought in my life," he says, "but I'm pretty fast!" (laughter) So he said he climbed into this ring and they put the gloves on him. He says, "And I dodged him for about 5 rounds…then he got careless…and I caught him right on the Adam's apple…and he went flat like this!" (laughter) "That was two pounds," he says, "then I picked up the copper kettle on the way home, gave it to my mother…you know for years she thought what a wonderful boy her son was." (laughter)

In our laughter with the comical grandfather, we realized that the gift of the copper kettle was not really what it appeared to be, nor was the prankster Grandfather always what he appeared to be. Rattler, in his artful telling, was able to take the comic shape of his own grandfather, who in turn was able to take the shape of his own youth, the modesty of mirth in the shifting of shapes. It was the laughter of imitation and incongruity. Thus, the transformative power of the storyteller allowed the comic to live in the serious and to reshape the day through laughter. The incidental misdeed of childhood had been long forgotten in the shared delight and transport of story.

In yet another artfully tumbling tale, this time of the *Old Mexico Ranch*, our Grandfather again spun upon and through the archetype of the comic. It was the story of Lord Charles De Laval (Beresford) and that individual's weakness for gambling. This Anansi character possessed both appetites and wit somewhat larger than life. And finding himself short of funds one summery day, he constructed a wager with the Prince of Wales:

> There's a promenade that goes right through…Hyde Park. It's only open…the Queen goes down there…it's only open to horses and pedestrians…saddle horses, you know. The Royal Guard rides through there, but you cannot have any wheeled vehicles on there, you know, no wheeled vehicles at all…no carriages…particularly in the 19th Century. And-uh, so anyway, I guess Lord Charles had-uh bet the Prince of Wales…that he could take a wheeled vehicle with horses and go through the park…100 pounds or so….Of course Edward immediately took him up on the offer of 100 pounds, that was easy. But what he wasn't aware of is that, of course, you've got to let one vehicle through, once a week, to pick up the garbage. (laughter)…So there came the Prince of Wales, riding around, and he saw this garbage wagon coming along, lo and behold, who was driving it but Lord Charles. (laughter) He finished his pick-up and held out his hand, like this. (laughter)

Rattler, from his storyteller vantage shape of trickster, joined me in a great weld of laughter. Scott-Maxwell (1968) writes that "as some dislike the paradoxical we forego the fun of admitting what we know, and so miss the entertainment of being mutually implicated in truth" (p. 142). Again, we laughed at the paradoxical and at the incongruity of things, of the wide gulf between appearance and comic reality. We laughed at the mischievous lord and the outwitted prince, but most of all we laughed for ourselves. By the tale, Grandfather gave me access to the inside of the trick. As Apte (1985) writes, "New individuals continue to emerge as clowns, fools, buffoons, and so on, primarily because fool-making is a continuing social process" (p. 235). And the collection of comic tales for Rattler, a cornucopia of anecdotal incongruities, comprised a kind of trickster cycle. Each of the "picaresque" characters became memorable for their unpredictability, whether it was the Albertan Happy Jack shooting flies on the kitchen ceiling of the ranch house or Lord Charles at the reins of a garbage wagon. That same delightful unpredictability came to characterize not only the "told about," but also the teller. I was never quite sure where our tricksterish Grandfather was going with the story. It was a matter of suspended disbelief. Instead, the unpredictability of the trickster figure was set against the predictability of a foil. Babcock (1985) writes that the trickster embodied "the fundamental contradiction of our existence: the contradiction between the individual and society, between freedom and constraint" (p. 163). We must hear of Lord Charles against the predictable Prince of Wales and Grampa against the professional challenger. Rattler's trickster cycle of tales then are of the individual who emerges from a larger context, even social constraint. Similarly, the storyteller, the shapeshifter, emerges, too, in the process of narrative. Perhaps it takes a trickster to find the exceptional in the context and cycle of the everyday for it is laughter that opens that door to narrative time travel.

Very often this archetypal shapeshifting of the storyteller becomes itself the story, again with the door to such trickery being opened with a laughter:

> There is a Japanese folktale retold of a fox that was known throughout the countryside for its ability to bewitch people. Few had been spared its mischievous ways. A death bed had once been filled with a tree stump, the chief's bathtub filled with mud and rotten leaves and the wine merchant's purse with a handful of leaves. This tricksterish fox was incorrigible. And one fateful day, a clever boy from the village was out walking in the mountains when the fox suddenly jumped out from behind a tree. The boy, however, paid no heed to the fox, but rather continued on his way. "Aren't you afraid that I'll bewitch you?" asked the fox. "Not at all," replied the boy, "for I have bewitching powers

also! Shall we have a contest and see whose powers are strongest?" The fox readily agreed and almost on the spot shifted his shape to that of a frog. "Surely you can do better than that...you still look like a fox-frog!" teased the boy. Then, quick as a wink, the fox changed himself into a snake. "Still not very good. You look like a fox-snake," the boy criticized. The frustrated fox then turned himself into a bird, daring the boy to shift better. "Oh, I could, but first you try one more change. Turn yourself into a fine meat dumpling and then jump into my hand," the village boy challenged. No sooner said than the trickster fox sat as a dumpling in the boy's palm! And just as quickly the clever boy popped the dumpling into his mouth and swallowed it whole...a fox in one bite! And that was the end of the fox! (Scofield, 1965, pp. 9–14)

Hence the trickster storyteller, in the bewitching of others, loses his/her own original shape. It is the inevitable process by which the storyteller becomes continually reconstituted in the retelling. This shapeshifting often becomes the story and the laughter a signal that another change has taken place. One cannot predict the next story or the next shape, but one can predict the narrative process by which it will occur. There may be white wolverine scars to show for it. Laughter lets us remember them. It gentles the memorable.

Dafna, herself in the archetypal shape of the laughing warrior, talked of this recollection and reconstitution that can live in the midst of our jollity:

> "If I ever forget Jerusalem, I should forget the use of my right hand," something like that...three times a day he was reminded of Jerusalem and looked to the eastern side. That's where Jerusalem is from Europe, when you look from Europe...he could not forget. And in every wedding, do you know that in every Jewish wedding the bridegroom breaks a glass? Well, why does he break the glass? It reminds everyone of the destruction of the Holy Temple....So you should never forget the destruction, even when he is so happy, he has to remember this particular moment in his past.

There are times when in the midst of our laughter we must remember. This I believe is the archetypal laughter of the warrior, of one to whom existence is no subconscious act. It is the laughter of those on the inside of a struggle, those to whom survival is a matter of the bones and not merely intellect. Dafna, our Israeli storyteller and shapeshifter, brought laughter into the arena of this struggle most often in her stories of the "outwitted." She told, for example, a remarkable story of a young Solomon and the fire. It was a story and a laughter that went back 3000 years to the narrative time of King David, Solomon's father. It, too, began with a dare and a wager whereby a rich man once said,

> "I'm going to give a great amount of money to anybody who would be willing to stand, on a cold winter day, in the midst of the water, the sea, for a number of hours." So this young man, who happened to live with his mother...they were very, very poor...said he would do it...and he went into the sea, even though it was very cold.

The evening hours ached by and the young man stood throughout the night in the winter sea. On the distant shore he was able to see his mother, waiting by the fire she had built. To his credit, he managed this incredible feat. In the morning, the young son went to the door of the rich man to collect his money:

> [The rich man said], "Oh no you can't because your mother, she lit a fire. She brought the wood."..."But her fire was on the shore, and it was my heart that kept me going!"

The rich man stubbornly refused to pay, and so the now upset young man went to King David, seeking justice. The King, however, sided with the rich man, and so the youth left the palace even more upset. There he met Solomon, the King's son. At the Prince's request, the youth told of this injustice. Solomon promised to help and asked the youth to return the following week:

> So Solomon asked his father to make a banquet...on a particular day...and Solomon went to the cook and said, "I want you to keep the pots and soups here and put the fire over there!" (laughter)

The day of the banquet arrived, the guests were seated, and the King clapped for the food to be served. When the soups and pots arrived, however, the King was enraged:

> "Oh uncooked meat! Uncooked soup! How dare you!" So his son Solomon said, "Hey, last week you said to this young man that he survived in the water because of his mother who had a fire on the shore. Well, that's the same as your food. If the fire on the shore could help this man, the fire over there could cook your food, couldn't it?" (laughter) King David said, "Oh Solomon, you are smarter than I am and you are right." King David apologized to this person, and he made the other man give him his prize. (laughter)

Both the guests at the banquet and the 3000 years of story listeners were brought to laughter and in that laughter found the justice of Solomon. Like a Kuloscap or a Nanabusho, Solomon demonstrated how to protect his people through wit. Whereas the wit of a Lord Charles brought comic relief, the wit of a "contrary" Solomon brought comic protection. Fortunately, King David was moved by the humor of the situation in a way that serious entreaty had failed to accomplish. The King moved to the side of the laughter and in doing so did himself justice. Kierkegaard similarly shared this parable and dream:

> Something wonderful has happened to me. I was caught up into the seventh heaven. There sat all the Gods in assembly. By special grace I was granted the privilege of making a wish. "Wilt thou", said Mercury, "have youth or beauty or power or a long life or the most beautiful maiden or any of the other glories we have in the chest? Choose, but only one thing." For a moment I was at a loss. Then I addressed myself to the Gods as follows: "Most honorable contemporaries, I choose this one thing, that I may always have the laugh on my side." Not one of the Gods said a word; on the contrary, they all began to laugh. From that I concluded that my wish was granted, and found that the Gods knew how to express themselves with taste; for it would hardly have been suitable for them to have answered gravely: "Thy wish is granted." (Oden, 1978, p. 125)

As listener, and like Kierkegaard, I, too, continually moved to the side of the laughter, like a King David, throughout my many storytellers. I laughed and felt the justice of the wolverine Kehkawhakes, the humor and justice of the village lad who swallowed the fox in one bite, the justice of a youth who suffered the gelid sea for his mother. In all these fine tales, the shapeshifter told of the struggle for equity and vindication and did it with humor, a requital through laughter. Laughter even made it possible to live through injustice. I learned, too, that like the trickster from which it came, the laughter could both create and destroy. Although it separated the human from the divine, laughter suggested a way back to the holiness. I think also in my own life that those moments most filled with spirit were invariably most graced by laughter.

As a youngster I remember our Red Deer River ranch. It was animated by mule deer, sun-baked bullsnakes and rattlers, hawks and prairie dogs. Along the river shores, not far from the corrals, there lived, too, little pockets of quicksand. There I jumped and laughed my little boy way through the heat wavering summer days. My jumping on quicksand turned my mother's hair grey, she said. And I always laughed when she said it.

On a 10-cent dare and at the age of 10, I jumped from the top of an old cottonwood to a black stock pond that waited below. It was a jump for my brother's crowd, a jump for an 8-cent orange crush and two red licorice. I did hit the scummy water below, and I did avoid impalement from submerged fence posts. And I learned something about laughter that day. I did not laugh in the climbing up, in the separation, but Lord how I laughed when my head finally burst up out of the water, like a pheasant from cover. Lord how I laughed then. Laughter was on my side then, after I had swallowed the fox in one bite.

To the laughter of the archetypal trickster and the archetypal warrior must be added the laughter of the shaman or healer. This is the laughter that either maintains the balance or mends the pieces back together again. In metaphor and for several of my storytellers, it was the sound of the drum for in that instrument there was combined both the medicine of the funny and the serious. Pesimwastches said it this way:

> The drum could be spiritual...the drum could be funny and enjoyable, and the drum can be serious at times....It gets serious when you're doing healing, when you're healing people. And in the ceremonies it helps....Then when you want to have fun, it laughs.

As the northern storytellers have taught me, there was a special reverence to the laughter, a special healing, when that joy was expressed from within the people and their ceremonies. Laughter was essential to the balance at these times, whether the ceremony was pure joy as in a handgame competition or something more serious and prayerful. Laughter became the drum and set a rhythm to the occasion. And like the interstice of silence, laughter was a joint production of the circle of the healer and the wounded. Again, in the act of laughter, the shapes shifted, and at its best, all involved became both healer and healed. By way of example, Grandmother Sakastenohk spoke of the round dance in her own community as a time of laughter and healing, the merriment of the drum:

> You don't hardly have a chance to dance, you older people (laughter)...so many young people are involved in it...nowadays you don't see any alcohol in the round dances, really, that's why we join in, you know. We're old and...they're happy to see us and we're happy to see them enjoy their lives the way it should be with us all....We join in with round dances....(laughter)

Even to be there, in the circle of the people and engaged by the laughter of the drum, was to feel better about one's world. To laugh was to take one's place as one of the people. Grandfather continued:

> When those round dances take place, you know…we use peace pipe, we use sweet grass, we get the elders to pray for people and also we get the speakers in round dances. You know, a lot of times I choose to speak to the people on both languages….There's more and more young people, they see for their own eyes, you know, what people do to have a good time, without alcohol….When they see young people singing in the centre, drumming…they want to be one of them….You know, I think that's the best counsel so far, I ever see, to our people…that's why we continue go to round dances.

Whereas alcohol separated and isolated and wounded through false hilarity, the laughter of the drum ceremony reaffirmed the individual as one of the people. The laughter was a vital part of the healing. As Sabochees had said, a life without laughter was no life at all. To be fully human was to laugh. Sakastenohk's young were able to recover their humanity through this laughter. And those who could bring others to such a state were indeed the great healers of that society, healers who could enable others to undertake the contrary:

> We must unlearn those things which we have learned; by learning them we have hitherto not known ourselves. We must learn those things we have neglected; without knowing them we cannot know ourselves. We must like what we neglect, neglect what we like, tolerate what we flee, flee what we follow. We must cry about the jest of fortune; jest about its tears. (Ficino, 1990, p. 48)

Indeed, Mosum, Sabochees, Pesimwastches and Sakastenohk all had that healing gift of story and laughter that enabled the listener(s) to consider the previously unconsidered, to learn what had been neglected, itself a trickster act.

That ability to heal with story and laughter, however, was not the single province of the grandfathers. It was alive and well in the person of Sparrow, our littlest storyteller. As listener and friend, I always felt much better for being at Sparrow's kitchen table. The joy of her telling person enabled me to see the world through Wesakychakian eyes. Her laughter was a medicine and a surprise and a twinkle. I found her "one liners," for example, to be a recurring and particular joy:

Barbies look a lot like humans they are way smaller.

We are learning how to draw...like a face with a long nose hanging over a brick wall.

We really sit on my little sister's bed, and...each of us gets to choose a story....They choose big storybooks....They want to choose the longest ones that stay up longer.

There's no such thing as an unsinkable ship.

Mom and Dad still do that to me...they'd go "now don't smile, now don't smile, don't smile"...and I turn around and smile.

I am a Jack in the Box, the leading role..."Better to mend than to bruise."

With Sparrow, laughter was a matter of perspective. Her delight in discovery of all things "neat" communicated itself to the listener. And as Sparrow's world revealed itself, I was able to rediscover the world, too, for the first time. Her laughter helped me to "unlearn the things I knew about." And because she chose to see the earth with such wide laughing eyes, she healed others by her vision. In the positive spirit of the creative trickster, our Sparrow went in search of her own eyes. Naturally, there was a story about this, one that I happily shared with her.

I first heard the story of *Wesakychak's Blind Journey* years and northern years ago. Our local culture centre had approached the community, elders and parents alike, for stories that would assist in the bilingual and bicultural education of the young. One very elderly grandfather, white whiskered and bespectacled, softly spoke the following tale:

> Wesakychak the Trickster was out walking early one spring morning when he came upon a flock of chickadees. They were busy playing a chickadee game...busy removing their eyeballs from their eye sockets and throwing them high up into the air. And when the eyeball came back down, the chickadees would fly under and their eyes would fall right back into their sockets. The birds were doing this one eye at a time. When our Big Brother Wesakychak asked them what they were about, they replied, "We are snowblind and our poor eyes feel burning hot and sore. By throwing our eyes up into the air we cool them off. They feel very good then!" (They were hoping to play a little trick on our Brother.)

Being who he was, Wesakychak just couldn't resist the game. "Go ahead," coaxed the chickadees, "just throw them up on to the willow branches, then shake the willows until they fall loose. You'll hear where they land. And Wesakychak did just that, but before his eyes could even land the chickadees had caught them and flew away. The Trickster had been tricked! Wesakychak continued to shake the willows and listen, shake and listen, but to no avail. A passing chickadee confirmed their loss and so our Brother Wesakychak set out on a blind journey in search of a muskeg spruce. And each time he bumped into a tree he would ask it what kind it was...first the willow, then the tamarack, and then the spruce. Indeed his blind journey was a difficult one, but at last Wesakychak bumped into a muskeg spruce, just what he had been looking for. Feeling down the side of the tree our Brother was able to gather a mouthful of spruce gum. He chewed and softened it carefully, then rolled the gum into a round ball and popped it into his eye socket. Ah, sight at last, and with one good eye he was quickly able to make another. Wesakychak was now able to look out upon his world, saying "future generations will experience the snowblindness in the spring." And Wesakychak said this to be so. The truth of this story can still be found by children in the early waking mornings...for then they shall still find little bits of spruce gum in the corners of their eyes. (Peechemow, 1987, Book IV, pp. 1–13, in translation)

The shapeshifter Sparrow was a trickster, too, in the tradition of the transformer Wesakychak. Just as our Big Brother went in quest of his eyes, so Sparrow walked out into adulthood, seeking her vision. She would bump into the trees along the way, too, and it was that bumping that so often became a laughter. Listening and laughing for me was an empathetic reaction to her discoveries. Sparrow's stories and laughter, both to her and me, were "good things to think with," what Levi-Strauss dubs "bonnes a penser" (Archibald, 1990, p. 73). Out of the snowblindness came our mutually constructed vision, with a laughter. Healing words marked Sparrow's engagement with life:

> I used to think I had brown eyes. I wear glasses and sort of the same color of hair....When I wash it [my Dad and I] look the same.

> I just see a poster in my mind, and then I think of [Terry Fox] as like he did all that for like everyone else.

Even at school like we have a Christmas tree in our classroom, and it makes me feel comfortable.

But boys in the class are so unmature....Like you say "excuse me" and they say "Why, did you fart?" Like "Why did you fart?" Now that, every single thing they say is like stupid...so you never say anything nice.

Through her ritual of stories and laughter, Sparrow opened something up. As Campbell (Osbon, 1991) says, when one tells stories, "part of you that you normally never really touch in everyday living comes out and you've opened something...that's why one of the really important things for any artist, especially for storytellers, is vulnerability" (p. 6). Laughter facilitated that opening and allowed the telling to become an act of faith. Our little friend stood out on the limb of the cottonwood and trusted to the waiting hands of the pond below. To tell was to trust. And it was laughter that enabled the inside and the outside to exchange places, the soundscape of the healer.

As a fourth archetype, my storytellers laughed also when they shifted into the shape of the soothsayer or ancestor. Some might suggest that there is a secret place in each of us, a sacred landscape perhaps, that belongs to the ancestors. Again, the door to that place is most often opened with a laughter. Campbell (Osbon, 1991) describes it as:

> Our old people, when they're talking about storytelling, they start with this place here, and they call that "the remembering place," because you can't, as a person, you can't remember very much....I can only remember 40-some years, okay...but this place can remember thousands of years if you open it up. (p. 6)

There was the sense of that "remembering place" in all of my storytellers and shapeshifters, regardless of age, gender, or ethnicity. Laughter seemed to invite the ancestors to the kitchen table. It secured the place and their visit. In the presence of the ancestors, the storyteller became soothsayer and slipped into the long-term memory of the listener. I remember, for example, the afternoon Sparrow informed me that truth was an animal that walked on four legs. We laughed, and I remembered. I remember also the elder Sabochees who when most in the midst of laughter spoke with such insight. To Sabochees, the old stories and the laughter were a gift from the Great Spirit. To neglect them was to say no to the gift of life, to not believe in the Great Spirit. For Sabochees, laughing with the old stories provided a connection to an earlier time, a time pre-ancestral, a time before remembering:

The old people used to say Wesakychak was around here, that man, a long long time ago…when there wasn't any people around, that time…just Wesakychak was around. That's what the old people say. And there were all kinds of Wesakychak's friends—all the animals, the birds, all the ducks and geese. That's what the old people say.

Wesakychak came to earth in the shape of the storyteller and took up habitation in this "remembering place" of the people. He was continually reshaped in the laughter of the shapeshifters:

> He represents not only the undifferentiated past but likewise the undifferentiated present within every individual. This constitutes his universal and persistent attraction. And so he became and remained everything to every man—god, animal, human being, hero, buffoon, he who was before good and evil, denier, affirmer, destroyer and creator. If we laugh at him he grins at us. What happens to him, happens to us. (Rodin, 1979, p. 52)

Thus, Sabochees, through his own tales of the trickster Wesakychak, was able to shapeshift and bring the listener face to face with the pre- and postancestral.

This laughter of the ancestral voice was consistently evident, too, in the talk and tales of Dafna. For our Israeli friend, the ancestral often took the form of the proverbial, a conversational genre that invariably elicited a smile or knowing chuckle. In an enchanting way, the proverbial was a formulaic response to an everchanging yet repeating context:

> I used to use them [proverbs] everyday in my class. For the situation there is always something someone said 2000 years ago. It's just amazing. They would come to me like that in every instance…where they were appropriate. They would just come to me. It is wonderful to show them and to feel that we're not inventing anything. They already thought about it 2000 years ago. (laughter)

Laughter in the same sense was proverbial, a kind of formulaic reaction to the context. And as the proverbial helped to organize thought along mnemonic lines, so, too, did laughter. Indeed, formulaic expressions made the recovery of thought possible. It just came. As Ong (1982) writes, the "more sophisticated orally patterned thought is, the more it is likely to be marked by set expressions skillfully used" (p. 35). For Dafna, the art of the proverbial meant living with the ancestors:

They are about every thing...happiness, about respect...like they say, "Who is a clever person? The one who learns from everybody." It sounds much better in Hebrew. (laughter) And then there is a question, "Who is a happy person? The one who is satisfied with all he has."

To this wealth of the proverbial in Hebrew, Dafna added also other proverbs from Yiddish and Polish folklore. It was with particular and ancestral pride that Dafna spoke of her own son's articulate way with a proverb. Indeed, Dafna laughed at the arrogance of a modern and western world so possessive of its thought. She bowed instead to the ancients:

Philosophically, we have to go back 3000 years ago...that's where it all started...what was ever is just a fragment of what was already there. And I am not talking only about Judaism, about the Greeks, about the Babylonians, the Egyptians...all the ancient people. They created the vast amount...and we only added some to it. (laughter)

Thus, the oral shapeshifter, Dafna, became soothsayer through not only the proverbial, but through the biblical as well. Her stories, both colloquial and ritual, were very often centered on biblical context and allusion, as we have heard. The stories invariably celebrated the humanity, weaknesses and strengths of the ancestral. And that humanity gave laughter. Dafna, then, was particularly drawn to the time of the Kings as a living and vital time in the narrative life of her people. These biblical characters were only made better by their humanity.

When a king had his nose stung by a bee, the listener laughed in empathy. When a young David questioned the need for "annoying" the spiders and bees, God promised that one day he would know. Like every listener, a youthful David sought insight into the mysteries of his God. And one day that purpose, that mystery, became evident:

King Saul was [still] ruling....He was chasing [King] David because he was afraid that [David] would take his kingdom from him. David was running away and trying to hide in places all over the country. King Saul used to send soldiers to find him....So one day David was hiding in a cave, and he heard the soldiers, not far around, and the soldiers were looking all over the place. But at night the spiders put a web over the entrance to the cave, and when the soldiers were looking at the entrance to this particular cave, they said, "Oh he can't be there, otherwise the spider web would be broken." (laughter)

The soldiers moved on, and I laughed with the shapeshifter, Dafna, that something so small and humble as a spider web could provide protection, even life itself, to one who would become so mighty. Perhaps it is similarly not surprising that something as modest as the spider web of laughter could also give life to a species. Again, much of the ancestral joy was in the correction of imbalance. A king found humility, even wisdom, in the quiet places that surrounded him. Arrogance became self-deprecation became respect. As Saltman (1986) says, the intimacy of story and shapeshifting is that

> it comes from the body, it comes from the human voice, and it is as lasting as the human voice is fragile from that single person because the stories have been handed down through millennia and polished by so many long dead human voices. There is that sense that we share, we are laminated into the past, our own past that we know or don't know by hearing those stories. (p. 3)

The sound of our laughter, I believe, was instrumental in polishing the old stories and laminating the listener into the narrative journey of a people.

Grandfather Rattler, too, was deeply laminated into the historicity of his land and people, as we have heard throughout his stories. And as with Sabochees or Dafna, access to that ancestral voice was very often through a laughter. It was a discretionary voice made memorable by its power of instruction and not mere entertainment. Rattler, for example, was particularly fascinated and charmed by the narrative doings of the British monarchy. His retelling, however, often had a ring of investigative journalism to it:

> When he got on the train to go to Bristol...he met this beautiful young lady, and-uh, of course, he put on his charm...and so they spent a night together at a motel in Bristol, and lo and behold she got on the boat with him and they crossed the sea together, and it wasn't long before he discovered that he had seduced his aunt. (laughter) And guess what happened? A child was born! (laughter) No inheritance...brought on by his own indiscretions...that's living history, you see. (laughter)...I had a little problem getting full research because it was kept hidden in all kinds of documents.

The trickster of insatiable appetite was ajar with the expectations of his society, and our own listener laughter echoed the mismatch. This laughter again polished an old story into an intimacy. The spider web of circumstance held even the mighty, just as it held the listener.

On yet another narrative occasion, Grandfather spoke of the political history of our province and in doing so further shifted into the shape of anecdotal historian. He described the initial Social Credit cabinet and specifically one of its first ministers:

> He was raised on the border of the reservation, the Blackfoot Reserve....His father was a rancher out there...of French-Canadian background...a fascinating person to talk to. He could bring to life that period, you know. How different they were! I see him every once in a while. I take him out for coffee.

And it was during one such coffee ritual that the now retired Minister told this story:

> I was a cabinet minister, and I led a palace revolt. Aberhart and Manning, both were pushing, trying to push this bill through....I thought it was a terrible mistake....I got the back benchers to support me, and when it went through the house it was defeated. (laughter) It was defeated, but of course, it wasn't a money bill or anything, so it didn't mean the defeat of the government, you see....There I was standing in the hallway when up came Premier Aberhart, and I said to him, "Sir...do you want my resignation?" And he looked at me and said, "What for?" and walked on. (laughter) "Oh," Aberhart said, "one more thing...it happens all the time in Whitehall!" (laughter)

In the artistry of the shapeshifter, Grandfather became the voice of both the living and the long dead. It was a voice, whether in the shape of a police scout or cabinet minister, that consistently broke into the formulaic rhythm of laughter. And again it was that laughter that made the remembering place such a refuge, a place that turned the foxes into dumplings.

Listening to my elder, polishing as we did his old stories with our laughter, took me back to another grandfather. I remembered our portable school in Wood Buffalo National Park and how it snuggled so nicely on the banks of the Lower Peace. At recess time, before and after school, I would walk the few feet to the river bank, and there I would sit on an old board-bench. Very often the old grandfather, Alfred, would sit there also, recently widowed and deaf, his rheumy eyes upon the river as it flowed by. We seldom exchanged words, the old man and I. We mostly sat and river stared together, our attention to the high water driftwood, the occasional beaver, the family skiffs departing on a hunting trip, and the voices of children at play. The river bench was our prayer wall, our ancestral time, beside time. It hollowed and fit in the right places. Early that spring and one afternoon recess, I remember shouting to the old man, "Tanzay Ni Mosum? How are you my grandfather?" "I'll be going out on the spring hunt soon," he replied with his old man voice, "by the inside channel...but I'll take my canes along." We laughed then, he and I, both shapeshifters.

My storytellers have taught me that there are times, ancestral times, when we laugh together on the inside channel. And although the shape of our laughter may shift from body of trickster to body of warrior to body of healer to body of ancestor, it all keeps the spirits glad. That old man and I were listening to the folkloral voice of the river. We listened under every rock for the laughing voice of Manitou. We listened for a trickster land to inhabit with our giant skunk stories and our side-splitting myths. And like a Prometheus, we listened for the love of our kind. We listened like foxes for the deliberate birth of laughter, for its arrival from a tear in the sky.

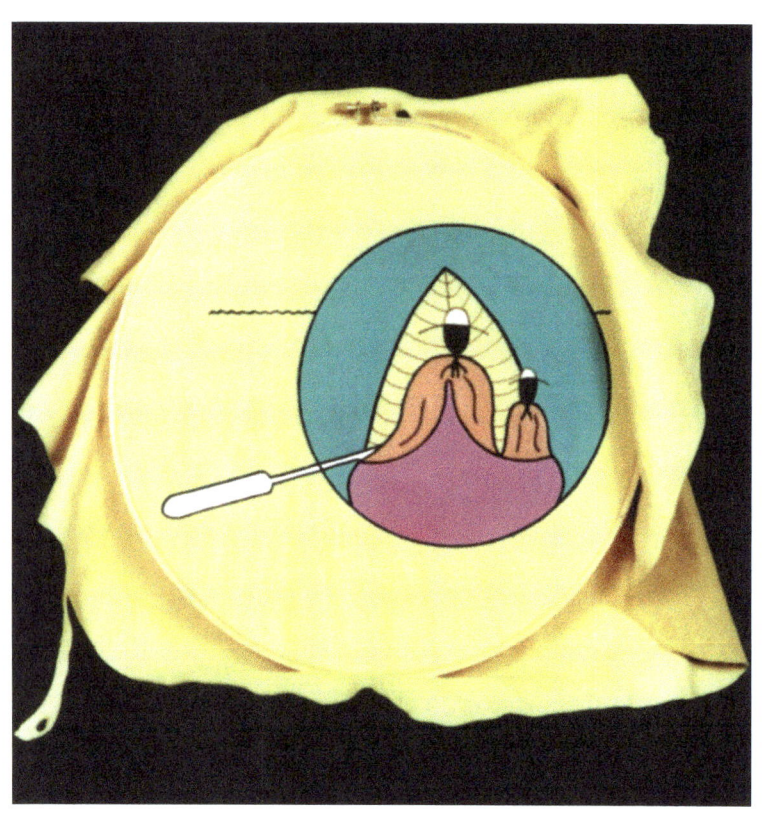

Deer Hide Painting:
Themselves Once More

Chapter 5
The Intergenerational Conversation

ELDERS: THEMSELVES ONCE MORE

The Old
who so gradually become themselves once more
and so gradually break up
like smoke, no one notices it, they are gone
into sleep
and light. (Bly & Jacobsen, 1980, p. 80)

What is an elder? I have heard that question posed by friends of every age, disposition and ethnicity. What constitutes elderhood? How will I know it when I get there, if I get there, or am I there? Is it a question that needs asking? Is it a question of who or what or where? Does the answer transcend the question? Perhaps, in quest of elderhood, we are wise to begin in that which itself transcends apprehension, a good story, from a reteller of tales:

> Once upon a Japanese moment, two mature frogs, one living in Osaka and one living in Kyoto, happened upon the same thought at the same time. Both felt a need to get out and see a bit of the country. Surely there was much more to life than the small creek home in Osaka or the winding ditch in Kyoto. And so both creatures, in

the same moment, set out for a visit to the other's town. It was indeed a long and arduous journey but in good time both frogs reached the mountain which separated their respective villages. Both frogs climbed slowly to the top of the mountain and there introduced themselves to the other. They stretched out luxuriously on the shaded green grass, cooled their round frog bellies and passed the time of day.

"You know this travelling is a difficult matter, being frogs and all," complained the frog from Osaka.

"I have an idea, my friend!" suggested the frog from Kyoto. "Why don't we both stand up on our tippy toes, supporting each other the while, and each study the objects of our destination from this mountain top?"

They did just that, standing as tall as possible, holding on to the other, and each staring off into the intended horizon.

"Nothing new there," grumbled the frog from Kyoto.

"Yes," agreed the frog from Osaka, "your town of Kyoto is really no different than my own village...might as well return home!"

And so both frogs, believing that the object of their travel was no different than the town they were leaving, shook hands and bowed each to the other and returned home. All the length of their days they each believed it. However, what we must remember is that the eyes of frogs are situated well back on their heads. Although each thought that they were looking ahead to their destination, each was only looking back to the town they had left. In fact, Kyoto and Osaka are as different as can be. (Lang, 1951, p. 213)

My storytellers have taught me that as much as I seek the prophetic, seek the vision and elder person of the future, I am in fact frog-gazing upon the places I have just left. As Keesing (1978) writes, "The world is changing too fast for prophets to prosper—I can only speculate" (p. 194). For just as our future seems to come from the ancestors, to be embedded in the storied lives of the old ones, so our past seems to reveal itself best in speculations of our destiny. My storytellers have taught me also that the reduction and categorization of narrative time, into story past, story present and story future is a difficult one, although certainly an inquiry into elderhood is a philosophical consideration of time and aging. And as we cannot step out of the narrative river long enough to frame it, we become somewhat victimized by our own scholarly attempts. However, by our stories, we can aspire to truth even in our fantasy (Le Guin, 1980/1981, p. 195). And by our stories, we are able to climb up on the knee of the particular elder and stare into his/her retiary words and folding hands. By the elder stories, we are at least able to find questions to the answers that we could not even imagine and stare back into the future. What is an elder?

At the northern kitchen table, every bit of story talk and every bit of story tale inevitably and in some way turned to the word and fact of elder. I sensed that the community concept of elder, inseparable from the concept of culture, was full of both living folks and their situations. Yet, as Faulkner (1958) writes, "We done got into the habit of confusing the situations with the folks" (p. 41). Thus, my northern storytellers taught me that elderhood was more about person and less about situation. It was "person" who was able to story a memorable life. And it was "person" who was able to survive, even in detail. Pesimwastches expressed it this way:

> What is an elder? And an elder had to answer that....An elder is a person that is able to remember all the people he has seen in the past and remember how long he has lived, what he's gone through. And then when you get to the age of an elder, you're able to tell things right into detail.

Pesimwastches then named the elders he has known, both male and female. For him to know the elders, particularly the ones who are no longer on the living side, was to be able to provide that vital connection between the ancestral voice and the daily voice, between where we were and now. Indeed, all of my northern storytellers, when asked of elderhood, first responded with the names of particular elders. Elderhood was not an easy conversation. As Scott-Maxwell (1968) writes, "Talking is too committal for a beginning. I had one friend who always carried some small objects of interest in his pocket, and on occasion would show them; the skull of an asp, seed pods of a rare shape. These make speech easy" (p. 30). With Pesimwastches, the names came out like objects of interest; the names provided a way into the talking and a way into the stories of these elders. We polished by naming, each elder and memory now a smile misted inward. In our conversations around the northern table, be the storyteller Sabochees, Mosum, Pesimwastches, or Nitotem, every discussion of elders would inevitably wind itself into this specific, the named. The word elder seemed to conjure up grandparents now gone, characters still treasured by their communities. In their naming, these elders remained the witnessed, the seen who had not yet reached the full ancestral stature of the anonymous. Someone, or someone's loved one, had once been in close contact with these elders. To still know their stories well was to celebrate their presence and to participate in the tradition of elderhood. It is through a knowledge of the stories that the ancestors are expressed by the elders of today. And just as modern scholars footnote their literary origins, so the storytellers of an oral culture give respect in memory space to the old ones whom they name:

> We lost the mainstream of our elderly elders. They're gone now, and…they're still with us. We talk about them everyday, you know. We're not afraid to talk about them. And this is what makes the next elders come out cuz they're able to talk about the previous elders.

Thus, an elder is one who remembers and tells of the elders who have gone by, tells of the newly ancestral. According to Pesimwastches, elderhood is not age specific:

> There are some people that we consider elders even before they reach the age of 40…because of their ability to be able to understand and, you know, assist in your past life with this life.

The elder's life had been a wonderful collection of the seen and the heard, a particular testimony to the survival of the people. The death of an elder then represented a celebrative state of mourning. The daily voice had become the ancestral voice:

> I wish I had more stories from this elder that passed away. I wish I had more time for this elder so that I could still pass the stories that she has told or he has recited….You know, not too long ago I was talking to Grandpa…he's passed away now, a couple of months ago…he was just telling me about.

As storyteller, the elder embodied the culture, the people. His/her words were living words and depended solely upon his/her existence for their expression. In a sense, his/her life had been a gift, and he/she had brought honor to that spirit of the living, through the sharing of his/her stories. As Campbell writes, "The privilege of a life time is being who you are" (Osbon, 1991, p. 15). The loss of an elder then is the loss of one who has finally come to terms with his/her own person. Sabochees, through the metaphor of the book, underlined this sense of loss at such an elder's passing:

An elder, he remembers a long time ago and he sees things, the bad...you have to respect an elder like that....If you lose one elder, anywhere in the community like that, it's just like you've lost a book, thick like that....That's what I heard an old guy say.

With the loss of the elder is the people's loss of "one who could see things." The narrative of the people will be less for it:

Like I told you, if you don't have any stories, you won't be any good....And the same thing, if we don't have any elders to tell the stories, if we don't have anything from long, long ago...if we lose that book, we'll get sick.

To Sabochees, the elders meant life. And as such, the elders deserved our highest respect:

You have to respect the elders, any kind of elder, a woman or lady, a man...because they know everything, even the medicine, all the roads on this earth.

Not only did the elders prepare us for our mortality, but by their aging gave flesh to our own daily shadows. De Beauvoir, in *The Coming of Age*, writes:

Let us recognize ourselves in this old man or in that old woman. It must be done if we are to take upon ourselves the entirety of our human state. (Cunningham, 1977, p. 9)

It follows then that respect for an elder is respect for oneself and the "human state." As Sabochees said, it is the elders who know "all the roads" and who have demonstrated the courage and energy to live in the present.

Sabochees felt that an elder also persevered in the face of doubt. And in the face of change, the elder represented the importance of tradition and a bush-life:

Some people don't believe that, even Indian people [i.e., that we're not alive without elders]....Some young people don't believe that...but that's why some old people won't stop. They're still trying to make people understand with the stories.

As traditional embodiment. the elder represented not only his/her people, but his/her time as well, a time when life's circular rhythms did not always include televisions and trucks and hockey games. Black Elk of the Oglala Sioux once said, "The power of the world works in circles" (Meili, 1991, p. 50). To Sabochees, elder time was more calm and circuitous, less busy, more purposeful. There was time to tell the stories of one's life:

> A long time ago, when you wanted to do something, it had to be a story. But now it is different, everything is different....When we stay [in town], we don't even know how long things are....It's just like 1 year is 5 years already. Even in the summertime you're driving around, maybe 3 times a day, and it's night already....If you stay in the bush half a year, you're going to be thinking about 2 years.

"Town time" for Sabochees was hurried, continually going in and out of existence, and often purposeless. Elder time, on the other hand, allowed one space to live circuitously, peacefully with family and self and the land. As I listened to Sabochees, his dark eyes remembering, I felt in the presence of both elder purpose and parable. His words gave me a sense of elder and circulative time. The tea cups were mostly full, baby grandson was in his ceiling swing and I was mindful of the words of Van der Post (cited in Travers, 1989):

> And hearing it [i.e., "once upon a time"], a great peace came upon me. I was beyond space and time, everybody was a neighbor—this universal feeling of propinquity which makes the mystics speak of the forever which is now. (p. 106)

Sabochees, the elder, was able to bring people into proximity, into a nearness of narrative time and space that allowed our communication to take place. Similarly, the person of the elder was able to draw near to others, not only through remembrance and relation, but through the fine art of respectful listening. And good listening, not just conversational pausing, takes time:

> They listen good, and even some people used to be like that, even young people....They go around to old people just for stories. That kind of person, when they get old, now that's when they'll be good with stories, like that. I believe that...some people listen to stories, sometimes a little, but not that much. When they get old, they're not able to tell stories because they didn't listen enough.

A good listener, our friend Nitotem also maintained, was able to respectfully draw near to others. Later there would be time, the elder time, to remember and relate. Within that act of propinquity, there was demonstrated not only the respect shown to the elders, but more initially the elder's own respect for the community and human state.

Thus, the elders listened; it was not simply a matter of being "listened to." As one elder tersely enjoined, "If you listen, then you'll know something" (Meili, 1991, p. 239). According to Nitotem, these elder sensitivities were all a matter of character:

> You have to have the respect, you have to have the character to be an elder....I know a number of people in the community...they're considered as elders and basically because of the way they conduct themselves, the respect they have of the community, of the people.

Individual elders and their stories projected a sense of completed character. Thus, the elders were perceived as having reached a more relaxed and finished state and not as bent on becoming, as the middle-aged. And as Mosum pointed out, there was a personal exchange of power taking place for as the elder's physical prowess began to slip there was a concomitant increase in spiritual power. That spirit came from the fact of survival. "A fine old age," wrote Gide, "can never be taken for granted. It represents perpetual victories, and perpetual recoveries from defeat" (Cunningham, 1977, p. 17). And having survived the many defeats and celebrated the many victories, it is only inevitable that the elder become the mythical and eternal spirit guide to others. To the young, the grandparent is always a grandparent, always a spiritual guide, and ageless:

> She's my grandmother, and it never really came to me, 'til she passed away, that throughout the years, I don't think in my mind, she didn't age at all 'til the day she passed away....I don't think she aged in the 30 years I've seen her. It's like she's always there.

And like his elder Sabochees, Nitotem sensed the unhurried and unfrenzied nature of Grandmother's circuitous life rhythm:

> They had to be busy at all times, too, but it was a different kind of being busy, a different way....I don't think there was a time schedule for people like my Grandmother....Then you had the whole day to do whatever you had to do.

Perhaps that is why, as Sabochees suggested, the elder was able to "see things," that is, they had the kind of time that allowed them to look. Campbell (1989) refers to this elder time as the capacity to live only in the day rather than being driven by possibilities of the day after or the day before:

> After a certain age, there's not a future and suddenly the present becomes rich, it becomes that thing in itself which you are now experiencing. (p. 95)

Perhaps an elder is someone who is now content to live below the surface of his/her own life.

Within the conversation and stories of the northern elders existed also a sense of the pioneer. The elder had come from somewhere else, both geographically and metaphorically. Sabochees, Nitotem and Pesimwastches had talked of those who travelled north to Harper Creek country. They were the pioneers, the "pedone," the foot soldiers. By their travels they had cleared the way of obstructions. As Sabochees had told it, these elders knew all the roads, literally and figuratively. They knew how to get from one place to another. They knew, particularly through narrative, of the bite of hardship and the laughter of accomplished survival. These elders had demonstrated both strength in the leaving and strength in the arrival. Their storytelling itself meant survival for within the later narrative journeys were the shared insights that would be needed by the next generation of travellers. The elders remembered and in doing so gave order back to the world. Through their remembering, life was "given shape that extended back in the past and forward into the future, a simplified, edited tale where completeness may be sacrificed for moral and aesthetic purposes" (Myerhoff, 1980, p. 77).

Not so very long ago, as chance and the purposeful signs would have it, I found myself in the company of the elder Sabochees as we toured an innovative teaching facility for Northern children with special needs. On two or three stops along our tour, the pool, the physio room, we noticed several ordinary adults working with Lynette. Lynette was a paralyzed child of 14, limited to blinking her right eye lid or flexing her wrist as a means of communication. A blink of her right eye meant "yes." Nearing the end of our tour, Sabochees and I were introduced to this imprisoned child. The instructor and Lynette were involved in a music therapy session. "She loves 'Kids on the Block,'" the instructor grinned. I was first introduced to Lynette and murmured, "Hi." I shuffled from foot to foot and thought "God have mercy," unsure, pained, at a loss. Sabochees, however, old trapper and elder from north of the 60th, hunter of moose and good stories, put his weathered arm around this child and gave her a big kiss. And until the end of the visit, old Sabochees remained comfortably at Lynette's side. In that ordinary act of caring, Sabochees gave one educated but unprepared human being a small lesson in elderhood. Elders were those who failed to notice the obstructions.

What is an elder?

The elders were those who had survived, be it middle age or the journey to a new hunting area, and lived to tell of it. Dafna, too, in coming to terms with the Jewish elder, spoke of those who were the first, those who cleared the Israeli way of obstructions. And like Sabochees, Dafna spoke with deep reverence. Again, there was connection in the elder life to the primary reality of the soil:

And you see, the renewal of Israel started with the land. That's how it started, just putting small villages all over the place and working the land...and they said, "Whatever we seed will be ours. If we cultivate the land, it will be ours." That's how they did it, spread all over small places, with so much hardship, but they did it.

Dafna described the elder pioneers as patient and stubborn and independent. They were the ones who courageously came "to places where there was nothing" and survived, those who drew their power from their own work (Dillard, 1982a):

All sorts of diseases, and how you call this, mosquito, malaria, terrible, terrible...with some families they lost most of their children...some families came with 10 children and they were left with one. If we have survived, it is just because of them, not because of the Tel Aviv people, it's not because of anybody else, just because of those people who stuck to the land...they literally stuck to the land. They are the heart.

Their survival became the unifying substance of story:

They carry the legend of our people. If there is a lot of disagreement in many, many areas, everyone agrees on that, those people who started settling our lands in the 80s and 90s of the last century and in the beginning of this century, they established Israel.

With what the elders carried, the character of the people was confirmed. The story of their individual survival, village survival, became the story of a founding people. And within her description of the elder giants, Dafna included also those early Russian pioneers who established the kibbutzim. Their life of equal opportunity was similarly livid with great passion and commitment:

> Work all day, and sing and dance at night....And at that time women did a lot of men's work, too. They not only worked together and shared everything, you know...whatever came in was for everyone's benefit....What these forefathers did, no one can do....Those are the giants.

Like Mosum or Sabochees, Dafna quickly became specific when she spoke of the elders. There was always a named connection to one's own life. Dafna's own daughter, for example, completed a "roots project" in Grade 7. It went to the heart of the "legends":

> She went to her grandpa's and grandma's and interviewed them....They told her the stories, and she went into the photo albums and picked up all sorts of photos from different stages in their life....They trace it many years back with all the names, the stories, and the pictures.

As Dafna told it, this was a year-long project for her daughter and one that culminated in a year-end celebration with the parents and grandparents as special guests:

> My mother-in-law sang a song for them and told them a story of the pioneering days in Israel, you know, at the beginning...just a wonderful celebration....I can see it now!

The elderly mother-in-law perhaps most symbolized for Dafna the pioneer spirit that was Israel, and in her person, she provided witness to a time of giants. It was one thing to survive, but quite another to sing of it. As a child, Dafna often wished that she, too, had been born in Israel, perhaps wanting geographic proximity to the elder and pioneer spirit of the land. Such pioneers deserved every respect, and just as she spoke of her elders with such veneration, so then did her own children:

> My children still respect very much their grandparents, very, very much, so...in the story sometimes, they will sit patiently and listen to

it for the 11th time, you know....And if someone is not feeling well, all of them will go, all of us will go everyday.

As the elder had cared for his/her family and people, so traditionally the elder was cared for during his/her advancing years. Like Sabochees, Dafna sensed a change in this tradition, and it concerned her:

> Up to say the last 20 years or so, there was a very strong feeling for the old....Like my parents, they couldn't have looked upon themselves as not taking care of their own parents, taking them home....They could not have seen themselves as removed from them.

To be close to the elders was to be close to the stories and the life energy from which the stories had been forged, again a matter of propinquity. This traditional consideration of the Jewish elders was, however, changing:

> You'll find many elderly people are sent to homes....It's a way of moving away the problem from your home, from your closeness, and this is a very saddening thing that I can see. This is a big change in what used to be the Jewish tradition.

Dafna, who deeply regretted never meeting her own grandparents, mourned a culture that could distance itself from its elders:

> [My husband] heard stories from his grandma [with whom he shared a room]. See, I never had a grandma or grandpa. They were dead before I was born. I don't even know what it means to have one. This is something I was always so upset about. I never had anyone like that.

Still, in her stories, if not in the days of her childhood, the elders figured largely in Dafna's narrated life. Like Pesimwastches, the elders provided spiritual guidance as the growing Dafna negotiated through the stories of her childhood: Solomon, Rabbi Akeevah, Tolstoy, the folkloral wonders of the brothers Grimm, the famous Israeli poets, and on and on, giants all. The countless stories enabled Dafna to stand on the tip of her toes and wonder about the landscapes that the words shaped. Whereas to Sabochees, the elders lived in their own unofficial words, to Dafna, the elders were also those who inhabited a literary land and thus escaped their own immediate passings. The elders were always giants in their ordinary lives, their days filled with passion and courage. They were the ones who gave so much care to others and asked for so little in return. They were the ones who were able to blend into the story of a people and let it tell itself, uncluttered by perception of self and ownership. The narrative was allowed to spin without glorification of their individual lives. As Rouse (1978) suggests, their story became "our own story, whatever it tells, for the mythic force that makes it, moves by the same laws of feeling that move us" (p. 1). It is enough that the story be told. I have an old feather-hatted friend, whiskered of northern chin and political of eye, who once whispered to me:

> You know every time you put another layer between yourself, your foot and the earth, you make it more difficult for the spirit of our mother to reach you. Sock, shoe, truck, tires, cement pavement...it all separates...even rocks have a hard time living in pavement. (Elder Adolphus, in conversation)

Dafna's elders had a way of feeling the spirit earth. They knew where to step. They seemed able to negotiate the separations.

What is an elder? To our "littlest storyteller," Sparrow, the elders were visitors, mostly specific and named. They were the grandparents and an ordinary part of what was perceived to be an ordinary life. As the elderly, they had lived a full story:

> Did you hear about that guy that my Grandpa saw when they were hunting? The guy that froze? In the canoe?

Sparrow's own life was intricately connected as listener to the narrative of the grandparents, their doings and their tellings:

> Grandpa...he saw lots of stuff, Grandpa....So much adventure, like adventure books.

Just as Grandfather Sabochees described elders as those who could see things, so the child Sparrow described her grandfather as one who "saw lots." And like Dafna, to Sparrow the traditional elders, this time Ukrainian and French, were also giants. They were the details of celebration in a small girl's life:

> It was for Ukrainian Day, and all the Russians are just about Ukrainian, and they performed something for us and then we performed something for them...and there were parents, and then we had pot luck after that for dinner and all sorts of perogies and meatballs

and cabbage rolls. They danced, and then they sang for us in Russian, and we sang in Ukrainian and French.

Like Dafna's daughter and her "roots" project, Sparrow's personal and public life was filled with acts of cultural and elder respect. Every important holiday included considerations of the grandparents. Every important family event and achievement was brought to the attention of the elders for their input and approval. The grandparents, all four within minutes of the family farm, were an almost daily presence in Sparrow's life. They were the ones who brought goodies and stories and tradition to the kitchen table. They brought importance and ceremony to the everyday. They brought kindness and seemed comfortable with Sparrow just as she was, fully enjoying the ongoing story of her childhood.

At times, however, the elderly to Sparrow were objects of great curiosity. They were always old. And they were sometimes odd, even frightening:

> Oh my God...the oldest lady in the world was celebrating her 118th or 119th birthday. Her eyes were like, they were pulled apart and really gross, and she was in a wheelchair, and she was smiling, and she...she didn't have like barely any wrinkles on her...that's old.

Sparrow's words often came in an extemporaneous rush, like the thaw of a spring northern creek. In her folkloral fashion, Sparrow was able to bring the oldest lady in the world, unwrinkled and smiling, into her own unrivaled common sense reality:

> I remember I used to hear...I think I heard from Mom...if you had your kids when you were 18 years old, you'd become 118 until you died. If you had it when you were 14, you'd go 114 years old. That's what I heard.

Thus, the joining of Sparrow to the world of the elders was at times clannish and personal, at times academic and curious, but at all times discursive.

I imagine our athletic Sparrow, her eyes a wrinkle, her ponytail a-bounce, our youngest storyteller; I imagine her stepping out from a bubble-faced crowd, stepping out onto a grass track, a running surface. Sparrow steps out from her surrounding kind and into the stream of runners who race by, swept up like a chopped motorcycle into the pull of a highway freightliner. I imagine that, in the beginning of her race, Sparrow's child legs to be in frantic motion for not only is she sprinting to catch the passing runners and their adult legs, but she is running also to catch the natural rotation of the earth.

Thus, I imagine our "littlest storyteller" to be at the one time engaged in the two runs: the one a burst and immediate, the other more inevitable and to the nature of her species. Now, what if we shift the metaphor? Replace the runners with the specific stories of our kind, the earth's rotation with the narrative stream and oral track that each Sparrow steps out into. Imagine Sparrow's youthful telling, its hurry up, its insistence on engagement, its wonderfully casual sense of space and time, its bursting ahead in sheer joy of dialogical movement. Perhaps as the telling goes on and the storied years slip by, the characters take on an ever-increasing roundness as they, too, shift from the hurried folkloral nature of a suddenly emerged teller to the more rounded drama and echo principles of adulthood. Imagine the child Sparrow's telling as just keeping up, mostly unmindful of the planetary narrative spin but still an integral and intense part of it. Imagine then the child Sparrow as herself elder, ever searching for the wonder point at which the foot race, the single telling becomes the wonder of that larger narrative spin, the wonder point at which 118-year-old pulled-apart eyes see all, the point at which the child temporal becomes the elder eternal, and we tellers all slip off into the shadows of our names.

Imagine, what is an elder? With Grandfather Rattler, the elders were as far ranging as his stories. They varied from grandparents to book publisher to cleric to healer to chief to priest to redcoat to homestead neighbor to explorer to academic, seemingly without end. And without exception, his elders were each of this land, Western Canada, deeply embedded in its rolling prairies and spring-high rivers and coulees. Thus, the trace character of each narrated elder was also to be found in the seams of character of the storyteller Rattler. Like Rattler, the elders were their own people and not about to be obstructed or confined. Within the context of the kitchen table, Grandfather shared this bit of sports and life philosophy:

> What I disliked about skiing is that you're totally confined...in the cross-country you're confined to a track, you know...but with snowshoes you can go anywhere...particularly with the bear-paws...no matter how deep the snow....Once you get that pace, you just keep going and going and going.

Each of his elders met this concept that I call the "bear-paw principle." They all found their own way, and as Sabochees might say, they knew all the personal roads that connected people and places. Of first and retelling importance to a youthful Rattler were the grandparents. They, too, were of the bear-paw principle, and like Dafna's Israeli giants, Sabochees's Cree grandparents, or Sparrow's Ukrainian ancestors, they were the "pedones," the pioneers. And with similar reverence, Grandfather spoke of his English grandparents, their emigration to Canada at the turn of the century, the adventures of their early homestead years along the Red Deer River and later in the "north country":

> My grandfather, you see, was a veterinarian, and he came out about 1903. He was a perfect person for the prairies even though he'd come from a very wealthy family in Lancashire, England...but he just didn't fit in. I'd say he'd make a perfect example of the remittance man, but he wasn't. He came out to homestead...actually he came out as veterinarian....On the cattle boat Pat Burns had hired my grandfather.

By the spring of 1907, Rattlers' grandparents and their children found themselves in a covered wagon "heading out" for Red Deer River country, slowly picking their way through the rotting carcasses of recent winter killed cattle. Two years later, the couple and their children moved into a nearby town and opened up two or three livery stables. Being a good neighbor was a matter of course:

> He said as many patients were human as were [animal]. He said some of the calipers he had for small animals worked just as well pulling human teeth....There was just trade, you know. No one had any money.

And feeling the south to be uncomfortably civilized, the grandparents moved on once again, this time to homestead in the north. Years and stories later, the couple opened a pleasure resort on a beautiful northern lake:

> He was 93....He was a pretty good age when he came to Canada, you see, but he spent all that winter building boats, and he got an infection in March in his kidneys....There was no penicillin available then, and he died of kidney infection....But the day before they took him in he was still hammering away on the boats.

The enduring grandparents lived in Rattler's wonderful medicine bag of stories. Their faces and adventures kept popping up like prairie crocuses throughout our storyteller's tales and talks. There was the story of Grandma and how she came by her copper kettle, Big Jack's haunted saddle and the livery barn, Big Mike and the Ghost camps, and in all these glorious tales there was a bigness and a proving up. Like Dafna's elders, these pedone cleared the way of obstructions. Their love, their laughter and their stories endured as they lived and narrated by the bear-paw principle, unconfined and just "kept on going." The stories of Rattler's grandparents suggested yet another fragile truth. Elders not only facilitate a propinquity in the species, but they are able to do so because they were themselves loved. All of them, they were loved. Although my elders vary widely, widely in age, disposition and race, they all deviate not one whit from that given; they were loved in an unconfined way, a "set the spirit free" way. Perhaps that is why Rattler's storied elders seemed able to give themselves to the thing, the homestead, the adventure, the struggle, the clan, the story. They evinced a kind of concentrated passion and were able, like Dafna's elders, to stick to it. They had focus. Rattler beautifully illustrated this in his "pin point" story:

> A friend and I had gone up in 1949 to Banff just before the University opened....We'd just taken a cottage in Banff, and we stayed there for a couple of weeks. My brother had promised me his car, but he could not get it to us right away....[Later] he phoned me and said, "My car is ready now, come and get it," so I took the bus out of Banff quite early that morning about 6 o'clock....When we got past Canmore, there was somebody standing along side the road....He looked like he must have travelled this way all the time, and the bus was fairly full. There was a space, so he came and sat beside me, and we started talking....He had the strangest packsack I'd ever seen, but it was his portfolio of pictures, you see.

More synchronicity here, where the myth meets science and coincidence takes on meaning. Rattler immediately recognized the well-known and elderly artist, and being a painter himself, they were soon immersed in art talk. The conversation then specifically turned to the amount of blues in the artist's mountain pictures and the manner by which he visualized his subjects:

> He laughed, and he reached in and pulled out this little card...and made a pinhole in it. And he said, "Look at those mountains through that." It was marvellous.

Rattler was greatly taken by the pinhole camera, this diffuser of blue mountain and golden stook field light. And Rattler's own stories of the elders were like that. They diffused the light, both elder and story. These stories made more public what the teller Rattler held private (Cohan & Shires, 1988, p. 1). Within the traditional net of elder stories, Rattler told not only of grandparents and kin, but also of friends and acquaintances. There were tales of the town starter Father Langevin, Old Bob the founder of Mule Days and Bill, the outspoken publisher:

> He might find a hundred reasons against and one reason for it, but that one reason for it, because he's visionary, will encompass the one hundred other reasons that were against...and go ahead and do it.

Like Sparrow's Ukrainian grandparents, they had pinhole focus and the passion that such concentration called forth. At their best, these characters were visionary and carried within their bones a sense of the generations to come. And by their storytelling nature, they were all teachers. Rattler recalled with strong and great fondness one such teacher elder. As the seven gods of storyteller fate would have it, the family crop, a bumper wheat crop, was hailed out, and so a young Rattler was unable to attend university in Louisiana and complete his engineering degree. Instead, Grandfather found himself in a 4-month war emergency course for teachers, thanks to the particular guidance of one kindly and elderly professor, Dr. Sansom:

> We'd sit outside the old church, right across from the hotel, we'd sit across and it was like Socrates and all his students would gather round and we'd talk and he was such an interesting....I explained my dilemma, and he said, "Oh no problem at all, come in and see me in the morning and I'll register you." So that was the beginning of my teaching career.

And years later, this same kind of elder presence in education would greatly influence Rattler's daily teaching story, this time in the person of a well-loved principal:

> Some of my fondest memories of teaching goes back to there because our principal was like an old grandfather. He's 90 now, and he's still active...he's considered legally blind, you know...still straight and strong. After he retired from teaching, he became a minister, hospital chaplain, because he loved working with older people as he said and sick people....He was sort of the grandfather of the school....I don't know how he did it...he just had this bearing about him.

Like Sabochees and his concern for elder time, Rattler found the presence of the grandfatherly principal to be calming and a step removed from the now budgeted and digitalized nature of western education. Both Dr. Sansom and the principal brought young people to the circle and more specifically brought the professional life of Rattler back to the elder and story circle of the Red Deer River country. Within their natures, and the nature of his grandparents, were the very insights into teaching pedagogy that our grandfather would need. Principles of bear-paws and pinholes come to mind.

Indeed, the circle of old ones that held Rattler in its spell was not limited only to kin and acquaintance. There was another dimension in Rattler's life that gave flesh to the concept of elder. That dimension was historical and folkloral. It was specific and for Rattler included such western personalities as Maskipitoon, Poundmaker, Gabriel Dumont, Anthony Henday, police scout Jerry Potts, Reverend John McDougall and Chief Crowfoot. These giants came alive in the details and in the telling. They were often conjured up from Rattler's story bag, and as if by the magic of once upon a time, each elder connected to the other. In the telling, they were full flesh, personal, and never reduced to the commonplace:

> Jerry Potts was born in Montana, yeah, his father was a factor at one of the forts along the Missouri....He was a marvelous interpreter...and of course...he just couldn't get lost. He led this party of North West Mounted Police through a blizzard some 60 miles, and they discovered that when he got to...probably Old Fort Whoop-Up, you know, when they finally got through this blizzard, they discovered that Jerry Potts had been snow blind through it all...yet he knew exactly where he was going. What it was, was sensitivity.

Each of those Rattler called elder, even those literary word blind, displayed this special sensitivity and sense of direction, pinpoint purpose, and perhaps none more so than the one whom MacEwan (1958) refers to as the chief of chiefs, Crowfoot (p. 23):

> Crowfoot's son was lost, he was killed by the Cree, so Crowfoot adopted a Cree boy, who became the Chief of the Plains Cree [i.e., Poundmaker]. What an incredible man Crowfoot was, too, because after that there was peace between the groups....He had insight.

And all the Rattler stories of elders now "gone into sleep and light" evinced this ability of the old ones to heal. Just as Rattler's words spun a connective and medicinal web, so the lives of the folkloral healed through laughter and courage and remembrance. As with Sabochees, the presence of elders now ensured the ancestors later. They provided liaison to the healing spirit of the place as they travelled like the sun and through the day. I am reminded of my trapper friend, Mooniyas, who skiffs his way down the Peace River, in most seasons, on his watery way to Big Slough probably, by plywood boat he pokes his way up every creek, to drop a fish hook, shoot a duck, or check for fresh moose tracks. Mooniyas travels like that, but always to return to the main river and channel, the Peace, always.

Rattler's like that with his stories of the elders, you see. He takes you up many narrative creeks along the telling way, he teases the fish of your interest with the hook of his artful telling, but always to return to the elder places and the main channel of the tale.

And for all of that, what is an elder? When our Arusha Masai friend and storyteller, Tololwa, spoke of elders, he spoke first in metaphor and second of specific person:

> The elders are seen more like, ok if you have a tree then probably...[the elder] is the trunk from which the branches grow out of...the ancestors may be providing the roots....Over here [i.e., in Canada], you might find the elder be seen as a kind of a dead branch breaking off a tree.

Like Mooniyas' river travel, there were branches and there were main channels. In the society of his childhood, Tololwa described the hierarchal circuitry of community relationships and life. The elders, and specifically his grandparents, had graduated to a position of respect and honor. That is just the way it was:

> My grandfather was almost like an institution, that the older they get the more respected they become....I guess because they get closer to the-ah ancestors. So maybe the closer you get to the ancestors, the more respected you are.

There are many similarities here to the culture of Mosum's youth whereby this loss of physical power and aging was counterbalanced by an increase in spiritual strength. The treatment of Masai elders was similarly ordained by tradition:

> According to tradition, the elders are supposed, you know, to be respected....Giving him, my grandfather, a place of his own, that was a sign of respect, almost as if that was his, his, as it were his sanctuary, and he deserved that. He deserves peace. He deserves, uh, to be listened to, you know. There is no question of mistreating the elders, of

course some people did that, but according to tradition, in principle, you're not supposed to do that. Tradition was on their side.

Tololwa's grandfather, like Sabochees, was able not only to see things, but to tell things. Everyone who lived with Grandfather on the coffee farm worked hard, as did Grandfather. At times he could be driving, "like a wounded buffalo," but also, at other times, he could break into a wonderful story. Talking in the Masai language was literally "eating one's words," and Grandfather was one who so loved to dine on words, to tell and retell the world to his children and grandchildren. Many of his stories came from those who visited him for they were not allowed to leave his company until they had told him one new thing. I am reminded of Dafna here and her own father who similarly learned at least one new thing each day. Yes, the Arusha Masai grandfather would tell of real life, as he had heard it and storied it to be, countless times:

> He would see a plane go by, and he would say, "Hmm, did I ever tell you about the British?" and then he would go into one of his stories about the British during the Second World War and, you know, planes going over the city of Paris and-uh some of the things had happened in history, but he would mix history with a lot of legend.

And as with Tololwa, the stories grew and took on a life of their own. Grandfather, like his grandson, was provoked to story by a stimulating world:

> He would see a man walking by with a funny hat and he would say, "Did I ever tell you about the man who got into trouble because of his hat?" Of course, he had told me the story 10 times, but I would say no, and he would tell me again.

Thus, a respectful and traditional response was given by a child to one grandfather who respectfully and traditionally told of life. To the grandchildren, wide-eyed and listening still, Grandfather was elder, and elder was story. In the eating of his words, Grandfather not only painted the world, he created it. And so, in the beginning of things and from the perfect void of silence came a grandparent's story.

Sabochees would call this beginning of things from the perfect void of silence "once upon an elder time." It was an elder time when story came from survival and breath, not script. Elder speech came from the earth and its winds, from a primary reality. It was probably never terribly neat, never terribly precise, but wandering and human. The elder speech did not list. It comforted and teased and divined:

> There are some elders who have the ability to be able to tell the nature of the seasons, the coming seasons, just by looking at the stars....The morning star would usually tell....I think it must be its relation to other stars, you know.

Being an elder had something to do with the full circle, Le Guin's hoop snake, Grandmother's hearth. It was never a tidy matter of two opposite and magnetic points or an exercise in dualities. It was full ellipse. The elder was animation for a certain kind of full living made for good telling, good animation.

And by all the above, I have travelled widely in words but always I hoped to return to the main discursive channel of "What is an elder?" The story talk and the story tales were both an elder celebration and an elder concern. For within the joy of the specific, Pesimwastches's grandma, Rattler's grandfather, within the courage of the lived words, there lived also fear. Can we imagine a time without our elders, a time of no "living national treasures" (Franck, 1980, p. 24)? And if we can imagine such an eventuality, what then? Can our world survive without the holy place called elderhood? Je-Nee expressed her concern this way:

> We don't have our [Korean] grandparents anymore in the same house, in the same home....The children doesn't have chance to listen to the story from their grandparents....When my grandma told a story and my kindergarten teacher told a story, they always told...it was so live, it was just real, real....I felt that real things was happening....When they told about tiger, they just imitate tiger's voice, and everything was just vivid, vivid.

Increasingly, the elders, as animators and pedone of so many cultures, are being exiled to the twilight zone of bridge, crib and Chun Gee. It is to be hoped that their eventual return from exile will itself be a good telling.

As a little sun-freckled boy, I would bicycle and coast my way to Grannie's for a visit. She would be stationed on the end of a large white sofa, her old legs curled under, somewhere in the middle of a cork-filtered cigarette and a tall glass of ginger ale. Grannie smoked Spud cigarettes. They smelled of "across the line." I would reach for the yellow and orange sugar candies. No limits. And then we would talk, Grannie and I, of creatures and characters. When she laughed, Grannie laughed full belly, from her under curled legs to the top of her grey "perm." Often, too, there would be a little chore on those visits. Grannie would have me open a jar, for example, just open a pickle jar with a tight lid. She started me on my career, actually, as opener of jars and explorer of sacrosanct places:

> The new ceremonies were not like the old ones; but he never said they were not complete, only different. (Silko, 1977, p. 233)

Deer Hide Painting:
They Say You Talk To The Angels

They Say You Talk To The Angels

It was an old, old, old, old lady
And a boy who was half past three;
And the way they played together
    Was beautiful to see.

She couldn't go running or jumping
And the boy no more could he
For he was a thin little fellow,
    With a thin little twisted knee.

They sat in the yellow sunlight,
Out under the maple tree;
And the game that they played I'll tell you
    Just as it was told to me.

It was Hide and Go Seek they were playing
Though you'd never have known it to be,
With an old, old, old, old lady
    And a boy with a twisted knee.

The boy would bend his face down
On his one little sound right knee,
And he'd guess where she was hiding
    In Guesses One, Two, Three.

"You're in the china closet!"
He would cry and laugh with glee.
It wasn't the china closet;
    But he still had two and three.

"You are up in Papa's big bedroom
In the chest with the queer old key!"
And she said, "You are warm and warmer.
    But you're not quite right," said she.

"It can't be the little cupboard
Where Mamma's things used to be,
So it must be in the clothes press, Grandma."
    And he found her with his three.

Then she covered her face with her fingers,
That were wrinkled and white and wee,
And she guessed where the boy was hiding
   With a One, and a Two, and a Three.

And they never stirred from their places,
Right under the maple tree—
This old, old, old, old lady
   And boy with the lame little knee.

This dear, dear, dear, dear lady
And a boy that was half past three.
(Bunner, 1917)

   Our daughter Siné and I sat at our Dunvegan kitchen table as Betty slowly recited these words, her thumb and fingers touching on each "old" to get it right. Betty cried near the end, and she said she was crying for 1959. Sometime that summer, in a shiplap-sided farmhouse surrounded by caragana hedges, the child Betty sat with her mother and grandmother. They were cutting up vegetables for the noon farm meal. The linoleum was green and white and clean shiny, and Grampa of the bushy eyebrows was out in the shop. Grandmother was loudly silent for she had several strokes years previously and could no longer speak. "Tell your grandmother what you're doing in school," mother coaxed. Betty paused, then a child's inspiration. "I know, we learned a poem….It goes 'It was an old, old, old, old lady.'" And as Betty recited, she touched finger to thumb four times, and by the second verse, Mom had joined in, their voices together in rhythm. The next verse, it was Grandma's turn, yes Grandma. Her whisper came in from the silence, growing stronger with each verse. Grandma joined in, and the three generations finished the poem together, as one voice. Betty said she remembers how her mother and grandmother cried and her not understanding exactly why. Since that summer noon so many seasons ago, Betty has become the mother, her mother the grandmother, and grandmother the ancestor. The new grandmother has had several strokes, too, and so as Betty recited for us, she too cried as she touched finger tip to thumb, four times. I knew exactly why.
   In that story of the intergenerational, we are given the connection of the very young to the very old. It is, I believe, the relationship of the storyteller to the listener, of those who need to speak and those who need to listen. My storytellers have taught me also that the parts are interchangeable;

indeed, they must change if the promise of conversation is to be fulfilled. We each of us sit in the noon sunshine, sit on green and white linoleum and cut up our vegetables, each of us both listener and speaker and one day ancestor. As Fulghum (1986) writes, "Nature so works it that everybody gets a turn at getting what they deserve in one way or another. And while the meek may or may not be blessed, some of them are prepared" (p. 44). When Grandmother lost her speech, she could no longer be listened to, yet she still found a part to play, behind her fingers that were "wrinkled and white and wee." Grandma found a way to prepare, just as listening to her story and her person, I, too, am better prepared.

This intergenerational conversation has been wonderfully told in the metaphor of story, in film and print. I am very often reminded of the movie *The Milagro Beanfield War*, lovingly directed by Robert Redford (1988). It is a story of ordinary events, of how something as mundane as water to a beanfield can initiate change, big change, human progress as opposed to industrial and economic growth. At one point in the filmy retelling, Herb, the sociology graduate student from NYU, approached the elderly and idiosyncratic Amoronteh with "They say you talk to the angels?" And the Mexican elder replied, "They are the only ones with time to listen." Throughout the telling, Amoronteh was visited by the Coyote Angel. At times, the angel teased the old man, cajoled, debated, advised, but always the Coyote Angel listened, just listened. Herb learned the sacrifice of this and by movie end had himself become something of a messenger, an angel. Perhaps every storyteller needs a Coyote Angel; they each create the other, "teller" and "told to." And I take every human being to be a storyteller. The very old and the very young seem to still have time as they sit in the "yellow sunlight, under the maple tree." As storyteller and Coyote Angel, they are able to take each other home again, "not to recover home, no. But to sanctify memory" (Fulghum, 1986, p. 26).

Perhaps of all my listening, it was most important that I listen to Sparrow. For her I became something of a Coyote Angel. I realized, too, how easy it was to go through my important days of grown-upness without ever really listening to a child. By my listening, Sparrow became a storyteller, a teller of sudden twists and turns. She told me of the big things, like angels:

> Normally, they don't dress in black or other colors, they just dress in white for good people. Some people say if you believe in going, if you believe that you go to Heaven when you die, they're going to take you up....Angels sometimes have these rings around their heads, and-uhm I'm not sure why, and they normally have blonde hair,

that's what I've seen, or brown hair, or white. And they also are very gentle and everything.

And then just as suddenly, she told me of ghosts:

There are no ghosts that maybe haunt you or anything, but I heard stories that they do…and you notice on the word ghosts that the "h" is silent, so you don't go g hosts! That's what I learned in Grade 2. (laughter)

As much as Sparrow loved a good story, be it *Home Alone 2* or a *Fear Street* novelette, she was comfortably situated in the theatre of the everyday. She saved things up for her Coyote Angel:

He and his friends were driving…you know where my Grannie and Grandpa live…well they were driving down that highway and they hit the ditch and they rolled it and…then it rolled again. And, right now he is in the University Hospital…and he's still in one of those kind of comas where they don't want you to wake up.

Everything, for Sparrow, held a story, and everything, a sister's cold, a new calf, Grandpa's fishy smelling truck, needed a telling. From time to time, however, I became the storyteller, Sparrow the listener, the angel. Then days later, I would hear the story back again, after it had been fully embodied and become a somatic event. By this narrative process, Sparrow and I once told of the three old men who were playing out their final folkloral hand in a shared hospital room: Ernest, Len and William. There was but one window, one visual contact with the outside world. And it was Ernest, a senior survivor, whose bed looked out from their hospital room and whose words often described that life beyond. Life moved on, and so it was that Ernest passed away and two days later Len was moved to the bed by the window. Len had his way with words and described in loving detail all he saw, the leaves turned up for the rain, the laddered fire trucks as they sped by, the young people holding awkward hands. William, ignited by the landscapes that he could only hear about, decided that it was his turn for the window and so

one night, like [Len] had a bad heart…and one night he was reaching out for his pills and [William] stole the guy's pills…and then [Len] died.

The next day, William was moved, at long last, to the bed by the window. Finally it was his turn. Not until the nurse left the room did the old man expectantly turn to the window

and noticed that there...noticed that there was just a wall there...there was just a brick wall....Oh, can you imagine.

Through Sparrow's words, I could imagine. By those words, she had become my window, my Coyote Angel. Again she had shown me how a brick wall could become a transparency, if one listened closely. And as much as Len needed to tell of things imaginable, William needed to listen. By the words, the listener became "warm and warmer." Some Coyote Angels knew these shortcuts. And I am not sure how, but it seems to me that the very young know what it is to want the bed by the window. They have a special sensitivity to the limited view and hardships of others. My "littlest storyteller" certainly knew what it was to look up to someone:

Did you hear about the guy that my Grandpa saw when they were hunting? The guy that froze? In the canoe? There were these live canoers going down the river and they...the canoe tipped or something. And they really froze in the water, and their ice jackets were solid frozen, and they were frozen, and they took them in to the hospital...my Grandpa took them in to the hospital....Grandpa, he saw lots of stuff.

Grandpa, for Sparrow, was in the bed by the window. His magical life held both the doing and the telling. He, like Coyote Angel, knew the shortcuts between words. Grampa knew how to hide things in the clothes press and in his words so that they would be found. It was a game of Sardines:

Better than hide and seek, I like the game called Sardines. In Sardines, the person who is It goes and hides, and everybody goes looking for him. When you find him, you get in with him and hide there with him. Pretty soon everybody is hiding together, all stacked in a small space like puppies in a pile. And pretty soon somebody giggles and somebody laughs and everybody gets found. Medieval theologians even described God in hide-and-seek terms, calling Him Deus Absconditus. But me, I think old God is a Sardine player. And will be found the same way everybody gets found in

Sardines—by the sound of laughter of those heaped together at the end. (Fulghum, 1986, p. 56)

Perhaps the middle-aged and the middle-minded play hide-and-seek best, while it is the young and old who prefer Sardines. They prefer to be found together, in the pile and with laughter. In listening to Sparrow, in slipping on the mythic guise of Coyote Angel, I found that pile as easy as "one, two, three." It was as easy as finding my Grandfather Willie who used to hide behind elm trees.

There was the Amoronteh and Coyote Angel in my listening relationship to Grandfather Rattler, too. But I would choose another metaphor, a different story, this time Hemingway's (1952) *The Old Man and the Sea*. In that tale, the elderly Cuban fisherman, Santiago, has been 85 days without a catch. Grandfather becomes an object of community derision, an anachronism, worthy only of porch and pipe. To the boy, Manolin, however, "There are many good fishermen and some great ones. But there is only you" (Hemingway, 1952, p. 23). The old man and the boy dearly loved one another, and oh how they talked, often about fishing, always about baseball and the great DiMaggio. They no longer fished together for Manolin's parents had insisted that the lad move to a luckier boat. And so on the eighty-fifth day of his trial, the old man, alone, weakened with age but still full of tricks, takes to the far fishing grounds. There Santiago hooked, finally, a fish. But it is no ordinary fish; they never are:

> And the fish came out. He came out unendingly and water poured from his sides. He was bright in the sun and his head and back were dark purple and in the sun the stripes on his sides showed wide and a light lavender. His sword was as long as a baseball bat and tapered like a rapier and he rose his full length from the water and then reentered it, smoothly..."he is two feet longer than the skiff," the old man said. (Hemingway, 1952, p. 62)

The wonderful story that followed is the story of one old man who refused to cut the line and let go. Instead, Santiago struggled with hunger and thirst, bleeding hands, fateful sharks; he struggled. And throughout those days of unbearable anguish, the old man took heart from his memories of the boy, from their talks together.

I, too, filled the Manolin part as my grandfathers talked of their fishing days, their refusals to cut the line. As Rattler, for example, set before me the narrative events of his life, we looked together for the pattern, the unifying themes. We looked for faces in the river driftwood and for fingerprints on the crocuses:

> One project among many, one that tempts me and might be tempting to others, is trying to find a shape or pattern in our lives. These are rich patterns, I believe, even if they are hard to discern. Our lives that seemed a random and monotonous series of incidents are something more than that. Life in general (or nature, or the history of our times) is a supremely inventive novelist or playwright. (Cowley, 1976, p. 70)

It was a collaborative act, Amoronteh and Coyote Angel, Santiago and Manolin, Rattler and Sparrow and all the others and I. In his search for pattern, Rattler held on to the giant marlin, held on to life. And that line was best crafted for him with story, sometimes relaxed, at other times vibrating with the tension. Appropriately enough, Rattler had a story for this, the life sustaining nature of the intergenerational relationship. It was the last story Grandfather told to me and began with an artful consideration of reincarnation:

> Suddenly in the 7th Century [reincarnation] appears not only in India through the Upanishads, but in Greece through Pythagoras and among the Druids....So it suddenly appeared this idea of reincarnation...but among Indian peoples it just didn't exist at all...except this one incident that took place at Three Hills that involved perhaps reincarnation. This is a story again told me by this old storyteller friend from Hobbema, and he was actually participating in it.

Not only did I hear a story of the intergenerational, but I witnessed the intergenerational dynamic in Rattler's relationship to the Hobbema elder and in my relationship to Rattler. Indeed, the folkloral voice by its very existence was an intergenerational one, a voice in pursuit of patterns. Years and years ago, the Hobbema storyteller had been travelling with his family along the traditional Great North Trail that led from Alaska and meandered southernly down through Alberta when

> they camped for the night at Three Hills, and there was a young boy there, a 4- or 5-year-old boy there, uhm-suddenly started screaming in the middle of the night....His mother went to him, and he kept

saying "over there," and he pointed to some brush on the side of the hills: "I'm dead! I'm buried over there! I'm buried over there!"

The next morning the family did some digging and sure enough they found a man buried under the brush, dressed in buckskins with his skull crushed. Uneasy from the incident, the family quickly moved on and sometime later reached a Metis encampment on the north side of Buffalo Lake:

> And when the boy got there, he suddenly ran over to this old lady and hugged her and started kissing her, and his mother said, "Who is that?"..."This is my wife."...At any rate, they showed the woman some of the buckskin they'd found, and she said, "I sewed that...that belonged to my husband. He disappeared on a hunting trip around Three Hills, many, many years before."

In Rattler's tale, the spirit lived on, by deed and by story, the spirit lived on. And through the dynamic of the intergenerational, the form changed, but the spirit remained changeless, even raging at times. Santiago, full of fury and tricks, brought the marlin in and gave its rapier to the boy.

And Rattler, he told stories and in his stories gave the rapier of pattern and so prepared the listener. As Powys writes, "In only one way can our mortal and it may be, our immortal life be bravely, thoroughly, and absolutely justified, and that way is by treating it as a story" (Cowley, 1976, p. 71). The spirit of the Three Hills hunter was the spirit of story, and story that needed a good telling.

I am reminded of another old man, Baptiste. Old Baptiste and I first met in the trade of my singleshot 12 gauge for his son's sled dog. After that we nodded our acquaintance often, at Harry's Trading Post and along the winter road. We developed in this way a friendship and a history. And from that friendship I was able to hear of Baptiste's spring hunt.

Some years ago, when the water had muddied from the spring melt and the high water sticks had moved on, Baptiste had moved his family to the river, back to the river. And on many evenings, old Baptiste, in woolen trousers and old time cap, would paddle his canvas canoe down river, down river for the beavers and the black ducks. One particular night, while adrift along the shore in the spring hunt, old Baptiste ran out of ammunition, .22 longs. But although the old man was out of shells, he still made the motions, with merriment, finger pointing at ducks at they flew by, slapping his hands together in Chipewyan fashion to indicate a probable kill. Drifting, drifting, he finger shot his way along. Then suddenly four black ducks exploded up from a backwater near the canoe. The old man's finger went up, and he tongue-clicked the shots. All four ducks fell dead to the water. They fell like river stones from the night sky. They fell beside the old man and his canvas canoe.

After that the old man was often served tea before he even knew he was thirsty, and he had a hard time catching up with his stories. The tea leaves in the bottom of his cup seldom said anything.

Rattler and old Baptiste taught me that the stories of the cut lines and confused tea leaves were important, too. These were the stories of the power that failed or was overspent. As much as the young drew inspiration and strength from Santiago, they drew caution from Baptiste. One had to come to terms with the imagined, for as Picasso said, "everything imagined was real, " especially from the bed by the window (Cowley, 1976).

My Grandmother Fraser lived also in the generation of tea leaves, no bags and little strings for her. And after we, as prairie kids, blew on and sipped our sugared tea, we would pass our melmac cups to Grandma. There she sat, rigidly upright, still skating at age 80 with her white hair up and her wire-framed glasses correctly on. She held our relationships, our fortunes and patterns in her wrinkled hands. Her words came like tongue clickings from old Baptiste's finger gun. And once Grandma said it, the words were loose. She held our fortunes in her firm words. Oh, how we listened, our freckles and eyes wide as Grandma recreated us by tea ceremony. We were the marlin on Grandma's narrative line.

It was Bateson who articulated a world viewed as relationship rather than objects, with relationships the essence of a living nature, and

> stories, Bateson would say, are the royal road to the study of relationships. What is important in a story, what is true in it, is not the plot, the things, or the people in the story, but the relationships between them. Bateson defined a story as: "an aggregate of formal relations scattered in time." (Capra, 1988, p. 78)

Like Bateson, Mosum presented his ideas to the young through the aggregate of story. In doing so, Grandfather revealed not only his guidance, but his love and his sensitivity to the relationships that connect us:

> We spent most of our lives outdoors, regardless of weather or season. Many times we walked on icy water or in rain, and many times we slept on the bare, frozen ground. Today, most of the elderly people, including myself, have rheumatism.

Most of the things we had were homemade. Everything we ate was fresh from the land, rivers and lakes. The meat was prepared by boiling or roasting, not frying. I believe all of this contributed to the health and strength of the people. The air and water were clean, fresh and sweet.

Transportation was provided by water, animals and man himself. Fire provided the energy for cooking, heat and light.

On many occasions, the people travelled for miles and always at their own expense. Sometimes they went to a Feast or Tea Dance, to visit a sick friend, or to mourn the passing of a friend or a loved one.

These are the ways I have seen and experienced. My parents lived and worked this way. I, too, followed in their ways and their footsteps.

By his stories, Mosum gave variations upon this central theme. His words and narrative journey drew a web from the young listener to the presence of the "old, old, old, old." The language of "High Cree" and the complexity of relationships only enhanced the message:

Things today have changed considerably. The modern ways have changed the way of life of the Indian people. Travel, communication and life itself is very fast.

There are rules and regulations that govern us. We must live and abide by these rules.

We have been given a land, a "reservation," with no jobs, no animals, and no choice. Our pride has been tarnished. We are a voice crying in the dark.

Most of the food we buy goes through a treatment process before it reaches the market. Our fields are sprayed, and our water purified before it can be consumed. No wonder people get sick!

It is sad to say that our ways are going, but true.

As much as Grandfather enjoyed storying the details, the firefighting for $3.50 a day, the stack of beaver pelts that were required to purchase a flintlock, the fur tokens valued at $0.33, the meat caches and the ever-present threat of wolverines, the central theme of his stories was always about the relationship between the young and the old and the growing concern for the present generation. That was Grandfather's main narrative channel:

Our young people are losing their heritage, culture and language.

I seldom talk of the old days to the young people because they do not listen, believe or understand. They are really lost—not knowing and not understanding the two cultures.

I sometimes fear I will lose my mind because of the simplicity of modern life. There is little physical work involved. Machines have taken over the work of men. We rely on material things for our daily needs.

Will the future generations say "Those were the good old days" when referring to our present generation? We will never know. Time alone will tell.

Grandfather, like Bateson, despaired of a reality filled with objects rather than relationships. By his stories, Mosum indeed encouraged the young to imagine another, a former way, a life made beautiful by the interweave of people and story. For Grandfather, this web of narrative lives formed a wonderful pattern, and one that intimately echoed the natural world that existed both within and without. The people moved with the seasons and in the seasons. It was all about balance. And imagine our elder's concern when he stood in witness of lives far out of balance, young lives now patternless, disconnected and alone, lives dispirited. Mosum, throughout his talk and tales, ever returned to the metaphor of the land, as did his people. Again, like Bateson, elder of another tradition, Mosum's words spoke to "the structure of nature and the structure of mind as reflections of each other...with mind and nature of a necessary unity" (Capra, 1988, p. 80). Thus, by his intergenerational act of story, Grandfather led the young from mind into nature. His words promised a cultural pattern that could connect.

Mosum also taught me an underlying truth of our storytelling species. Good storytellers give what they have and they have what they are. Good stories, memorable stories are deeply embedded in the tellers, and there is a spirit web that connects story mind to story matter. Good storytellers, in their intergenerational act, give what they are, aggregates in time. Our

Israeli wordsmith, Dafna, told this story of Hassidic origin. It beautifully illustrated the narrative enactment by which we connect to our kind, our God, and the manner by which we give what we are:

> There is another story about the day of Atonement which is the most holy of holy days....And the synagogue was crowded with people in this remote village in Eastern Europe...and all of the people were singing and praying on a very, in a very dedicated manner, and all of a sudden out of this praying, out of the books, of course, a strong whistle cut the mumbling of the prayers. And everyone was just startled! On the holiest of days someone was standing and whistling...and there was a peasant boy, a Jewish peasant boy who used to herd the cows. He never learned to read, he never learned a word, but he so wanted to talk to God, and this was the only way he knew. So he whistled, and everyone thought "now we are doomed and the Rabbi will be so upset."...But the Rabbi said, "We have to thank him because thanks to him God will listen to us this Atonement Day."

In our conversation that followed, Dafna praised the child for his heart and "purest intention." The elder Rabbi understood this passion of the child, understood what it is for the young to seek contact with their God and a place in the mystery, in the pattern. And through the story, Dafna was able to cut through the listener's own state of mumbling silence and reveal something of the relationship of the unlearned to matters of the spirit. When one gave what one had, as in the whistle of the peasant boy or the little food sacrifices of Amoronteh to Saint Jude, one received in kind. This was the circularity of the intergenerational and of all living phenomenon. One became the path by travelling on it, as the Buddha said (Chatwin, 1987, p. 74). By storyline, the elder found the child, the child discovered the elder, and a relationship, a pattern, was confirmed, with story as a primal state of giving. Giving gave connection. Dafna told this story:

> In Israel, they support, and even after they get married, you wouldn't believe it, the mother will come with two bags of whatever, she cooked this and she made this and she went to the market and she saw such a wonderful piece of whatever and she had to buy it. I still remember the fights my husband had with my parents when we first got married....Everytime they came, they had something for us. It could be a rocking chair. It could be a new lamp. It could be a new

set of dishes. And he was so upset. He said, "But we should get it on our own! Why do you bring all this stuff?" And they didn't know what he wanted from them, they were so used to this giving and giving and giving...and then he gave in. He caved in. He couldn't say anything anymore. (laughter)

Even today, Dafna assured me, the giving continues, especially to the grandchildren. Such giving, as Bateson would say, had little to do with objects and everything to do with relationships. The acceptance of a gift was in fact the acceptance of a relationship, a part in the weave. Dafna told also of an older generation's painful gift of story:

> I think only after they had children and the children grew up that they started to talk about the war. Some of them did, but most did not talk about the war for years, 25 years at least....For many years it was just "let me live my life, reconstruct my life, and start a new beginning, and I don't want to remember it." Only much later when they had settled and had a family that they started.

Bateson's definition of story as "an aggregate of formal relations in time" defined also the storyteller. This human aggregation of relationships unfolded, engaged, and connected the young to the old through time. Dafna demonstrated so many times that the narrative, connective line ever-spiralled back and forth through the centuries:

> I would say that most people do take the shape of their surroundings. I know I am very different here than I am over there. You probably do to survive, I guess. But you cannot always be totally different than you really are. There is always the real you in you, no matter where you are.

The "real you" for Dafna embraced a people and their stories. The "real you" was filled with the ancestors, the ones who had given so much, the ones who told for all they were worth, the ones whose stories pierced the air like a whistle during prayers:

> All of the Israelites, that's how we call ourselves, are friends. We have that expression which means all of the Israelites are friends; but it's more than the sense of "friends," you know...like this togetherness that one will give everything for the other. The other will give everything for the next.

Thus, we are bound by our givings into the patterns of our people. The old occupy a space, a bed by the window, that they in time might will to the young. And as Kornhaber and Woodward (1981) write, "Each time a child is born, a grandparent is born too" (p. xi).

Throughout my listening time, and particularly as Coyote Angel to the grandparents in my study, Rattler, Mosum, Sabochees, Pesimwastches, the Sakostenohks, I was revisited by yet another metaphor of the intergenerational, this time Mitchell's (1962) story of *The Kite*. It is the foothills tale of Daddy Sherry, almost 111 years old, the great-great-grandfather to young Keith. It is the story of a cranky and creative old man who had precious few heroes:

> His heroes would have to be warm and close and—home-made—not a detached shadow or voice summoned by electronic button—shared all at once by everybody. I imagine there were plenty of times when he got himself into a tight corner and had to be his own hero. (p. 200)

Daddy Sherry, however, greatly loved 11-year-old Keith. Neither was a shadow to the other, detached or summoned by button. They each took delight in the other, just the way they were and not for what they would some day become. They were both players and approached each day for the first time.

And at the kitchen tables of my own storytellers, I sat in witness to that same kind of intergenerational enchantment. They were really there for each other, and yet nowhere on their cards of vital statistics would it say so. I can hear yet Pesimwastches drumming to his grandson, see Sabochees pushing the baby swing, and Mosum laughing at the antics of a grandchild. For each other, grandparent and grandchild, they were homemade and unconsciously engaged in the emotional attachments that would bind them together for a lifetime. They provided an island, each for the other, and one that existed only by relationships. Sartre (1977) writes the following about his grandfather:

> I was his wonder because he wanted to finish life as a wonder-struck old man. He chose to regard me as a singular favor of fate, and a gratuitous and always revocable gift. What could he have required of me? My mere presence filled him to overflowing. He was the God of Love with the beard of the Father and the Sacred Heart of the Son. There was a laying on of hands, and I could feel the warmth of his palm on my skull. He would call me his "tiny little me," in a voice

quavering with tenderness. Everybody would exclaim "That scamp has driven him crazy."...I depended upon him for everything: what he worshipped in me was his generosity. (p. 14)

For many, the grandparent-grandchild relationship lasted, endured, retold as it was time and time again. Neither party to the love would accept anything less. For his 111th birthday, Daddy was given the most wonderful of gifts, a homemade kite, and with his old head back against a rock, the kite string in his gnarled hand, he flew it. Lord, how he flew it:

> There were thousands of ways of holding the string...gently, tenderly, fearfully, bravely, stubbornly, carelessly, foolishly. Some dropped it without warning; others were given terrible vision ahead to the time that they must drop it soon. With some it was knocked from their grasp by another; through the ages many men had engaged in contests to knock it from each other's grasp; states broke it regularly with rope or poison gas or knife or bullet. With dance and chant and taboo and ritual, with fairy tale and song and picture and statue, with pattern of word and note and colour and conduct, they tried to insist that they did not hang on simply for the blind sake of hanging on. It was for such a short time that the string was held by anyone. For most of his hundred and eleven years Daddy had known that, and knowing it, with his own mortality for a touchstone, he had refused to settle for less. Quite simple after that. Time and death and Daddy Sherry insisted: never settle for anything less. (Mitchell, 1962, p. 210)

While the middle-aged imagine how the world might be and busy themselves with theory and shadows of compromise, the young and the old, Amoronteh and Herb, Santiago and Manolin, Daddy and Keith, lived close to home, in the sunshine and tight corners, connected and heroes each to the other. My storytellers have taught me that it is a narrative string that holds the kite aloft and pasted against the sky. It is the string by which Anansi travelled to earth and brought stories to all people, and it is the string that gloriously connects our temporal sounds to an eternal silence. Hugo wrote:

> [The Child] talks. She says things whose significance she does not understand. God, the good old Grandfather, listens, filled with wonder. (Kornhaber & Woodward, 1981, p. 1)

God, the grandparent, the Coyote Angel, the one who listens to the young...I am reminded of the occasion of my parents' 56th wedding anniversary. Our cowboy clan, the three generations, gathered at the Dragon Palace for Chinese food. And the high moment of the meal came in Grandmother's fortune cookie. It read: "Your love is like a tasty mess of noodles." Grandmother loved that and laughed with heartiness. Fifty-six years ago my parents were married at Fort McLeod. The entire ceremony cost $12.50, as they tell it: $2 for the preacher, $1 for the witness, $6 for the ring, $3.50 for the hotel and meal. It was the opening ceremony to a relationship which has survived whiskey, saddle broncs, chinook winds, rattlesnakes and river ranches, stockyards and irrigation and growing children. They have survived the metaphors to become the metaphor itself. Today, these grandparents are deeply attached to wild geese, prairie flowers, longhorn cattle, grandchildren and each other. And although they are each proud individualists, their prairie days beat with one heart. They tease and laugh a lot, often with belly abandon. Their old stories, each a friend, are polished in the ears of the grandchildren. And as they listen, big-eyed, the little ones find even themselves in that "mess of tasty noodles":

> Insofar as we account for our own actions and for the human events that occur around us principally in terms of narrative, story, drama, it is conceivable that our sensitivity to narrative provides the major link between our own sense of self and our sense of others in the social world around us. (Bruner & Haste, 1987, p. 94)

It is narrative that indeed makes our transactional and intergenerational lives possible. Grandma's anecdotes enwebbed the young into that "mess of tasty noodles" we called family. Each lived by narrative relationship in the other and participated with an intensity and mutuality that even survived aging. As Kornhaber and Woodward (1981) transcribed from an interview with Paul, a young grandchild:

> Grandma is here all the time, but her body is shrinking. She seems to be getting smaller and smaller, a little bit every day. I mean, Grandma's body is getting smaller, but Grandma is not shrinking. Just her body. (p. 220)

Young Paul's sense of self and his enduring sense of Grandma were wonderfully bound up together. The intergenerational conversation and connection is an affirmative one. It provides a home in the midst of chaos: "If one affirms life, one must affirm the whole, the 'going-under' as well as the 'going-over,' the pain as well as the pleasure, the midnight as well as the high noon" (Caputo, 1987, p. 283). The grandparent-grandchild relationship does just that. It affirms by its enduring rhythm and situates each of us as separate as our notions of self allow, under one sun and in one shadow.

Finally, Je-Nee told this folkloral story of the shadow tree, a high-noon narrative that goes to the heart of the intergenerational:

> Well, in the old times, there was a very greedy old man...he doesn't want to share with other people...very rich...and there was a big tree, big gyoko tree in front of this greedy old man's home.

As Je-Nee had told me on other occasions, nature teaches us how to share, how to give, but this old man had been blind to its teachings. And so when a wise young man came along and seated himself in the shade of the gyoko tree, the old man woke up from his nap and screamed,

> "Get out of here! This is my tree, this is my shadow...my great-great-grandfather had planted this tree, so that makes it belong to me." This young man smiled and nodding, "Oh, I see," and asked the old man, "Are you interested in selling this tree to me?"

The greedy old man could not resist and thus sold the gyoko tree to the youth for a handsome price. Some time later, the young man returned to his gyoko tree and rested in its shadow:

> Um-as the sun moved from east to west, the shadow moved from east to west, accordingly, and this young man followed the shadow....So he went in to the old man's front yard, and he went into the old man's house and then living room...finally the old man's bedroom. (laughter)

> The old man was enraged at the youth's intrusion and demanded an explanation: "You sold the tree so the shade belongs to me. So I just followed the shade, the shadow you know."

Because of their embarrassment and the laughter of the villagers, the old man and his family left their home and community forever. And as for the gyoko tree, from that day on, everyone was welcome to its shadow. Its shade belonged to all:

They sat in the yellow sunlight
Out under the gyoko tree;
And the game that they played I'll tell you
Just as it was told to me.

Deer Hide Painting:
Birth of Trickster

Chapter 6
And If The Fiddle String Hadn't Broke...

SUMMARY AND CONCLUSIONS

> In leaving something unsaid the beholder is given a chance to complete the idea and thus a great masterpiece irresistibly rivets your attention until you seem to become actually a part of it. A vacuum is there for you to enter and fill up to the full measure of your aesthetic emotion. (Okakura, cited in Sawada & Caley, 1990, p. 110)

It is the dandelion and poplar tree and jackfish I like best. That is both the survivor and the teller in me. And I do like people, in all their many faces and masks, substances and shadows. I do like people. But I prefer to meet them on their own narrative turf, situated comfortably somewhere in their holy land of kitchen tables and belly laughter. I do like people. In my wishing song and prayers that they and their species go on and on and on, that our babies forever feel a kindly river breeze, I choose to celebrate. Not only does this celebration fill me with hope, but it gives me research strategy and courage in the face of what some call the hopeless. I am mindful of Mitchell (1981):

> I had thought that Austin was the only victim. All of us were. We simply hadn't noticed the adult footprints in our child caves, but they were

there all the time, left by guardian trespassers. They entered uninvited because they loved us and they feared for us. Often they entered only to tidy up for us, or simply out of curiosity to find out what we might be doing in there. They wanted only to make it safe for their vulnerable young, to clear it of danger. They did not know, nor did we, that they could be carriers, unintentionally leaving serpents behind, coiled in a dark corner, later to bite and poison and destroy. (p. 177)

I know as a species we are self-referential, and I know that we fill the child caves with our own footprints. I know that we often take the hoop snake of narrative and leave it coiled and poisonous, waiting to bite. My storytellers have given me these sensitivities by the privilege of their privately constructed sounds and silences. They have taught me of the honest and hopeful nature of ceremony. They have taught me also how to follow when a good story leads the way. Thus, by way of summary and conclusion, I prefer to begin with a tale, one that celebrates more than it coils. It is a story that leaves each of us to "enter and fill up to the full measure" of our aesthetic emotion:

A long time ago, a stone sculptor we'll call Hanooch, sat chipping on his stone sculpture, chipping, chipping, chipping away. "Why is it that everyone but me seems to be having such a good time?" he thought. "Here I sit chipping, chipping away on the soapstone, growing weary from the tip of my hammer to the tip of my toes."

Just then a procession came past his house. The parade was led by the Bay Manager, seated atop his magnificent red four-wheeler. He was politely followed by servants to the left and friends to the right. And everyone was willing to act on the Manager's most remote whim. "He must be the most powerful thing in the world, the whole world," whispered Hanooch, "I would love to feel like that just once." Almost unknowingly, the sculptor began to sing his wishing song:

Haiaiaiaiai, hai ah me,
If Hanooch only, the Bay Manager could be?

Suddenly a spirit voice called out from the northern sky, "Be thou the Bay Manager!" And what a feeling it was...for there suddenly was Hanooch astride his new four-wheeler, royally easing his way down the gravel road, servants lined up to the left and friends to the right, all ready to do his bidding. But after just a few moments our friend Hanooch began to grow weary and the sweat began to drip from his fur capped forehead. "You know, maybe there is something more powerful than a Bay Manager outfitted in his Bay Day specials and that something is the Sun. Why all my servants and friends look hot and uncomfortable!" Again, almost unknowingly, Hanooch began to sing his wishing song:

Haiaiaiaiai, hai ah me,
If Hanooch only, the Sun could be?

Suddenly a spirit voice called out from the northern sky, "Be thou the Sun!" And what a feeling it was...for there suddenly was Hanooch in the sky, beaming down upon the northern woodlands. But because our friend had never really been a Sun before, he shone much too brightly and with much too much heat. Soon all the tiny flowers in the bush were burned up and the people were caused great discomfort, whereupon a sheltering Cloud passed between the Hanooch-Sun and the earth. The shadow of this Cloud brought relief from the sunshine. "Hey," called out Hanooch, "maybe there is something more powerful than the Sun and that something is the Cloud." Almost unknowingly, Hanooch began to sing his wishing song:

Haiaiaiaiai, hai ah me,
If Hanooch only, the Cloud could be?

Suddenly a spirit voice called out from the northern sky, "Be thou the Cloud!" In that same instant Hanooch became his wish, the Cloud. He then began to rain down upon the land. And because he had never really been a Cloud before, he rained much too much. Soon the creeks overflowed into the rivers and the rivers overflowed into the seas. It was a time of great flooding and hardship for both the animals and the people...except that is for the stone. The soapstone sat oblivious of sun and cloud and rain. "Hey, wait a minute," thought Hanooch, "maybe there is something more powerful than the Cloud and that something is the Stone!" Almost unknowingly, he began to sing his wishing song:

Haiaiaiaiai, hai ah me,
If Hanooch only, the Stone could be?

Again, suddenly a spirit voice called out from the northern sky, "Be thou the Stone!" In that instant, Hanooch became his wish, the Stone. What a wonderful feeling of power it was too, until our friend the

Hanooch-Stone saw a familiar looking man coming his way. Suddenly the man took out his sculpting hammer and began to chip chip away at the Hanooch-Stone. The hammer sent sharp tremors throughout Hanooch's rock body. "Oh no," thought Hanooch and he quickly began to sing his wishing song:

Haiaiaiaiai, hai ah me,
If Hanooch only, the man could be?

And suddenly a spirit voice called out from the northern sky, "Hanooch, just be Thyself!" In that moment Hanooch became himself, and that was power enough. (Shedlock, 1951, pp. 179–182)

Our friend Hanooch is back, as are we. We have travelled as researcher and reader through the sun, the cloud, the stone of story. And we are back. Having attempted the narrative circle, Le Guin's hoop snake, we return with power enough. We have made the journey at the risk of leaving danger still coiled and waiting in the caves of childhood. Like Rosie, the hen, we are back in time for dinner (Hutchins, 1968). But having made the Hanooch journey, it is perhaps the narrative time now to reconsider the story particulars that held us like a fish hook.

To bring the research home, I chose a strategy of narrative interweave or narrative collage. The aesthetic of collage allowed the particular its own particular significance, but it also enabled the specific to participate in a surrounding reality. It was my hope and intention that within the solution of story the different voices would both collaborate and collide: "Every text, says Barthes, is a mirror of citations. We are all a plurality of other stories, including our own" (Rosen, 1986, p. 236). Thus, my particular storytellers existed as oral vortices in the surrounding river of ancestral folklore, teacher autobiography, scholarly theory, and deer hide paintings. I wished to celebrate diversity and interconnectivity in the comfort of the folkloral and traditional. This methodology has depended upon the researcher becoming a storyteller, thereby intimating the possibilities of a storytelling metaphor for our instructional lives. Perhaps we best learn about the telling through the retelling.

It has been my hope as well that this interweave of story would provide a comfortable and formulaic departure into reflection. Particular stories and story rhythms have a way of aligning themselves into the fabric of a larger tale. That is both the joy and the challenge of literacy: to transpose the enlivened and episodic orality of the storytellers into the interiority and sequentiality of the written word. Such research becomes the art of ventriloquism.

Bringing the research home had everything to do with words, that whirling interplay of sound and silence. The language of this inquiry was as varied as the theorists who peopled it. On occasion I have chosen four words when perhaps one would have been more to the scholarly point. I am forever under the spell of the seven Gods of oracy. It is my habit to speak then write. On other occasions I have chosen words for their very imprecision and suggestibility. Such language is an occasion. I wish the reader to inhabit a coherent place between the experience of the narrative and its telling. My hope is that interpretation is as much an act of mutuality as the sounds and silences that convey it. I have sought out words that seemed to bump the personal up against the professional and ideally confuse the distinctions. I believe that it was this diversity of words that animated the spirit of the study. It was words that suggested "a universe that displays local phenomena built on a nonlocal reality" (Herbert, cited in Combs & Holland, 1990, p. 15). They lead us into the secret places of the storyteller and to those hidden places that connected the stories. The words pursued themselves.

In the first theme, we touched upon the constituents of orality, what Ong (1982) celebrates as the psychodynamics of an oral culture. This theme represented a voyage into the orality of the kitchen table and more specifically into the expression and lives of our particular storytellers, Dafna, Sparrow, Rattler, Pesimwastches, Sabochees, and Mosum, and the later circle of Je-Nee, Tololwa, Sakastenohk and Nitotem. My research inquiry, which originally set out to focus on four very different storytellers, quickly grew to twice that number. I relearned one important lesson. There is no such thing as "one northern storyteller." The truth I sought in four lives became not only the particulars in story celebration, but more important the interweave and that orality created in the mix. I also learned that as much as I wished to leave the storyteller lives unpicked and uncoiled, there were soon times when their oracy stood in the service of my own cerebration and raging. At other times I followed my own stories in the service of others. I believe the storytellers and I, by acts of spontaneous orality, created one another. In doing so, our talks and tales always connected, from one thing to the other, from the last comment or story to the next, from one life to another. It always connected. On closer view, every act of storyteller orality, every conversation was replete with what I call syllable connectives or conjunctives. And the conversational aim was certainly contextual and communicative, not grammatical. Thus, at many times, transcription lent itself more to a poetic genre than prose. In my storytellers' words, telling was an additive act. Each part of the story formulaically hooked into the rest, just as the many stories together became the compounded teller. Words and gestures and silences added up into the associate engagement we call story. I found it fascinating, this manner by which a Dafna or Rattler or Sparrow got the narrative moving and then kept it moving. Each part of the telling contextually triggered something else. I felt that if I listened to Pesimwastches long enough, for example, I would become party to the entire narrative and quantum web that binds together all peoples. I was not only listener, I was relation. This sense of association and connectivity, however, was made more memorable or lasting through the Hanooch-power of repetition. Many of the tellers, and particularly Sparrow, echoed the principle of three. It was never just old; rather, it was old, old, old. Again, it was not the grammatical that drove the narrative fuse. Rather, it was more often conversational context and passion that kept the iterative loops looping. As idiosyncratic as the teller might be, each of my storytellers depended upon a kind of oracy that was both formulaic and traditional. Thus, the iterative and the conjunctive gave not only memorability to the event, but also the power to the moment. And I sensed that much of that power of the oral act came from its naming ability. When Sabochees named a particular place, he located it, not only geographically, but in narrative time as well. All of my storytellers proved similarly sensitive to this denominative act. To be able to call up the name was to specify the silence and wrestle down the unnameable. Again, I sensed in our oracy the manner by which words named and stories named and even entire lives or a people named. Storyteller silence became visible in the naming.

To the connective, repetitive, and denominative nature of our tellings, I included in the discussion a fourth constituent of orality. This was the empathetic and the means by which the person of the teller projected into the person or persons of the story. Dafna, for example, was able to slip magically from the person of teller to school teacher to spouse to mother to scholar to story character and back to teller, all within storyteller moments. Indeed, for all my storytellers, reality was a place of retelling and recovery, inviting, shifting. By simply listening, just listening for the sake of Heaven, I, too, was able to participate and move into the souls of the stories. An awareness of the constituents of our kitchen table orality has since made my own narrative and empathetic shuffles that much more possible. Le Guin (1981) writes:

The old violinist
has crossed the gulf of the decades
on a highwire of catgut. Consider
the lovely devices of living
to which we are driven, driven. (p. 3)

The storytellers, together in the intimacy of their folkloral and oral states, invited me out onto the highwire of narrative. They invited me most particularly to the other side, to the part of their person less professional and public. Metaphorically then, my next research stop was at the storyteller hearth, the place of story. I was repeatedly invited in to the landscapes of my storytellers' lives, and that geography invariably held within it a hearth or fireplace. Thus, in the second theme, we circled around the Tanzanian grandmother's hearthstones, the South Korean dahk paper floor and coal fire, the Israeli bonfire and candle, the staff room teapot, the Albertan box heater, the Cree hunting fire, moose meat cooking and dripping from a green stick. And throughout the narrative visits, it became apparent that traditionally the place of fire was the place of story. Each held the spirit of the other, story and fire. The most extraordinary stories were told in these most ordinary of places, at the hearth. Story and warmth and food seemed to be a ceremony that went to the very soul of every people. And for each of my storytellers, their retold childhood was the first place of just such ceremony and spirit. By their words they looked into a long ago fire and remembered. Each told of the comfort they felt when held by the flames and ancestral words. The suggestion was also that slow cooking meant for good storying, whereas fast food meant fast stories. Thus technology, by hurrying our ordinary lives, reshaped the narrative patterns by which we told of and accomplished our humanity. Still another feature of the childhood hearth was the relationship of that storytelling to one's dreaming times. Je-Nee, for example, told of falling asleep on her grandmother's knee and then dreaming of tigers and princesses and mountain guards. Childhood was indeed a wandering through the caves of the conscious and unconscious, fantasies and realities that both arrived at and departed from the hearth. It appeared that a full life, a full narrative life, was one that itself was dreamed of and told. Life told of itself at the hearth. It was where the elements of our humanity met, wind and fire and water. Is it any wonder that we now go to such lengths to bring the places of fire, the hearths, to our own institutions? We are "driven to such devices of living." Is it any wonder that we seek our ceremony in such unhurried, spirited and everyday geographies? We can live in these magical places; we need not just tell of them. Pellowski (1977) tells about one Taos storytelling practice:

> Each boy would bring with him two sticks of firewood. All would sit around the walls, and each in turn would tell a story. (p. 103)

Thus, we make a gift to the fire, and the fire responds with a story. I, too, brought gifts and firewood to the storytellers, and they and the fire responded with gifts of hazelnut coffee and cookies, hot bannock and mint tea, olives and sambusak, and the warmth of story within story within story.

Having reflected upon the characteristics and the place of an oral way, it was perhaps inevitable that I happened upon that which itself cradles such sound, and that is silence. I chose to talk of silence, as inimitable a task as that may be. And just as inevitably, I was driven to the metaphoric in an attempt to describe what I termed the interstice of silence, the ribbons of stillness that wrap and separate the sounds of this journey. It is one thing to reach for the light but quite another to find the words to delineate that gesture. My storytellers made it possible; for by their unique telling ways, they each exposed something of the psychodynamic of silence. Mosum, for example, in his traditional and Cree way, intimated the silence of good telling. This white space was an essential part of the story performance. It was mutually constructed by both the teller and the listener and at all times was full. Mosum's silences were not an absence or a lacking but rather an opportunity. They were a place to visit. And as many years as I have counted myself a sympathetic educator of English as a second language, I only then came to appreciate the phenomenon of "second language sounds" wrapped into a "first language silence." It was a small conceptual leap from this kind of performing and elliptical silence to what I would call reverent silence. These were the white spaces of conversation still untouched by sound, somatic events that praised and comforted and gave courage. Often these were the reverent places where the spirit most lived, in the knowing eye of the true friend, where the snow fell unwatched, and in the birch bark company, where the fire of the ancestors curled up to the moon. These were the storyteller silences that promised something within, often just an attitude and pause that connected something eternal to anything particular.

When Dafna talked of the quick animation of good Israeli conversation, she brought us to another shape of silence. These were such storyteller times when silence was indeed an opportunity missed, more object than act. A good life was one that filled the larger silences, the white surrounding spaces, with song and poem and laughter. Life came in the sound and the telling. And thus those most lacking in power, those who wished themselves into stones and any other shape most occupied the silent places. Their occupation was one of subordination and not reverence. Sparrow quickly learned of the relationship of sound, particularly school sound and authority. There are those who control the silence, just as there are those controlled by the silence.

Whatever the shape of the white spaces, be they spiritual or spiritless, oral hesitation or prolonged quiet, they came deeply contextualized. Sound and silence, hand in glove, lived together and not as phenomenon apart. As participant-observer and friend, I tried to imagine how this exercise of sound and silence varied from the communicative perspective of an oral culture to that of a literate one. Just as sound has changed so dramatically over the past few centuries, from natural to motorized, so, too, has our silence. And as much as I wonder at my ancestors' words and sounds, I wonder more at their silences. Were they any closer in their clan and in their privately constructed silences to the white space of eternity? Were they as driven by the noisy discovery of the self? Did their oracy keep them at the quiet centre of things? To what extent did their emerging syllables create their own silences? It was perhaps appropriate that all my questions to the ancestors were, themselves, met by silence. In *Solomon Leviathan's Nine Hundred and Thirty-First Trip Around the World*, Elephant nodded and said, "That is why I recommend simply going ahead. You might try to avoid fog, but really that doesn't matter. Even in the fog one can imagine the horizon" (Le Guin, 1983, p. 29). And perhaps most of all, when in the silence, one can imagine the answering sounds.

The fourth stop in our thematic consideration of orality was to the island of the written word, itself a silent and separate place. Again, I began with a metaphor, writing as an act of transubstantiation whereby the blood and body of oral sound was converted into the space of the written word. My storytellers first helped me appreciate how we attempt to recover by symbol what is naturally lost by sound. Thus, by acts of symbol presentation and literacy, we hold on to our words for dear life. And by recording, whether by microcircuit or quill, we promote an interiority, a way of travelling to the inside of selves and things. To all the storytellers, however, the literate act was much more than a simple recording of sounds. It was a state of being, and therein lay the dilemma. For as much as literacy celebrated the species, at times it also measured them. Thus, there was that expressed relationship between human worth and literacy. This interplay of the written and the spoken played itself out in each storyteller person. Some wrote and wrote beautifully, for example, that they might talk of it at the kitchen table. Others laughed and raged and talked that they might later write. The ever shifting nature of this interplay between the spoken and the written made it impossible to classify the storytellers or their peoples along some hypothetical continuum. Fortunately, expression was never divorced from life. It was never enough to "just be lettered" or "just be well spoken." It was never enough to store things away and commit one's learning to the bulletin board. All of the storytellers wanted room for their elbows, room for their stories, however they be told and however they be lived. In Sidney's words, "Well, I've tried to live my life right, just like a story" (Cruikshank, 1990, p. 1). I believe that more than anything else, the written word provided a predominant metaphor by which my storytellers told of their lives. Thus, as much as the personal life shaped the telling, shaped the storybook, so the genre shaped the life. Remember Sabochees, a true spirit-master of the oral, who referred to the death of an elder as the loss of a "real thick book." The challenge may be, given the power of the metaphor, to imagine a world wherein those things oral mean more, not less. It should be enough to remember. There are still things that a listener can teach a reader. In the same breath, an electronic reality is no less real for being electronic, nor is its orality any less spoken for having been scripted. As Hanooch might say, it should be enough to live one's life within one's own metaphors. Language may have got us up onto our feet, but I believe it is our metaphors that will keep us upright. Be they written or oral, they enable us to see in the round, to perceive the shadow within the substance, and to join together into the binding spell of the present.

In this collaborative narrative, what began as orality quickly then became metaphor. I became fascinated by those themes and metaphors that seemed to drive my tellers and perhaps me. I am reminded of Frost's (1967) words for people who wait along the sand and just such shores:

> They cannot look out far.
> They cannot look in deep.
> But when was that ever a bar
> To any watch they keep? (p. 132)

Perhaps, as much as what I listened for, it was my listening that was the significant event. But regardless of significance, I listened, and I listened for holiness. And having grown sensitive to the whisperings of the seven Gods of oracy, I first heard what I termed the metaphor of story as a holy land. By the denominative act of orality, my storytellers each told me of a special place, a particular place and geography, that they each took to be holy. For Sparrow, the holy land was a small island on the Athabasca River. It was a remembered place of sand and sunshine and water. It was where the family went during the very best of times. Dafna, too, told of a particular Israeli beach, white white sand and blue, blue sky and father in hand, father with beautiful long hair, father reciting Russian poetry. Rattler's rememberings transported me to the badlands of southern Alberta, hoo doo country, the Blackfoot "Garden of Eden." Again, it was a remembered place of Red Deer water, riverbank sand, and eyefuls of Alberta sunshine. For the Northerner, Sabochees, the holy land was Harper Creek, the place of his birth and yet again a place of water and sun and sand. Sabochees described it as a place of plenty where one could see everything, even a vision. People were simply a part of the rhythm of the life that encircled the place. To Tololwa, our professional storyteller, the holy land was an open country where his father used to teach. It was an unconstricted place through which the river ran all year round, even in the dry season. It was a place where thorns became little boy toys. Thus, for all of my storytellers, this wide variety of particular holy lands held three things in common. First of all, these holy places were all characterized by sunshine, sand and flowing water. They all spoke of outside places, noninstitutional, spiritual but not religious, places of primary reality. Second, again without exception, their holy lands had all been attained first in childhood. Thus, these spiritual places were not somewhere else and certainly not some remote island accessed only through years of formal education and experience. They did not lay waiting at the far corner of some salary grid. Instead, they were found in the context of home. And third, again without exception, the holy lands were all under siege. Adult footprints intruded upon the caves of childhood. Serpents were left coiled in secret places. For Sparrow, by way of example, the Athabascan island could no longer be visited because of the pulp mill effluence that choked it. Dafna watched her wandering white sand disappear under housing developments. Rattler, too, spoke of the need to protect our holy places, hoping that we would reverse the current trends of converting holy sites into gravel pits, digging for gold in Napi's bones. For Sabochees, I felt the deep pain of a holy land that was now situated too close to visit, yet too far away to live in. Thus, there was this siege of all the particular holy lands. Narrative could take one back and, I suspect, repeatedly did, but sometimes even that was not enough. I found it disconcerting that our most private and holy of places had so little to do with our public and institutionalized lives. Perhaps these particular places were simply the metaphoric water that flowed through the adult years. Our childhood bones seem to understand about holy places. Who, but an adult, could work so slavishly to recover what was never lost? Le Guin (1981) beautifully writes:

> A tree that blossoms in the wilderness
> in some April beyond history
> and farther west than all the pioneers
> is in no way less
> though there be none to bless
> and no woman stand in tears
> under the whitening flowers. (p. 33)

And although story could not fully recover those holy places situated as they were in some "April beyond history," story enabled revisitation to occur. Indeed, what most characterized the telling, characterized as well those sacred sites. Surely, no one would leave a holy land just that they might tell of it.

I listened, and I listened for hope. A consideration of particular holy lands seemed to lead inexorably to the metaphors that carry and themselves embody hope. Sparrow, for example, conversationally turned from what threatened her holy places to the particular and hopeful ceremonies of her own kind. Here was a young child who could imagine scenes of planetary suicide. Yet she always came back, in talk and tales, to the ordinary ceremony and protection of family, to Christmas Eve and the bedtime story. There were storylines that coursed through this young person, narrative threads that joined Sparrow together. And in doing so, both the story and the little girl telling gave me a personification for hope.

With Rattler, too, there was similarly this interplay between the public and the private stories, between the informal talks and the formal tales. The result was an incredible "layering on" of narrative from which the listener could always reach out and grasp a conversational thread. In the story of *The Spirit Stones*, for example, we were left to take hope from simple unconfining acts whereby the nature of a holy landscape became the nature of a spiritual being. Hope for the telling Rattler was in the uncovering of the tale as much as in the originary experience. One could suffer a rattlesnake on the bedroll for the later story and laughter it would mean.

Like Sparrow and Rattler, Dafna lived in particular metaphors and in these metaphors found hope. Hope lived in the passion of the lit candle, the enduring students who became a part of her life, the mother who taught her to laugh and skip, the father who insisted on learning one new thing each day, the family that met daily in the heart, the animated conversations and friendships, the train rides and moments of good chocolate. Hope lived in these routines and particulars, in the blend of the old stories and the new stories. Indeed, for all my storytellers, hope lived in particularity and in the passion of its telling. Dafna took great hope from this conviction that all peoples, and themselves all storytellers, seemed to share a life wish.

Mosum despaired. For years he had watched his holy land being ground up in the crucible of progress and development. For years our elder witnessed a growing imbalance between the things of the spirit and the things of the store. He wondered at what shape the new elders would take. In a soft voice and a conversation gentled by many silences, Grandfather spoke of his own particular youth. It was a time characterized by distance and rhythms and a strong sense of the "we, the people." And when I asked Mosum of hope, given all of these histories, he spoke of the Great Spirit. It was God who could make sense and justice of the stories. Prayer meant hope. It was prayer that ultimately would connect what Grandfather had heard to what he had seen to what would be.

In all the storytelling and our talks of hope, there was this search for agency, this search for the finger of God that wound up and truthfully coiled each tale. Thus, I thematically moved on from the metaphor of hope and prophecy to the metaphor of fidelity. How was it that my very diverse storytellers came to the metaphor of truth? What was the narrative relationship of fidelity to agency? I listened and listened for truth:

> I think about my past and try to change
> Into a singing metaphor a silent heart,
> A frail red parrot perched within its cage
> Repeating what it hears and cackling without change
> All that ear hears and tongue speaks. I form in thought
> The singing form that forms the silent heart. (Mandel, 1966, p. 469)

I wondered how it was that we transformed with fidelity our silent hearts into singing metaphors. Was storyteller truth but an accident of the telling, or was it a prerequisite to the event? My search sought something more than "frail red parrots perched within their cages." When I repeatedly asked Sparrow if her stories were true, she laughed with young consternation and told me that truth was when the animals walked on four legs. Truth was when Cinderella's glass slipper turned back into a chimney sweep's shoe. Truth for Sparrow was in the telling. It allowed us to inhabit the questions without answering them. Truth was where the fantasies of adulthood bumped into the realities of childhood.

Dafna, too, talked of the truth found in places where the points and polarities overlapped. There was a confluence where science and story met, weaving in and out, each of the other. She talked of "truth in life," of the mother and child who went into hiding for 6 years, fleeing from village to village. And on many occasions when the child was hungry and restless, the mother would nourish the youngster with story upon story. Truth did not live anywhere else. It was not removed for Dafna, but rather, it was "in solution." Fidelity was not any less for being particular and local. Good stories, stories told with fidelity, sustained. They metaphorically conveyed the truth of relationships.

Storyteller truth for Rattler was similarly in the telling. Fidelity meant getting to the bottom of the story and exposing those narrative tendrils of connectivity that fastened our lives together. Truth was never a straight line for Grandfather:

> But you know, the truth's like a green-broke horse. You can come running out of the barn and throw on a saddle, leap on its back and plant your heels in its side, but you never know which way it's going to run or who it's going to kick. Sometimes it's better to walk up slow, you know, with a carrot or an apple. Let it smell the saddle for awhile, before you pull the cinch and slide up. (King, 1989, p. 176)

Thus, Rattler teased and circled in, giving shape to the story and truth as he word slid his way along. One heard little corroborative truths along the way. Life was an oral winter count and not be to hurried. Fidelity was an exercise of memorability, getting the details and the names right. With Rattler, it was not a case of arriving at truth, for the listener was there all along. Truth was in the handling. And it had everything to do with the trusting relationship of the storyteller to the story listener, green-broke horse to rider.

Pesimwastches found truth in the relationship he had to his culture. Fidelity was not the sole province of the artful and well performed. Instead, truth was a gift, an understanding most often found in one's relationship to the elders. It came from an attitude of "let's look at" and "let's think about it." Truth came quietly here and more often than not on the heels of good laughter. This sense of northern fidelity did not separate people into cerebrative camps. To Pesimwastches, truth was contiguity.

And as the stories continued on, "my silent heart became filled with singing metaphors." Shapes of holiness and hope and fidelity first separated off then merged back together. The particulars combined in a folkloral way to give a sense of life as a metaphor in pursuit of itself. If, indeed, learning has anything to do with holiness and hope and fidelity, then surely the storytelling form suggests a bridge by which young silent hearts become singing metaphors. That may be a "truth in life," a story as agency. As the elder Roncco said,

> If you go through things like I did and you don't get killed, you're going to learn something. (Heynen, 1990, p. 49)

I suspect that survival creates its own kind of metaphors for truth, and laughter.

Very often, as researcher and writer, I was brought to the oral and the metaphoric by an act of laughter. And so it was laughter that I came to in my third chapter and specifically in the theme of story as a laughing matter. Our conversational laughter was set against the traditions of both the funny and the unfunny. Thus, there were those philosopher kings and those cultures that viewed laughter as an unworthy act, uncharitable scorn, the preoccupation of a vacant mind. Life was no laughing matter here. But in glorious counterpoint to the unfunny stood the tradition of the funny in both human thought and ceremony and certainly in all my storytellers. Thus, many other cultures praised the act of laughter, laughter as an aid to digestion, a positive preoccupation when in the vicinity of vice, laughter as an antidote to disease, a liberation and a balancing. Our laughter has been a presence, regardless of the tradition. And as much as story lives in storyteller breath, so laughter lives in story. There is something both ancestral and prophetic about our mirth. It joins us together and allows for an intimacy in the telling. Very often, too, it was laughter that opened the way for a truth. My storytellers were full of humor. They laughed a lot and in doing so connected their silences and their syllables together. Our laughter, like our silence, was mutually constructed, and it came in moments of psychological shift. When Rattler, as high priest of mirth, lovingly told his story of *Willow Flight*, he and I laughed and laughed and laughed. A moment of terror for one younger brother became a moment of joy for one now elder storyteller. A private loss had become a narrative gain. Rattler's stories were always filled with this laughter of incongruity. Very often the high expectation of the listener roared off into the laughter of the unexpected. Rattler's giggles came round, like an evening duck to a river channel. They eddied by and caught me in their current. Long, long moments of expectation suddenly puffed into nothing. And after an afternoon of this, Rattler in story and laughter, my sides ached with the medicine. I had been cerebral-charged by the most healthful of sounds. I had learned to languish in the mismatch of conceptualization and perception. Control did not seem so very important when there was such joy to be had in misadventure.

Sparrow's laughter was staccato, behind the eyes, and it came in moments of reconciliation. Her laughter helped her come to terms with the full irony of her situation, with the "weird." Like a sparrow, her giggles hopped from one branch to another, from one context and situation to the next. Laughter wrapped up into the folkloral gave our little friend both resolution and relief.

With Dafna, a good laugh was a moment of passion, a sharing with those on the inside. Like Tololwa's holy land, her laughter was unconstrained, her long black hair thrown back, the peals catching everyone in their flight. I learned from Dafna that laughter can connect a people to their culture and religion, that it can bridge chaos and perfection, tradition and change, hope and despair. Perhaps laughter is, indeed, subliminal metaphor, bringing story and characters face to face with their own humanity.

It was Pesimwastches who most embodied the ritual laughter of the "contrary." His wonderful full-body guffaws carried the listener beyond "heavy thoughts." Laughter was for him a celebration of imperfection. It was Pesimwastches's pleasure to share this gift of silliness that the Great Spirit had so thoughtfully provided. The stories and laughter of Pesimwastches, Mosum and Sabochees all kept you at the fire and in the circle. Their humility so very often began and then ended with a laughing.

Tololwa's laughter was a full rich voiced affair. It reminded me that laughter is relationship, that when we really set it loose, it leaves on a hero's journey of 1000 faces, out on a hero's cyclic journey of separation, initiation and return. Kipling once said that "no one in the world knew what truth was till someone told a story" (Rouse, 1978, p. 81), and that may be true. And perhaps no one in the world knew what a story was till someone laughed. They are inseparable, story and laughter, provocation and expression.

Just as laughter sets out on the heroic journey of 1000 faces, I set out to more fully understand the faces and archetypes that make us laugh. All of my storytellers made me laugh by their shapeshifting. Like a Wesakychak or Coyote, they shifted throughout their tellings, shifted by word, character, gesture and time. Each storyteller as shapeshifter led me from Badger laughter to ancestor truth. Within the wonderful and iterative story of *Misisikak, the Giant Skunk*, for example, Sabochees pulled me through this trickster cycle of laughter. At times in the telling, Sabochees was the comic trickster, converting winter landscape into the silly spring of belly laughter, and at other times he became the shape of warrior, one who laughed in defiance and opposition. In subsequent retellings and contexts, our elder laughed and transformed himself first into healer and later into ancestor or soothsayer. These were the shifting shapes of the storyteller—storyteller as comic, warrior, healer, and ancestor—that continually repeated themselves in the laughter of the telling. To laugh was to amuse, to defend, to remedy and to prophecy.

I found myself caught in this Anansi web of storyteller laughter, time and time again. In the guise of comic teller, for example, Rattler would fill the narrative air with picaresque characters and unpredictable situations. I held my listening breath as the interplay between constraint and freedom played itself out. By denouement, Grandfather had shifted me to the inside of the trick. Thus, as the comic teller shifted shape, so, too, did the laughter. It was inevitable that the storyteller and listener become forever reconstituted in the telling.

Dafna, in the laughter of the warrior, led me into the narrative time of the Kings. We laughed at the mighty, at royal noses that grew puffy from the sting of a bee, at meats that failed to warm from distant fires, at flowing robes that sipped from the soup bowl. We laughed at incongruity and found our own kind of protection in the comic. It was laughter that enabled justice to prevail. It was laughter that first separated the human from the divine and then so struggled to mend them together again.

In the northern story tradition, laughter very often took the shape and sound of the healer. It was the drum of laughter that not only called people together, but kept them together. Good story and good ceremony meant good laughter. Thus, laughter came again as a joint production of the healer and the wounded. As Sabochees said, to become fully human was to laugh. The sounds of our happiness were themselves the healing notes that led the individual from neglect to grace. When people danced together, be it tea dance or round dance, they were able to bring one another to laughter and in to the circle of the people.

Sparrow, in her Wesakychakian and shapeshifting way, similarly brought delight to those in her company. Her wide laughing brown eyes healed others by their look. I always felt better for her telling presence, its joyous animation. By the gift of laughter, Sparrow invited me to unlearn the things I knew about and was, indeed, able to open things up, things that needed the air and sunshine and laughter.

All of my storytellers possessed also the remembering place that allowed them to take the shape of the ancestor. It, too, was a door opened by laughter. Sabochees could talk of a time when the animals could speak, Dafna of a time when the temple still stood, Rattler of the little people of the plains, and Sparrow of a time before storybooks. This was the folkloral laughter of praise. It deeply laminated the listener into the landscapes of the ancestral. The voice of the storyteller moved from one of entertainment to instruction. Old stories were polished by our laughter into intimacies. Here truth began with a laughing.

By all this shapeshifting, all the foxes that turned into dumplings, my storytellers moved and laughed their 1000 faces across the holy land of narrative. And at the time, we did not look into the tea cup of our laughter for a pattern. We simply laughed and laughed for the sake of Heaven. At times, we bit the tail of laughter until the blood ran. And at other times, our laughter was more of a whisper and gentle courtesy. Like Sabochees now, I cannot imagine a life without laughter. I cannot imagine a life without the elusive mystery and power of our mirth sounds. What breath is to story, surely laughter is to life:

> Coyotes have the gift of being seldom seen; they keep to the edge of vision and beyond, loping in and out of cover on the plains and highlands. And at night, when the whole world belongs to them, they parley at the river with the dogs, their higher, sharper voices full of authority and rebuke. They are an old council of clowns, and they are listened to. (Momaday, 1966, p. 55)

The hoop of narrative and the 1000 faces of my storytellers brought me finally to the fourth mountain, to the elders. And having stopped at the islands of oracy, metaphor and laughter, I was now back to considerations of the originary substance, the elders. As friend and educator, I have lived most of my professional life in small northern communities, in communities where the elders themselves were regarded as holy lands. It was inevitable that my reflection, whatever its original shape, would come around to the grandparents of my own kind. In what fashion was story itself an intergenerational conversation? What does it mean to be an elder, or what I referred to as a Coyote Angel, in this world? Norman (1982) gathered, translated and shared this striking word image:

> Wild turkeys
> dance
> on a mound of earth
>
> and the moles
> under them
> say
> "We know the earth
> is loud
> with turkeys again."
>
> But you,
> not-yet-born,
> when I tap my fingers
> on the mound over you
>
> do you know who dances? (p. 128)

In our grandparents' words, I sensed that tapping over us, and I wondered at who dances. I wondered at those shapeshifters we call elders.

To Pesimwastches, the notion of elder was inseparable from notions of culture. Together they meant memory and survival. And when I asked Grandfather about elderhood, he quickly responded with the particular names of those he called elder. Most of the old women and men he named were now gone to the other side. Pesimwastches, however, assured me that although they had completed this living walk, their presence was still very much felt. They lived in story yet. And by being talked about, they enabled the new elders to come out. In other words, elders were those who connected the ancestral to the living. They are the metaphor, the human bridge, the connectors of resemblances and rememberings.

Sabochees also talked of elderhood and again began with the particular names of those his community considered elders. To this Grandfather, elders were a living treasure. The stories meant little if anything without them. Their presence, their shapeshifting and storytelling meant life. Their lives were a celebration of tradition and hope in the face of misdirected change. Sabochees also regarded his own elders as the embodiment and manifestation of a different kind of time. Gentle and unhurried, elders did not live in the future. They were not busy arriving. Their sense of narrative time allowed instead for both remembrance and relationship. By being good listeners, the elders were able to draw near to others, masters of propinquity.

Nitotem, again from the vantage point of the particular, in this case his grandmother, talked of character. He remembered his grandmother as changeless, always there, busy but not hurried, able to see things that others might miss. In fact, Grandmother was still there.

The northern storytellers, Pesimwastches and Mosum and Sabochees, all expressed yet another attribute of their elders. The grandparents had all come from somewhere else. They were the "pedone" and by their travels cleared the way of obstructions. Others could follow now. The elders had known hardship and misadventure, but that only added salt to the meat of a good tale. When they smoked and remembered, they gave words and order back to the universe. Their narrative storylines criss-crossed the northern bush. If one knew the old stories, one could travel and be at home anywhere.

Dafna, too, talked of the particular and of the pioneers when she considered elderhood. Dafna spoke with deep reverence about those who came before, those whose lives became such a story of the land. It was their hardships and struggles and survival that would become the enduring legends of the people. Dafna, who never knew her own grandparents, set great store in elders such as her mother-in-law. These giants provided a fixedness and hope in a landscape swept by the winds of diversity and change.

Sparrow, like me, wondered at the fingers that tapped on the mound. To Sparrow, the old had always been old. Grandparents were a natural part of the landscape and of the reality she called her life. They knew lots, were idiosyncratic and sometimes even weird. Grandparents made the special times even more special. They seemed to be a little more accepting and a little less correcting than other adults. Grandparents, too, knew what it was to live in the margin.

Like all shapeshifters, Rattler spoke both specifically about his grandparents and more generally about the picaresque characters who once inhabited his holy land of the prairies. They all lived now in the fourth dimension of his story world. As Sabochees said, the old ones knew the first roads that connected people to places. They had endured and lived now in the medicine bag of Rattler's stories. Their faces and adventures popped up like crocuses in the springtide, their adventures characterized by both focus and passion. The image of grandparent drifted like the Carbon Ghost throughout Rattler's tales. It gave body to what could be.

It was Tololwa who described the elders as the trunk from which the branches could grow, or even the roots. It concerned Tololwa, indeed all my storytellers, that some societies now regarded the elders as old branches in need of discarding. When Tololwa spoke about elderhood, he, too, spoke in the particular of his grandparents. To the young Arusha Masai child, the grandparents not only told story, they were story. Their persons made for good telling, and their lives were a narrative ceremony that carried the young along. The elder words teased and comforted and divined. And as Je-Nee would add, the grandparents' words made everything "vivid, just vivid." The little ones could well imagine who tapped on the mound and who disappeared into the stories and light.

Cameron (1986) has this to say about her grandmother, Klopinum:

> Sometimes, when the other Aunties came to visit, Klopinum would start a story, then nudge me sharply, and I knew I was expected to continue it for her. It was not expected that I use the very same words she used, but it was expected that whatever words I chose, the rhythm was to be as strong and as regular as the waves or my own breathing, and the heart of the story be unchanged. (p. 18)

I came to believe that the elders are those who start the stories then give us a good sharp nudge. As listeners, we are now expected to continue on with a rhythm as strong and fragile as life itself. More than mere storytellers and sound shapeshifters, the elders are the listeners and ancestral ear. They are the Coyote Angels, the ones who listen for both the sounds and the silences.

It was my pleasure to become something of a Coyote Angel to Sparrow and the others. My listening made a storyteller of her as she peopled our visits with ghosts and angels and new calves and people who wore their pants on backwards. I would start a story, a folktale, and then disappear into Coyote Angel. I became Santiago to her Manolin, and we never talked of ordinary fish.

Rattler, in the spirit of *The Old Man and the Sea*, held me like the marlin. I sat hooked as Grandfather teased with narrative line. As listener and holder of tea cups, I became part of the pattern, part of the narrative leaves that he nonchalantly scattered about for the young. I became as much fascinated by the connections between the stories as the stories themselves. Rattler nudged me into this conversation of relationships.

Mosum, like Rattler, celebrated a reality of relationships rather than objects. He talked to the young of a life made beautiful by the interweave of people and story. For Grandfather, these narrative lives formed a pattern that echoed the natural world. Mind and nature were the two sides to one storytelling act. In becoming a Coyote Angel, one brought together story mind and story matter.

Dafna talked of this giving that so characterized the elder lives. The "real you" was the one who would nudge and give and tell for all he/she was worth. By storyline, the intergenerational connection between the elder and the child was confirmed. It was the Coyote Angels who sent out their listening embraces, like a whistle during prayers. They held the kite as long as it would fly by their grasp and then passed the string over to a younger hand.

To my storytellers, God, the grandparent, the Coyote Angel and the youngster were each the hero to the other. They cared for and polished the old stories together at the kitchen table. They lived together in the sunshine and the tight corners. It was their one folkloral voice that I heard negotiate its way through the silence and the chaos. Their mutual sensitivity to narrative held them fast in oral concert.

Finally, I have heard voices, and it was these folkloral voices, the storytellers, who have enabled me to imagine, to conceive of inner voices, to search again. They did not prescribe. They simply told of their holy lands. And because of it, I can now imagine a metaphor for our professional lives: the storyteller as teacher, the teacher as Coyote Angel. More specifically, I can now imagine a teacher training program that encourages and celebrates the story and storyteller in each of its students. One can apprehend the pedagogical connection between an oral past and a literate future. The implications may speak to all people of culture. I have witnessed also a vibrant orality in the most literate of storytellers. If I have learned anything, it is that our orality drives the day, and as much as we represent our persons in print and quark, we remain inhabitants of our gestures and spoken words. It seems only reasonable that our professional practice be informed by the verbal round dance of our most natural selves. I can well imagine the ordinary classrooms that extend beyond themselves to include the holy narrative lands of childhood, classrooms that journey beyond the interiority of the written word and the written voice. Surely, a sensitivity to storytelling, specifically, and to the inner workings of orality, in general, would only enhance our instructional practice.

The elders seem to call for classrooms and class days filled with the primary and ancestral reality of wind, water, and earth. It is not enough that our grandchildren complete photocopied worksheets on the environment. It is not enough that they learn to reason from a posture of air-conditioned comfort. The elders speak of the narrative places where the background sound is natural and not motorized. It is not enough that the grandchildren learn to manage.

The storytellers and their words implicate. Indeed, I can imagine the secret places where I now live. I can imagine myself in the moments of silence and in the imaginings of others. I cannot imagine, however, being untold.

I, too, have experienced those travels into silence and the pure joy of a folkloral song. I have witnessed the particular and deep silence of Nose Creek country, the kind of silence that comes from 30 degrees of frost and a knee height of snow. There was something deeply spiritual about our teaching time in Nose Creek, and that became most obvious to me when I was cutting a clean snow line with a pack of trail hungry sled dogs. There is a recipe for these kinds of critters. Take the long-winded tendons and howl of a wolf, cross them with the Arctic flesh of a husky, add a smell of oiled harness, and you have yourself a bush dog. Betty and I had multiplied this formula by seven, and the result was a dog team that flew through the mystery of the northern bush each evening after school and on the winter weekends.

I remember one particular sun high Saturday in January. I slipped into my winter garb of high Cree moccasins, beaver mitts, red string on my wrist and army woolens, and enough chewing tobacco to dam a small creek. Another half hour and "the boys" were in an untangled line with Old Genghis harnessed in the lead, snarling and snapping out his divine rights. Axe, rifle, matches, extra socks and moccasins, teapail and tea, and it was the narrative time to hit the Nose Creek superstate! One last pass putting legs into harness, unknotting the drag rope from a tree near our trailer and "Marche! Hie! Hie! Marche! You fur bags! You tail wagging sons of the Spruce! Hie! Hie!" Genghis and company blasted out of there like the Cranberry partners from their chairs. And there may be a better feeling in life than hanging on to a catwalking old birch toboggan and inhaling the incense from seven well-fed sled dogs, there may be, but I doubt it.

It took more than a mile on the frozen Nose Creek before the dog transport settled down into anything resembling a rhythm. Half a mile further and I swung the boys off the crystal covered ice and up into the preliminary foothills of Nose Mountain. Genghis and crew were young, the snow fast, and before long I had wound about 7 miles back into the big spruce country. From my toboggan and carry-all, the trees looked to be as high as the very stars. The next 3 miles went even faster when the boys and I picked up the fresh scent and tracks of a small winter herd of elk.

But over a hot enamel cup of mint tea, I decided that my old triggeritchin' 30.30 would have to wait for another day. The illustrated night of a full moon was quickly settling down on the spruce foothills of the Nose. "Amazing how a change of direction can alter a critter's energy," I pronounced to no one in particular as we set out for home and supper. And in praise of privately constructed silence, I can imagine no finer expression of that than a blanketed toboggan ride down a quiet trail and under a January cold moon. But just after the first return mile, I spied something move, about 100 yards to the left of the trail, a fat spruce hen ruffled up on an old beartorn log. Well, if there is one thing that will bring a bush man to his less poetic senses, it is the thought of sharing his carry-all with some fresh meat. That spruce hen would make a fine gift for Kokum, our Grandmother, back at the village.

"Whoa! Whoa boys! Whoa!" and the team excitedly pulled over for a trail mark. I quietly turned my toboggan on to its side to act as an anchor if the dogs got spooked. Two or three steps into the bush, 30.30 shell levered into the chamber and shoulder pause and "Crack!" One spruce chicken minus one spruce chicken's head.

Normally I would have whooped and drum stomped for joy over such a shot. But all celebrations were short lived when I realized that Genghis and Company had set out for the canine comforts of home with no intention of pulling any unnecessary weight. Their frightened reaction to the 30.30 blast had bounced the old Chipewyan toboggan back upright, and it now looked like the disappearing ghost ship of the Ancient Mariner. No point in bellering "Whoa!" for that would only add gas to their canine fire. And there is no dignity in throwing a spear of words after an escaping dog team.

Home meant a 9 mile walk at probably 30 below. It could be worse, I supposed. And so with spruce chicken dripping red blood on the white snow and empty 30.30 on my shoulder, I set out for the fire and frying pan of Nose Creek. I made good mocassin time on the packed trail. The minutes passed. All at once then, I got a feeling, a sensation. Something or someone was watching me. No longer did I feel like a part of the bush but now only a passer through. I was sure that something was watching me. I was sure of it.

After reaching the snowy top of the next rise, I quietly stopped, then eased around and studied my back trail. There they were: wolves. Maybe 30 of them. The whole clan! And 30 hungry wolves have a way of making you think about life in general, and then specifically right now! My bullets had disappeared with the careening toboggan. One headless spruce hen in my possession, I did the only thing a sensible human being could do: I kept walking, stiffly. I had no quarrel with the wolves, and I desired none. Kind of a gentleperson's agreement was all I asked. It had something to do with the odds.

After topping the next rise, I noticed my honored company only one hill back and gaining. They came on like grey streaks of cold steel and with me the magnet. I kept walking. And when I reached the bottom of the next draw, the shadow platoon studied me from that same hill behind. I wondered if it was time to sacrifice my spruce chicken to a higher cause. Nope. There was a comfort in hanging on to it. I kept walking.

But before I got many steps further, I came to a quiet halt. I looked up from the trail to see that the wolves had fully circled me. They seemed to be awaiting my pleasure, their eyes gleaming out from behind spruce trees as high as the stars. The circle grew imperceptibly tighter, and I found myself at the hub of a hoop of wolves—one coal black raven flew squawking over the silent drama below. The wolves sat, eyes fixed on me and the spruce hen, their tongues out. And suddenly a medley of wolf howls broke loose that would make the songs of hell sound like a chickadee. Thirty wolf throats combined into a chorus and fiddle string that shattered the winter silence of the spruce. Then just as abruptly, there was silence again. Complete. Not a sniff or a lick. Silence....

In the still calm of that extended moment, I wondered at the seven Gods of story. Would they bring me to such narrative treasure never to retell it? And I wondered, too, of my empty toboggan and Betty's reaction to it. Would it stay empty long? Then there was Monday morning and our one-room school of eight students. What was to become of the mystery and truth of their lives? Would life allow them their own narrative turf, ownerships of their own metaphors? Would they learn to give hope by their celebrations as they came to inhabit childhood caves filled with adult serpents? Would their tellings have just the right mix of sound and silence in the oracy that filled the measure of each day? Would they learn about the teaching that begins with a telling of the eternal truths that live at the kitchen tables and in the particulars? Would they learn about the iterative patterns that spin in their own words? Would they fully experience the fiddle string that is oracy and the narrative threads of connectivity that binding-spell a people together? Would they learn about the devices of living, about the catgut highwire that calls to the storyteller in each human being? Would they bring their babies to the hearth fires and rock them to sleep with the old stories? Would they learn about the wind and the water and the fire and the honor that goes into each tale? Would they dare to stay in their holy land and listen for the silent truth that walks on four legs? Would it be enough that they remember? That their metaphors be marked by holiness? That the details of their life corroborate its fidelity? Would their silent hearts be filled with singing metaphors? Would their laughter piece together the honey gatherers of this life? Would their joy teach the people how to fly? Would their laughter flow like an inside channel through their narrative landscapes? Would they shapeshift and become, too, the Coyote Angel that listens? Would their elder baskets be full of the secrets of the stars? Would they wonder at the fingers that tap a rhythm on the mound over us? Would the self be power enough?

Would they learn how to start a story...
    then give a sharp nudge...
        would they learn of the wolves...
            and old storytellers that ghost into the night...
        for
                in the beginning was
                    and was not sound...

Bibliography

Alford, E., & Harris, C. (Eds.). (1992). *Kitchen talk*. Red Deer, AB: Red Deer College Press.

Anderson, L., Aubrey, I., & McDiarmid, L. (1979). *Storytellers' rendezvous*. Ottawa: Canadian Library Association.

Anonymous. (1946). *The arabian nights* (E. Goodenow, Illus.). New York: Grosset & Dunlap.

Anonymous. (1975). The fall. *School Magazine, 1*, 237–242.

Apte, M. L. (1985). *Humor and laughter: An anthropological approach*. Ithaca, NY: Cornell University Press.

Archibald, J. (1990). Coyote's story about orality and literacy. *Canadian Journal of Native Education, 17*(2), 66–81.

Aristotle. (1967). *Poetics*. Ann Arbor: University of Michigan Press.

Ashton-Warner, S. (1986). *Teacher*. New York: Simon & Schuster.

Babbitt, N. (1975). *Tuck everlasting*. New York: Farrar, Straus, Giroux.

Babcock, B. (1985). A tolerated margin of mess: The trickster and his tales reconsidered. In A. Wiget (Ed.), *Critical essays on Native American literature* (pp. 153–185). Boston: G.K. Hall & Co.

Baker, D. (1981). *Functions of folk and fairy tales*. Washington, DC: Association for Childhood Education International.

Baker, R., & Draper, E. (1992). If one thing stands, another will stand beside it: An interview with Chinua Achebe. *Parabola, XVII*(3), 19–27.

Barthes, R. (1972). *Mythologies* (A. Lavers, Trans.). New York: Hill and Wang.

Barthes, R. (1973). *The pleasure of text* (R. Miller, Trans.). New York: The Noonday Press.

Baughman, M. D. (1979). Teaching with humor: A performing art. *Contemporary Education, 51*(1), 26–30.

Bierhorst, J. (1985). *The mythology of North America*. New York: William Morrow & Company.

Bly, R., & Jacobsen, R. (1980). Four poems (R. Bly, Trans.). *Parabola, V*(1), 78–80.

Brown, J. E. (1979). The wisdom of the contrary. *Parabola, IV*(1), 54–65.

Bruchac, J. (1987). Striking the pole: American Indian humor. *Parabola, XII*(4), 22–29.

Bruner, J. S. (1962). *On knowing: Essays for the left hand*. Cambridge, MA: Belknap Press of Harvard University Press.

Bruner, J. S. (1990). *Acts of meaning*. Cambridge: Harvard University Press.

Bruner, J. S., & Haste, H. (Eds.). (1987). *Making sense: The child's construction of the world*. London: Methuen.

Buber, M. (1964). *Tales of the Hasidim: The early masters* (O. Marx, Trans.). New York: Schocken Books.

Bunner, H. C. (1917). One, two, three. In *The poems of H.C. Bunner*. New York: C. Scribner's Sons.

Burton, W. (1962). *The magic drum: Tales from Central Africa*. New York: Criterion Books.

Cameron, A. (1986). *Dzelarhons: Myths of the northwest coast*. Madeira Park, BC: Harbour Publishing.

Campbell, J. (1949). *The hero with a thousand faces*. New York: Princeton University Press.

Campbell, J. (1972). *Myths to live by*. New York: Bantam Books.

Campbell, J. (1989). *This business of gods*. Caledon East, ON: Windrose Films Ltd.

Capra, F. (1988). *Uncommon wisdom: Conversations with remarkable people*. Toronto: Bantam Books.

Caputo, J. (1987). *Radical hermeneutics: Repetition, deconstruction and the hermeneutic project*. Bloomington: Indiana University Press.

Carpenter, E. (1972). *Oh what a blow that phantom gave me!* Toronto: Bantam Books.

Carpenter, F. (1937). *Tales of a Chinese grandmother*. Garden City, NY: Doubleday, Doran & Company.

Chafe, W. (1985). Some reasons for hesitating. In D. Tannen & M. Saville-Troike (Eds.), *Perspectives of silence* (pp. 77–89). Norwood, NJ: Ablex Publishing Corp.

Chatwin, B. (1987). Dreamtime. In *Granta 21: The Storyteller* (pp. 40–79). Cambridge, GB: Granta Publications.

Clandinin, D. J. (with Connelly, F. M.). (1991, April). *Cultivation and awakenings: Living, telling and retelling our stories*. Paper presented as part of a Division K Invited Symposium on The Content and Character of Teachers' Knowledge at the annual meeting of the American Educational Research Association, Chicago.

Cohan, S., & Shires, L. M. (1988). *Telling stories: A theoretical analysis of narrative fiction*. London: Routledge.

Colum, P. (1927). *Storytelling: New and old*. New York: Macmillan.

Combs, A., & Holland, M. (1990). *Synchronicity: Science, myth and the trickster*. New York: Paragon House.

Connelly, F. M., & Clandinin, D. J. (1990). Stories of experience and narrative inquiry. *Educational Researcher, June/July*, 2–14.

Cooper, S. (1990). Fantasy in the real world. *The Horn Book Magazine*, 3(66), 304–305.

Cousins, N. (1981). *Anatomy of an illness as received by a patient*. Toronto: Bantam.

Cowley, M. (1976). *The view from 80*. New York: The Viking Press.

Crites, S. (1975). *The narrative quality of experience*. Soundings.

Cruikshank, J. (1990). *Life lived like a story*. Vancouver: University of British Columbia Press.

Cunningham, I. (1977). *After ninety*. Vancouver: J. J. Douglas Ltd.

D'angelo, F. (1982). Luria on literacy: Cognitive consequences of reading and writing. In J. C. Raymond (Ed.), *Literacy as a human problem* (pp. 154–169). Alabama: University of Alabama Press.

Davis, V. I. (1982). Literacy: A human and a legal problem. In J. C. Raymond (Ed.), *Literacy as a human problem* (pp. 37–54). Alabama: University of Alabama Press.

Dewey, J. (1934). *Art as experience*. New York: Minton, Balch & Company.

Dillard, A. (1982a). *Living by fiction*. New York: Harper & Row Publishers.

Dillard, A. (1982b). Prelude: Teaching a stone to talk. In J. N. Powell (Ed.), *The Tao of symbols* (pp. 19–27). New York: Quill.

Dillard, A. (1991). *Pilgrim at Tinker's Creek*. New York: Harper's Magazine Press.

Doggett, G. (1986). *Eight approaches to language teaching*. ERIC: Clearinghouse in Language and Linguistics.

Eastman, M. (1936). *Enjoyment of laughter*. New York: Harper.

Eastman, M. (1972). *The sense of humour*. New York: Octagon Books.

Edman, I. (Ed.). (1928). *The works of Plato*. New York: The Modern Library.

Edmonds, I. G. (1966). Time for old magic/Agayk and the strangest spear. In *Trickster tales* (p. 216). New York: J.B. Lippincott Company.

Ellison, R. (1947). *Invisible man*. New York: Random House.

Estés, C. P. (1992). *Women who run with wolves: Myths and stories of the wild woman archetype*. New York: Ballantine Books.

Farella, J. (1993). *The wind in a jar*. Albuquerque, NM: University of New Mexico Press.

Faulkner, W. (1958). *Uncle Willy and other stories*. London: Chatto and Windus.

Ficino, M. (1990). Holy laughter. *Parabola, IV*(1), 48–53.

Fox, M. (1991). *Creation spirituality*. San Francisco: Harper San Francisco.

Franck, F. (1980). Living ancestors. *Parabola, V*(1), 24–31.

Frost, R. (1967). Neither out far nor in deep. In L. Trilling (Ed.), *The experience of literature*. New York: Holt, Rinehart and Winston.

Fulghum, R. (1986). *All I really need to know I learned in kindergarten*. New York: Ivy Books.

Gadamer, H. -G. (1986). *The relevance of the beautiful and other essays*. Cambridge, Great Britian: Cambridge University Press.

Garfield, L. (1985). *The wedding ghost*. Oxford: Oxford University Press.

Goody, J. (1977). *The domestication of the savage mind*. Cambridge, Great Britian: Cambridge University Press.

Gregory, R. L. (1977). Psychology: Towards a science of fiction. In M. Meek, A. Warlow, & G. Barton (Eds.), *The cool web: The pattern of children's reading* (pp. 393–398). London: The Bodley Head.

Grimm, J. -W. (1944). *The complete Grimm's fairy tales*. New York: Pantheon Books.

Hallett, M., & Karasek, B. (Eds.). (1991). *Folk and fairy tales*. Peterborough: Broadview Press.

Hamilton, V. (1985). *The people could fly: American black folktales*. New York: Knopf.

Hardy, B. (1978). Narrative as a primary act of mind. In M. Meek, A. Warlow, & G. Barton (Eds.), *The cool web: The pattern of children's reading* (pp. 12–13). New York: Athenium.

Harman, H. (1962). *Tales told near a crocodile*. London: Hutchinson of London.

Havelock, E., & Herschell, J. (1978). *Communication arts in the ancient world*. New York: Hastings House.

Hekman, S. (1984). Action as a text: Gadamer's hermeneutics and the social scientific analysis of action. *Journal for the Theory of Social Behavior, 14*(3), 333–354.

Heath, S. B. (1982). Protean shapes in literacy events: Ever-shifting oral and literate traditions. In D. Tannen (Ed.), *Spoken and written language: Exploring orality and literacy* (pp. 91–117). Norwood, NJ: Ablex Publishing Corp.

Hemingway, E. (1952). *The old man and the sea*. New York: Charles Scribner's Sons.

Heynen, J. (1990). *100 over 100: Moments with 100 North American centarians*. Saskatoon, SK: Western Producer Prairie Books.

Hutchins, P. (1968). *Rosie's walk*. New York: Aladdin Books.

Illich, I., & Sanders, B. (1988). *The alphabetization of the popular mind*. San Francisco: North Point Press.

Jerusalem Bible. (1966). Garden City, NY: Doubleday & Company, Inc.

Kant, I. (1949). *Critique of practical reason: And other writings in moral philosophy*. Chicago: University of Chicago Press.

Keefer, J. K. (1990). Arks and tunnels. In *More than words can say. Personal perspectives on literacy* (pp. 114–121). Toronto: McClelland and Stewart.

Keesing, R. M. (Ed.). (1978). *Elota's story. The life and times of a Solomon Islands big man*. St. Lucia: University of Queensland Press.

Keillor, G. (1985). *Lake wobegon days*. New York: Viking Books.

Kendon, A. (1985). Some uses of gesture. In D. Tannen & M. Saville-Troike (Eds.), *Perspectives of silence* (pp. 215–234). Norwood, NJ: Ablex Publishing Corp.

King, T. (1989). *Medicine River*. Toronto: Penguin Books.

Klein, G. (1986). Is being two days now the pot turn down. *Children's Literature in Education, 17*(1), 53–60.

Koestler, A. (1964). *The act of creation*. London: Hutchinson & Co. Ltd.

Kornhaber, A., & Woodward, K. (1981). *Grandparents/grandchildren. The vital connection*. New York: Doubleday.

Kroeber, K. (1992). *Retelling, rereading: The fate of storytelling in modern times*. New Brunswick, NJ: Rutgers University Press.

Laboucan, J. B. (1987). Masquematuay. In *The Grouse's Pouch Kit* (pp. 7–13). Fox Lake: Little Red River Board of Education and the Kayas Cultural Centre.

Lang, A. (1951). The two frogs. In M. Shedlock (Ed.), *The art of the storyteller* (3rd ed. rev., pp. 213–215). New York: Dover Publications.

Langeveld, M. J. (1983). The stillness of the secret place. *Phenomenology and Pedagogy, 1*(2), 181.

Langton, J. (1973). The weak place in the cloth: A study of fantasy for children. *The Horn Book Magazine, XLIX*(5), 433–441, 571–579.

Leeming, D. A. (1990). *The world of myth*. New York: Oxford University Press.

Lefcourt, H., & Martin, R. (1986). *Humor and life stress: Antidote to adversity*. New York: Springer-Verlag.

Le Guin, U. (1975). *A wizard of earth sea*. New York: Bantam.

Le Guin, U. (1979). Why are Americans afraid of dragons? In S. Wood (Ed.), *The language of the night: Essays on fantasy and science fiction* (pp. 39–45). New York: Putnam.

Le Guin, U. (1980/1981). It was a dark and stormy night; or, why are we huddling about the campfire? In W. J. T. Mitchell, (Ed.), *On narrative* (pp. 187–195). Chicago: University of Chicago Press.

Le Guin, U. (1981). *Hard words and other poems*. New York: Harper & Row, Publishers.

Le Guin, U. (1983). *Solomon Leviathan's nine hundred and thirty-first trip around the world*. New York: Philomel Books.

Le Guin, U. (1989). *Dancing on the edge of the world: Thoughts on words, women, places*. New York: Grove Press.

Lessing, D. (1988). *The Doris Lessing reader*. New York: Alfred A. Knopf.

Lincoln, K. (1983). *Native American renaissance*. Berkeley: University of California Press.

Long, D., & Knight, B. (1979). *The laughter book*. Don Mills, ON: Mission Book Company.

MacEwan, G. (1958). *Fifty mighty men*. Saskatoon, SK: Modern Press.

MacLachlan, P. (1982). *Cassie Binegar/Patricia MacLachlan*. New York: Harper & Row.

Maltz, D. N. (1985). Joyful noise and reverent silence: The significance of noise in pentecostal worship. In D. Tannen & M. Saville-Troike (Eds.), *Perspectives of silence* (pp. 113–137). Norwood, NJ: Ablex Publishing Corp.

Mandel, E. (1966). Children of the sun. In C. Klinck & R. Watters (Eds.), *Canadian anthology* (pp. 469–470). Toronto: W.J. Gage Limited.

Matsumoto, M. (1988). *The unspoken way. Haragei: Silence in Japanese business and society*. Tokyo: Kodansha International.

Meek, M. (1991). *On being literate*. London: The Bodley Head.

Meili, D. (1991). *Those who know*. Edmonton, AB: NeWest Press.

Melville, H. (1930). *Moby dick*. New York: Random House.

Mindess, H. (1971). *Laughter and liberation*. Los Angeles: Nash Publishers.

Mitchell, W. J. T. (1980). *On narrative*. Chicago: University of Chicago Press.

Mitchell, W. O. (1962). *The kite*. Toronto: Macmillan of Canada.

Mitchell, W. O. (1981). *How I spent my summer holidays*. Toronto: Seal Books, McClelland–Bantam Inc.

Momaday, N. S. (1966). *House made of dawn*. New York: Harper & Row.

Morreall, J. (1983). *Taking laughter seriously*. Albany, NY: State University of New York.

Myerhoff, B. G. (1980). Re-membered lives. *Parabola, V*(1) 74–77.

Nanooch, A. (1987). Son-of-a-Paskisikun. In *The Grouse's Pouch Kit* (pp. 19–25). Little Red River: Little Red River Board of Education and the Kayas Cultural Centre.

Neihardt, J. G. (1932). *Black Elk speaks: Being the life story of a holy man of the Oglala Sioux.* New York: Pocket Books Press.

Neilsen, L. (1989). *Literacy and living: The literate lives of three adults.* Portsmouth, NH: Heinemann.

Nietzsche, F. W. (1968). *The portable Nietzsche.* New York: Viking Press.

Nigg, J. (1982). *The book of gryphons.* Cambridge, MA: Apple-Wood Books.

Noddings, N. (1986). Fidelity in teaching, teacher education and research for teaching. *Harvard Educational Review, 56*(4), 496–510

Norman, H. (1982). *The wishing bone cycle. Narrative poems from the Swampy Cree Indians.* Santa Barbara, CA: Ross-Erikson Publishing.

Norman, H. (1990). *Northern tales: Traditional stories of Eskimos and Indian peoples.* New York: Pantheon Books.

Oden, T. (Ed.). (1978). *Parables of Kierkegaard.* Princeton: Princeton University Press.

O'Hagan, H. (1960). *Tay John.* Toronto: McClelland & Stewart.

Ong, W. (1982). *Orality and literacy: The technologizing of the word.* London: Rutledge.

Osbon, D. K. (Ed.). (1991). *Reflections on the art of living: A Joseph Campbell companion.* New York: Harper Collins Publishers.

Pearson, C. (1986). *The hero within.* San Francisco: Harper.

Peechemow, J. (1987). Wesakychak's blind journey. In *The Grouse's Pouch Kit* (pp. 1–13). Fox Lake: Little Red River Board of Education and the Kayas Cultural Centre.

Pellowski, A. (1977). *The world of storytelling.* New York: R.R. Bowker Company.

Pevere, G. (1992). The rites of Frum. *This Magazine, 26*(3), 12–15.

Pirsig, R. M. (1991). *Lila: An inquiry into morals.* New York: Bantam Books.

Plato. (1945). *Plato's examination of pleasure (Philebus).* Cambridge, Great Britian: The University Press.

Polkinghorne, D. (1988). *Narrative knowing and the human sciences.* Albany, NY: State University of New York Press.

Purves, A. C. (1990). *The scribal society.* New York: Longman.

Raymond, J. (Ed.). (1982). *Literacy as a human problem.* Alabama: University of Alabama Press.

Redford, R. (Director). (1988). *The milagro beanfield war.* Universal City Studios.

Ridington, R. (1990). *Little bit know something: Stories in a language of anthropology.* Vancouver: Douglas & McIntyre.

Rodin, P. (1979). Holy laughter. *Parabola, IV*(1), 48–53.

Rosen, H. (1985). *Stories and meanings.* Sheffield: National Association for the Teaching of English.

Rosen, H. (1986). The importance of story. *Language Arts, 63*(3), 226–237.

Roszak, T. (1986). *The cult of information: The folklore of computers and the true art of thinking.* New York: Pantheon Books.

Rouse, J. (1978). *The completed gesture.* New Jersey: Skyline Books.

Ryga, G. (1970). *The ecstasy of Rita Joe.* Vancouver: Talon Books.

Sacks, S. (Ed.). (1978). *On metaphor.* Chicago: University of Chicago Press.

Saltman, J. (1986). The magic of storytelling [CBC Radio Broadcast]. In *Ideas.* Montreal: Canadian Broadcasting Corporation.

Sartre, J. -P. (1977). *The words* (B. Frechtman, Trans.). New York: Fawcett World Library.

Saville-Troike, M. (1985). The place of silence in an integrated theory of communication. In D. Tannen & M. Saville-Troike (Eds.), *Perspectives of silence* (pp. 3–18). Norwood, NJ: Ablex Publishing Corp.

Sawada, D., & Caley, M. T. (1990). Shibusa: An aesthetic approach to ecosophical education. *The Trumpeter: Journal of Ecosophy, 7*(3), 107–110.

Sawyer, R. (1942). *The way of the storyteller*. New York: The Viking Press.

Schafer, R. M. (1969). *The new soundscape: A handbook for the modern music teacher*. Scarborough, ON: Berandol Music Limited.

Scofield, E. (1965). *A fox in one bite: And other tasty tales from Japan*. Tokyo: Kodansha International Ltd.

Scott-Maxwell, F. (1968). *The measure of my days*. New York: Penguin Books.

Serwer, B. (1970). *Let's steal the moon*. Boston: Little, Brown, and Company.

Sewepagaham, A. (1987). Remembering the ways. In *The Grouse's Pouch Kit* (1–29). Fox Lake: Little Red River Board of Education and the Kayas Cultural Centre.

Shakespeare, W. (1966). *Complete sonnets and poems*. New York: Airmont Publishing Company, Inc.

Shanker, S. (1965). *Semantics: The magic of words*. Boston: Ginn and Company.

Shedlock, M. (1951). *The art of story-telling*. New York: Dover Publications.

Sheridan, J. (1991). The silence before drowning in alphabet soup. *Canadian Journal of Native Education, 18*(1), 23–29.

Shor, I., & Freire, P. (1987). *A pedagogy for liberation*. Boston: Bergin & Garvey Publishers, Inc.

Sidney, Sir Philip. (1950). *The defence of poesie*. Heidelberg: Carl Winter.

Silko, L. M. (1977). *Ceremony*. New York: Penguin Books.

Sinclair, L., & Rosenbluth, V. (1986). The magic of storytelling [CBC Radio Broadcast]. In *Ideas*. Montreal: Canadian Broadcasting Corporation.

Stafford, K. (1986). *Having everything right: Essays of place*. Lewiston, ID: Confluence Press.

Stoller, P. (1987). *A sorcery's shadow: A memoir of apprenticeship among the Songhay of Niger*. Chicago: University of Chicago Press.

Swarthout, G. (1975). *The shootist*. New York: Doubleday & Company.

Tan, A. (1989). *The joy luck club*. New York: Putnam's.

Tannen, D. (1985). Silence. Anything but. In D. Tannen & M. Saville-Troike (Eds.), *Perspectives of silence* (pp. 93–111). Norwood, NJ: Ablex Publishing Corp.

Todorov, T. (1977). *The poetics of prose*. Ithaca, NY: Cornell University Press.

Toelken, B. (1979). *The dynamics of folklore*. Boston, MA: Houghton Mifflin Co.

Townsend, J. R. (1987). The life journey. In B. Harrison & G. Maguire (Eds.), *Innocence and experience: Essays & conversations on children's literature* (pp. 138–147). New York: Lothrop, Lee, and Shepard Books.

Travers, P. L. (1989). *What the bee knows: Reflections on myth, symbol, and story*. Wellingborough, GB: Aquarian Press.

Van der Post, L. (1961). *The heart of the hunter*. New York: William Morrow and Company.

Widdows, P. F. (Trans.). (1992). *The fables of Phaedrus*. Austin: The University of Texas Press.

Wilder, T. (1955). *The bridge of San Luis Rey*. New York: Washington Square Press, Inc.

Wrightson, P. (1991). Deeper than you think. *The Horn Book Magazine, LXVII*(2), 162–170.

Y Maestas, J., & Anaya, R. (1980). *Cuentos*. Sante Fe, NM: The Museum of New Mexico Press.

Yanagita, K. (1972). *Japanese folk tales*. Taipei: Orient Cultural Service.

Zong, I. -S. (1952). Folk tales from Korea. New York: Grove Press.

Index

Active recording, 22
   (*see also* Clandinin; Connelly)
Adventure
   accident, ceremony, and, 44 (*see also* Story/Stories, Rattler's)
   imagined (*see also* Story/Stories, Sparrow's)
Alford, E., 47
Anansi
   Nyame box, 16
   and webbed stories, 4
Anaya, R., 14, 47
Ancestors, 1, 54, 59, 69, 80, 98, 103, 109, 122
Ancestral
   act, 15
   campfire, 16
   face, 11
   gods, 53
   imitation, 33
   line, 145
   manner, 20 (*see also* Story/Stories, Mosum's)
   and the modern, 103
   place, 4, 127
   shadow of, 103
   silence, 80
   template of good teaching, 3
Anderson, L., 177–179
Anonymous, 115, 116
   (*see also The Arabian Nights*; Story/Stories, New Guinean)
Apte, M. L., 207
The Arabian Nights, 115, 141
Arcana Microcosmi (Nigg), 2
Archetypal laughter
   of the Heyoka, 11
Archetype (Jungian), 139
Archibald, J., 214
Aristotle, 178
Ashton-Warner, S., 57
Aubrey, I., 177–179

Babbitt, N., 23–24
Babcock, B., 207
Baker, D., 138, 146

Baker, R., 14, 44
Barthes, R., 17, 20, 110
  (*see also* Gesture/s)
Baughman, M. D., 9, 191
Bierhorst, J., 16
Birth/Re-birth, 7, 40, 44, 104, 125, 127, 130
Bly, R., 223
Brown, J. E., 201
Bruchac, J., 195
Bruner, J. S., 21, 136, 262
Buber, M.
  listening for the sake of Heaven story, 27
  (*see also* Heaven)
Bunner, H. C., 247–248
Burton, W., 12

Caley, M. T., 268
Cameron, A., 286
Campbell, J., 11, 24, 58, 92, 125, 169, 191, 196, 226, 230
  (*see also* Folklore/Folkloral form, ritual of in manners; Holy land/place/s; Teaching moments, great teaching of all the greatest teachers)
Campfire/s, 16, 19, 20, 24, 47, 48, 52, 53, 54, 55, 59, 61, 145
  (*see also* Le Guin)
Canadian, 5, 10
Capra, F., 255
Caputo, J., 262–263
Carpenter, E., 97–98, 122, 131
Carpenter, F., 85–86
Chafe, W., 74
Chatwin, B., 258
Childhood
  act of replenishing silence, 73
  (*see also* Story/Stories, Sparrow's)
  behind the curtains, 79
  branding tales (Sewall's), 49
  dream reality of, 61, 120
  (*see also* Dreaming time; Story/Stories, Je-Nee's, Pesimwastches')
  first step, 79
  as holy land, 18, 115–132
  Korean (*see* Story/Stories, Je-Nee's, childhood floor culture)
  names and naming, 40, 104
  night, 51
  secret places of, 21
  sense of story, 138
Circle/d/s, 1, 3, 5, 24, 37, 47, 61
  need a fire, 55
  perfect, 48 (*see also* Campfire/s; Le Guin)
  and professionalism/slowing down, 57
  (*see also* Ashton-Warner)
  of stones without entrance (death), 58, 143–144
  theme of open, 58
  transformation/transubstantiation
  (*see* Transformation/Transubstantiation)
Clandinin, D. J., vii, 17, 22 144, 154
Classroom/s
  around the campfire, 52
  management, 56
  and metaphoric life, 6–7
  mission/residential, 28, 41, 97 (*see also* Story/Stories, Pesimwastches')
  Platonic fashioned, 20
  and silence, 3
  and sound and silence, 24 (*see also* Silence/d/s; Teaching moments)
Cohan, S., 238
Colum, P., 4
Combs, A., 135, 151, 163, 271
Connelly, F. M., 17, 22, 144, 154
Conversation
  active recording of, 22 (*see also* Clandinin; Connelly)

definition of, 18
   instead of interview, 20
   intergenerational, 10–11
   interplay of story and, 140, 144
   space, 142–143, 149
   taking of time, 54
Cooper, S., 164, 166
Cousins, N., 180
Cowley, M., 253, 254, 255
Cree (*see also* Story/Stories, Cree)
   formulaic silence, 71
   High, 28
   the "masquematuay" of the, 16, 135
   Swampy, 9, 62
   Wesakychak Trickster, 9, 36 (*see also* Trickster/trickstering/tricksterish, elders)
   Woodland, 58
   (*see also* Story/Stories, Sabochees')
Crites, S., 21
Cruikshank, J., 275
Culture
   clash dynamic of sound and silence, 72, 97, 104
   and nature interplay in stories, 4
Cunningham, I., 227, 229
Curriculum building projects, 22–23

Dance/dancing, viii, 6, 52
D'angelo, F., 89
David and Goliath, 138–139
   (*see also* Story/Stories, Sparrow's)
Davis, V. I., 90
Death, 3, 8, 22, 39–40, 42, 51, 57–58, 69, 74, 93, 122, 143
Dewey, J., 186
Dialectical balancing act, 22
   (*see* Clandinin; Connelly)
Dillard, A., 65, 74, 105, 140, 144
   (*see also* Silence/d/s; Prayer/chant)
Doggett, G., 194

Draper, E., 14, 44
Dreaming place, 124
Dreaming time, 5, 24
   (*see also* Childhood, dream reality of)
Drum/s, 2, 3, 6, 24, 61

Eastman, M., 180
Edman, I., 172
Edmonds, I. G., 29–30
   (*see also* Story/Stories, Inuit)
Elder(s), 223–264, 283–287
   ability to draw near to others, 228–229
   age specific, 226
   "bear-paw principle," 236–238
   to be respected, 241
   with children and grandchildren, 17, 19, 58, 61, 148
   completed character, 229
   connection between ancestral voice and daily voice, 225
   death of, 93
   embodies the culture, 226
   ensures ancestors, 240
   freedom, 11, 90–91
   as giants, 232
   have focus, 238
   historical, 240
   holy land, 125
   hope, 149
   in-waiting, 7
   knows all roads, 227, 234, 242
   and laughter (*see* Laughter; *see also* Cree; Gesture/s; Oral additives; Story/Stories, English, High Cree, Pesimwastches', Rattler's; Trickster/trickstering/tricksterish, elders)
   memory, 92
   most elderly, statesmanlike, 20 (*see also* Story/Stories, Mosum's)
   names and naming, 39–40, 104

one who sees things, 227
  as pioneer, 230, 232
  prophecy, 150–151
  respect for, 130, 151
  spiritual guide, 162, 233
  story within story, 149
  struggle, 94
  surviving and telling about it, 231
  time and aging, 224–225
  in training, 192
  as a tree trunk, 241
  treasured, 225
  (*see also* Grand/fathers/mothers/parents)
Elements as place, 47 (*see* Place/s)
Ellison, R., 12
Estés, C. P., 51, 52, 204
Ethnocentricity
  and metaphoric postures of fidelity, 7
The Exchange of Powers Between the Wolf and the Dog, 36
  (*see also* Story/Stories, Pesimwastches')

Failed stories, 255
The Fall, 116
Family of the moment and family of humankind
  interplay in stories/storytelling, 21
Farella, J., 20
Faulkner, W., 225
Ficino, M., 212
Fidelity, 157–174
  in the telling, 161
  move with the generation, 171
  pre-understanding, 172–173
  (*see also* Truth)
Fish and game of it, 177–178
Fit of generation to story, 171
Folklore/Folkloral form
  bridging life and art, 7, 30

and the crosscultural educator, 17
  escape, recovery, consolation, 138, 142, 145 (*see also* Baker)
  first, 1–2, 99 (*see also* "In the Beginning Was and Was Not")
  as fragments of belief, 12 (*see also* Grimm)
  around the hearth, 48–49
  impulse, 14
  ritual of in manners, 58, 92 (*see also* Campbell)
  mythic riches of, 13, 24
  place, 11 (*see also* Place/s)
  poetic, 121
  as a primary act, 13, 29 (*see also* Hardy)
  private/public, 13
  as repetitive, 24 (*see also* Redundancy/Repetition)
  as therapeutic/medicine (*see* Pellowski; Storytelling, overview of; Therapeutic/medicine stories)
  third person nature of, 13, 139
  understanding of/engagement in, 13
  the very act of telling, 13
  voice, 13, 15,
Food, fire, and story (*see* Memorabilia)
Four elements as place (*see* Place/s)
Fox, M., 151
Franck, F., 243
Freire, P., 136
Frost, R., 276
Fulghum, R., 249

Gadamer, H. -G., 16
  poetic language, ethnicity and truth, 24
Garfield, L., 10
Genesis and the beginning of silence, 65
  (*see also* Illich; Sanders)
Gesture/s

acrylic deer hide, 20 (*see also* Interpretive story paintings)
body, 76–78, 127
caress, 10 (*see also* Story/Stories, *Grandpa Willie and the rock saddle*)
children/grandchildren, watching his hands, 19 (*see also* Story/Stories, Sabochees')
with eyelids, 76
eyes and fingers, 76
finger tracing, 17
move with word and, 7, 33 (*see also* Laughter; Oral accounts/Orality, connective journey; Story/Stories, Sewall's definition of)
mutual and joint production of, 77
pointed with his lips, 76
pure (Barthes), 20
silence of, 74–75, 77
upturned hands, 76
yardstick swinging, 8
(*see also* Story/Stories, *Mary Ann and the yardstick*)
Gift giving, 20–21, 23, 106, 138, 143, 149
The golden fish, 121
Goody, J., 35
Grand/father/mother/parents, 10, 17, 18, 19–20, 28, 31, 32, 36, 37, 38, 39, 40, 43, 48–51, 55–58, 60, 61, 69, 70, 73, 74–75, 69, 87–92, 96, 131, 138–143, 148–149, 150
Great Forest Book, 169
Great Spirit, viii, 93, 115, 128
Gregory, R. L., 100
Grimm, J. -W., 12, 13, 140
(*see also* Folklore)
Gryphons
living in the Canadian middle as, 5
metaphor of, 2

search for storytellers who live and tell of, 3

Hamilton, V., 136–137
(*see also* Stories/Story, African, about hope)
Hardy, B., 13, 14
(*see also* Folklore)
Harman, H., 78–79
Harris, C., 47
Haste, H., 262
Havelock, E., 5, 14
(*see also* Oral accounts/orality)
Heath, S. B., 91–92
Hearth, 273
Hekman, S., 172
Hemingway, E., 252
Herschell, J., 5, 14
Heynen, J., 11
High fidelity, 157–174
Holland, M., 135, 151, 163, 271
Holy day (Jewish Sabbath), 52–53
Holy land/place/s, 277–278
called childhood, 18, 117–119, 130
lost and revisitation cycle, 116, 118
need for, 16, 112
a northern place/community, 19, 55
not some other place, 24 (*see also* Campbell)
story is a, 115–132
and silence, 65, 69, 70–71, 129
secret and, 115
transformation/transubstantiation (*see* Transformation/Transubstantiation)
and water/elements, 47
Honor/able, 24, 47, 48, 61
Hoop snake, 2–3
(*see also* Le Guin; metaphor)
Hoopedness of the storytelling act, 23, 53

Hutchins, P., 270

Illich, I., 65–66, 80
  (*see also* Genesis and the beginning of silence)
"In the Beginning Was and Was Not" (Sewall), 1–2
Injustice, 159
Intergenerational conversation, 10–11, 223–264
  as affirmative, 262
  reincarnation, 253–254
  they say you talk to the angels, 247–264
Interplay in stories/storytelling
  being and speaking Cree, 92, 148 (*see also* Literacy)
  conversation and story, 140, 144
  culture and nature, 4, 33
  culture of orality and specific cultural ways, 29
  the exceptional and the ordinary, 21 (*see also* Bruner)
  family of moment and family of humankind, 21
  formulaic and privately constructed silence, 71, 80
  intergenerational, 10–11, 49
  the known and the unknown, 7, 81
  of literal/literary/literate/metaphoric/oral, 14, 37, 49, 68, 85–112
  past and future, 18, 54, 81, 108, 144
  past and present, 120
  pause and significance, 6, 19, 24, 31, 67–68 (*see also* Narrative joy; Narrative time of pause)
  poetic and prosaic representation, 30, 31, 35
  possession and person, 21
  public (professional) and private, 16
  reality and representation, 16, 17, 58

sound and silence/s, 7, 22, 24, 32, 65–82, 104, 117, 122 (*see also* Silence/d/s)
strangers into family, 49, 52 (*see also* Interplay in Stories/Storytelling; Transformation/Transubstantiation)
universal and local, 138
Interpretive story paintings, 20
  (*see also* Gesture/s, acrylic deer hide)
Interview (*see* Conversation)

Jacobsen, R., 223

Keefer, J. K., 99
Keesing, R. M., 224
Keillor, G., 164
Kendon, A., 77
Key words, 38–39
  (*see also* Names and naming)
King, T., 279
Kitchen table, 3, 5, 13, 15, 16, 17, 18, 21, 28, 29, 31, 43, 47, 48, 52, 53, 61, 87, 119, 124, 131, 137, 151
  (*see also* Methodological concerns)
Klein, G., 4
Koestler, A., 188
Kornhaber, A., 260, 261, 262
Knight, B., 179
Kroeber, K., 129

Lang, A., 223–224
  two frogs story, 223–224
Langeveld, M. J., 117, 119, 120
Laughter, 177–198, 280–283
  access to knowledge, 202
  acid test of life's performance, 186
  ancestral voice, 218
  archetypal; Heyoka, 11
  camp clowns, 184

and Chipewyan Prairies' pursuit of truth, 9
of the circle, 47
contrary, 192
in the person of the Hare, 195
definition, 180
directed inward, 185
gives balance to the unlaughable, 182
God's greatest gift, 191
learning and survival, 195
in lieu of perfection, 178
as light, 44
lives in story, 180
mediates the telling, 191
and memory, 189
as a metaphoric bridge, 7, 9
and Navajo sense of balance, 178, 191
as oral additive, 32, 33
and relationships, 178
secures justice, 182
as shapeshifter/tricksterish, 8, 9, 19, 20, 56, 58, 90–91, 94–96, 122, 123, 126 (*see also* Nanooch; Story/stories, and laughter, Pesimwastches', Rattler's)
and silence, 67, 70, 72, 107, 147–148
tradition of the unfunny, 178–179
and triangulation, 9
Zoroaster, 179
Leeming, D. A., 203
Lefcourt, H., 179, 180
Le Guin, U., 2, 11, 13, 20, 48, 104, 111, 122, 139, 142, 225, 272, 277 (*see also* Circle/d/s, perfect; Metaphor, hoop snake as; Campfire)
Lessing, D., 187
Life
as high energy and passion, 188
(*see also* Laughter, acid test of life's performance)
Life-rescue

through stories and metaphor, 7
Lincoln, K., 9
Listen/er/s, 7, 9, 18, 19, 20, 21, 27–28, 41, 42, 48, 49, 58, 61, 68, 74, 76, 77, 78, 98, 120–121, 122, 123, 124, 127, 141, 142, 149
Literacy, 85–112
Long, D., 179
Love, vii,
for the illiterate, 96–97, 111
listener and, 21
for neighbor, 147

MacEwan, G., 240
MacLachlan, P., 8
Maltz, D. N., 69
Mandel, E., 279
Martin, R., 179, 180
Matsumoto, M., 69
McDiarmid, L., 177–179
Meek, M., 99
Meili, D., 228, 229
Melville, H., 22
Memorabilia
symbols of food, fire, and story, 47–62
Memorability/Memory
body engagement, 77
child's first narrative, 51
elder's, 92, 94, 125
oral accounts/orality and, 5, 6, 33–35, 51, 79, 93, 120, 121
past and future, 19, 81, 144
past and present, 120
and redundancy/repetition (*see* Redundancy/Repetition)
storyteller's, 49
and struggle, 94 (*see also* Ong; Redundancy/Repetition)
Stafford's description of, 6
teacher's life (*see* Teaching moments)
Metaphor

bridge, 112
book, 226–227 (*see also* Literacy)
campfire (*see* Campfire/s)
circle (*see* Circle/d/s)
death of an elder, 93–94
gift, 128, 143, 149
gryphons, 2
holy land, 115–132
hoop snake, 2–3, 122 (*see also* Le Guin)
hope, 135–154, 278
human language, 38, 93 (*see also* Story/Stories, Jennifer's)
interplay between the literal and, (*see* Interplay in stories/storytelling, of literal/literary/literate/metaphoric/oral)
interiority of, 7, 139
knowing and manipulation of, 7, 148 (*see also* Nietzsche)
and life-rescue, 7
as lived-in, 6
medicine of, 94, 115–174
night, 51, 59–60, 116
the rattlesnake of, 6
as ruffled grouse, 8
of scale, 190
of storyteller as teacher, 3, 7
as god(s), 17
story as, vii, 7, 29
Metaphoric life
of the classroom, 6, 24
open circle theme, 58 (*see also* Story/Stories, Rattler's)
through sound and silence/s, 7, 22, 24, 32, 65–82, 104 108, 117, 122, 129, 132 (*see also* Silence/s/d; Teaching moments; Transformation/Transubstantiation)
survival, 146–148
Metaphoric power

to create holy/special places, 116, 128
loss and revisitation of, 94, 116, 118
to give pause and ethical significance, 24
to recognize ethnocentricity, 7
to stand on one foot, 146
to walk on one leg, 7
(*see also* Names and naming)
Metaphoric landscape
ancestral voice and, 11
holy land (see Holy land/place/s)
inhabited by young and old, 11
Metaphoric talk to tale, 139, 144
Methodological concerns, 17, 22, 30–31 (*see also* Active recording; Interplay in stories/storytelling; Kitchen table; Story/Stories; Translator's presence)
Mindess, H., 180
Mitchell, W. J. T., 149, 267
Mitchell, W. O., 260, 261
Momaday, N. S., 10, 11
Moment/s
authors as participants of the, 42
first folkloral, 1
family of the, 21
and memorability/memory (*see* Memorability/memory)
of a poem, vii
personal telling, 3
teaching (*see* Teaching moments)
traditional, 24 (*see also* Toelken)
Morreall, J., 179, 180, 182, 194
The Mourning of a hunter's spirit, 36 (*see also* Story/Stories, Pesimwastches')
Myerhoff, B. G., 230
Myth/ic, 11, 12–13, 24, 16, 65, 74, 132, 164
(*see also* Grimm; Pevere; Schafer)

Names and naming, 6, 9, 21, 22, 33, 37–41, 44, 73, 104
Nanooch, A., 95–96
Narrative ceremony, 4, 5, 9, 13, 14, 20–21, 23, 40, 44, 48, 54, 55, 59, 60, 87, 117, 145
   (*see also* Gift giving; Names and naming; Anaya; Pellowski; Y Maestas)
Narrative joy
   of ballpoint pen, 105 (*see also* Story/Stories, Dafna's)
   exuberance, 35–36 (*see also* Story/Stories, Sparrow's)
   one who lived with such, 57 (*see also* Story/Stories, Rattler's)
   a special pause, 31
   of writing, 112
Narrative pluralities, 18, 19–20
   (*see also* Story/Stories, Pesimwastches', Rattler's)
Narrative production, 21
   (*see also* Polkinghorne)
Narrative time of pause, 19
Navajo Night Chant (in Momaday), 11
Neihardt, J. G., 23, 118
Neilsen, L., 22
Nietzsche, F. W.
   knowing and the manipulation of metaphor, 7
Nigg, J., 2
Noddings, N., 161, 164
Norman, H., 9, 39, 62, 201, 204
   The cranberry partners, 201–202
   (*see also* Names and naming; Story/Stories, Swampy Cree)
Northern home/s, 20, 55
Northerners Nitotem/Sakastenohk, 20, 60–61, 150

Oden, T., 210
O'Hagan, H., 21

One room knife, 43
   (*see also* Story/Stories, Rattler's)
Ong, W., 5–6, 16, 28, 31, 33, 37, 41, 61, 77, 87, 103, 216, 271
   (*see also* Oral accounts/Orality, literacy and, Ong's definition of, repositories of; Oral additives; Redundancy/Repetition; Story/Stories, body engagement)
Onomatopoeia, 33
   (*see also* Shanker)
Openness,
   in the Greek notion of truth, *aleltheia*, 21
Oral accounts/Orality
   authority of, 20, 40
   and artistry, 3, 7, 30
   centrality of human beings, 80
   characteristics of, 29–44
   child to elder/child in elder, 11, 42, 110
   as connective, 5, 6, 14, 30, 32, 41 (*see also* Ong; Oral additives)
   creation and conservation of knowledge, 14 (*see also* Havelock and Herschell)
   culture of, 29
   as denominative (*see* Names and naming)
   elusive to capture, 29
   and empathetic projection, 41–44
   first folkloral moment of, 1–2
   and gestural engagement (*see* Gesture/s)
   and imitation of nature, 33
   and interplay of stories of long ago, 16, 31 (*see also* Interplay; Oral accounts/orality, additive)
   and laughter, 7, 9, 18–19, 32, 33, 44, 71–72, 106, 107, 122, 123, 126, 141–142, 147–148 (*see also* Cree;

Gesture/s; Oral additives; Story/Stories, English, Cree, Pesimwastches', Rattler's; Trickster/trickstering/tricksterish, elders)
as life-rescue, 7
literacy and, 27–28, 85–112
and memorability/memory (see Memorability/Memory; Redundancy/Repetition)
as a mode of action, 37 (see also Ong)
and narrative hoops, 11
Ong's definition of, 5
and pausing between friends, 6 (see also Oral additives; Scott-Maxwell; Silence/s; Teaching moments)
power of (see Names and naming)
and public/private experience, 7
repositories of, 16 (see also Ong)
style of thinking, 5, 87
and technology (see Technology)
as therapeutic/medicine (see Pellowski; Storytelling, overview of; Therapeutic/medicine stories)
time of primary, 15
Oral additives, 31–33, 41
(see also Gesture/s; Laughter; Oral accounts/Orality, connective as; and empathetic projection; Story/Stories, definition of; Silence/s/d)
Osbon, D. K., 215, 226
Painted eyebrow, 85–86
(see also Carpenter)
Passion/s, 19, 32, 33, 35, 54, 71, 94, 106–109, 123
(see also Story/Stories, Dafna's, Sparrow's)
Pause/s, 3, 6, 19, 24, 31, 32
Pearson, C., 196
Peechemow, J., 213–214
Wesakychak's blind journey, 213–214
Pellowski, A., 13, 15

(see also Narrative ceremony; Storytelling, overview of)
Pevere, G., 16
Pirsig, R. M., 119
Place/s, 4, 11, 16, 19, 21, 24, 38, 39, 41, 42, 47–62, 69, 93, 96, 104, 112, 117, 118, 124, 127, 129, 130, 131, 132
Plato/Platonic, 20, 39, 178, 196
Polkinghorne, D., 21
(see also Narrative production)
Prayer/chant,
Cree, 130
give thanks (Sewall), 16
in Hasidic Judaism, 3–4
for holy places, 16, 112, 115–132
Mission school and, 97
Navajo Night Chant (in Momaday), 11
religious storytelling, 15, 125
silence and, 65, 69, 70–71, 72 (see also Dillard; Pellowski; Storytelling, overview of; Silence/d/s)
"Sunrise on Narrative Hill" (Sewall), viii
women and, 108
(see also Story/Stories, Dafna's)
Purves, A. C., 109
Raymond, J., 96
Redford, R., 249
The Milagro beanfield war, 249
Redundancy/Repetition, 24, 33–37, 41, 44
Remembering place, 215
Research ceremony, 17, 87
Responsibility, 42
Ridington, R., 97
Rodin, P., 216
Romeo and Juliet, 38
Rosen, H., 142, 146, 270
Rosenbluth, V., 4
Roszak, T., 173

Rouse, J., 91, 97, 234
Rumplestilzkin, 39
Ryga, G., 22
Sacks, S., 7, 148
Saltman, J., 218
Sanders, B., 65–66, 80
Sartre, J. -P., 260
Saville-Troike, M., 68, 72, 73
Sawada, D., 268
Schafer, R. M., 3, 65
   silence as perfect sound, 5, 32
Scofield, E., 207–208
Scott-Maxwell, F., 3, 207, 225
Secret places, 172, 220
Self/Selves
   narrative and recovery of, 5, 7, 18, 87
   within culture, 150
Serwer, B., 104–105
Shakespeare, W., 38, 87, 104
Shanker, S., 33, 38
Shapeshifter, 201, 220, 283
   struggle for equity and vindication, 210
Shedlock, M., 268–270
   Hanooch, 268–270
Sheridan, J., 47, 79–80
Shires, L. M., 238
Shor, I., 136
Sidney, Sir Philip, 6
Silence/d/s, 271, 274–275
   after stories, vii, 70, 129
   and celebration, 21, 24, 32, 67, 94, 97, 142
   classroom and, 3, 79
   completed narrative, 160
   as a cultural view of universe, 69–70, 73
   and culture clash, 72
   first language patterns of, 73
   formulaic, 71
   of holiness/holy place/s, 65, 69, 70–71, 129
   and laughter, 67, 70, 72, 107, 141–143, 147–148
   mutual and joint production of, 70, 77
   mystery of, 73–74
   need for, 151
   as pause between friends, 3, 6 (*see also* Scott-Maxwell; Silence/d/s; Teaching moments)
   paintings visualized the, 21
   the perfect sound of, 5, 32 (*see also* Oral additives; Schafer)
   privately constructed, 3, 71, 80
   as a sacred place, 69
   shape of (deeply contextualized), 74
   sound/s and, 22, 24, 32, 52, 65–82, 104, 108, 117, 122
   use of, 75
   and women's subordination, 72, 108
   wordless communication (Japanese), 69
   (*see also* Matsumoto)
Silko, L. M., 244
Sinclair, L., 4
South Korean
   bridegroom and the spirits of story, 14–15
   colleague Je-Nee (*see* Story/Stories, Je-Nee's)
   story bag, 16
The spirit moans, 33, 77
   (*see also* Story/Stories, Pesimwastches')
Spiritual guide, 162
   (*see also* Elders)
Spontaneity (*see* Story/Stories, Rattler's, shape of silence, Sparrow's)
Stafford, K.
   definition of memory, 6
   rescue, 7

Story/Stories
  adventure (imagined) (*see* Story/Stories, Sparrow's)
  African,
    about hope, 136–137, 149 (*see also* Hamilton)
    about silence, 66–67, 78–79 (*see also* Harman; Van der Post)
    aggregates in time, 257
    Agnes and loss of leg, 6–7
    American, 107
    Anansi and webbed, 4 (*see also* Anansi)
    Arusha Masai, 28, 40, 48–49, 52, 54, 59, 132
    birth/re-birth in (*see* Birth/Re-birth)
    as body engagement (*see* Gesture/s)
    boy and the fox story, 207–208
    as celebration, 15, 21, 22, 24, 32, 44, 51, 54, 92, 94, 126, 142
    Central African honey gatherer and sons', 12
    Chinese (*see* Painted eyebrow)
    Cinderella, 159
    corroborative act, 168–169
    creation (Spanish), 47 (*see also* Anaya; Y Maestas)
    Cree, 16, 19–20, 28, 58–62, 71, 92–94, 148 (*see also* Cree)
  Dafna's
    Atonement Day, 258
    background, 28
    bluebird of fidelity, 164–165
    body gesture, 76, 77, 127
    David and the spiders, 217–218
    empathetic projection, 42
    first day of teaching story, 189–190
    first story place, 52–54
    The gift of the bee, 190–191
    gift giving, 258–259
    The golden fish (Israeli poem), 121

    Hebrew past and Israeli future, 19, 54, 108, 144, 208
    holy land, 119–122, 123, 127, 130, 132
    Israeli bonfire, 61
    Israeli train travel, 147–148
    jumping rope, 188–189
    laughing warrior, 208
    metaphors of literacy (ballpoint pen/book), 105–112
    Moulon's robe, 191
    passion/ate,
      as medium of transformation/transubstantiation, 54, 71, 106–109
      as oral additive, 32, 33 (*see also* Oral additives; Passion/s)
    polarities, 163
    proverbs, 216–217
    redundancy/repetition, 34, 41
    silence of holiness, 70–71
    Solomon and the fire, 208–210
    story as truth, 164
    story as sustenance, 163–164
    survival and continuance of a people, 163–164
    women's subordination, 72
    writing as a holy undertaking, 71, 108–110
  definition of,
    Polkinghorne's, 21
    Sewall's, 21–22
  English, 28, 93, 107
  Failed stories, 255
  Fish and game of it, 177–178
  Fit of generation to story, 171
  French, 28, 107
  The golden fish (Israeli poem), 121
  grandfather, 18, 19–20, 28, 31, 32, 36, 38, 39, 40, 43, 48–49, 55–58, 70, 73, 74–75, 87–92, 96, 131, 138–

143, 148–149, 150 (*see also* Story/ Stories, *Grandpa Willie and the rock saddle*, Pesimwastches', Sabochees', Rattler's)
grandmother, 10, 17, 40, 48–51, 52, 60, 61, 69, 79, 131, 138, 154
Grandpa Willie and the rock saddle, 10
great grandfather/parents, 20, 103 (*see also* Story/Stories, Mosum's)
Hanooch, 268–270
Hasidic Judaism, 3–4
Heaven, 27, 28, 29, 30, 36, 41, 44, 65, 85 (*see also* Buber)
Hebrew (*see* Story/Stories, Dafna's)
High Cree, 28
high fidelity, 157–174
about hope, 135–154
Inuit, 29–30 (*see also* Edmonds)
and interplay (*see* Interplay in stories/storytelling)
Japanese, 69, 112 (*see also* Yanagita)
Je-Nee's,
    background, 28
    childhood floor culture, 50–51
    dream and fantasy, 51, 60, 61 (*see also* Northerners Nitotem/ Sakastenohk)
    kitchen table, 20
    Korean coal fire, 61
    Korean calligraphy, 68
    metaphor of night, 51, 59
    Old woman and the tiger, 154
    wise young man story, 263
    (*see also* Story/Stories, English, Korean)
Jennifer's, 37–38
Jewish, 104–105, 109, 110, 111, 147
Korean, 28, 50–51, 54, 61, 68
    as a laughing matter, 177
    and laughter, 7, 9, 18–19, 32, 33, 56, 44, 57, 58, 66, 71–72, 77, 88, 89, 90, 92, 94–96, 106, 107, 122, 123, 126, 141–143, 147–148 (*see also* Cree; Gesture/s; Laughter; Oral additives; Story/Stories, English, High Cree, Pesimwastches', Rattler's; Trickster/trickstering/tricksterish, elders)
learning by, 93
Longfoot
    suicide story, 173–174
Mary Ann and the yardstick, 8
metaphor (*see* Metaphor)
Mosum's
    background, 28
    most elderly, 20, 67
    elder hope, 149
    eyelid gestures, 76
    growing concern for present generation, 257
    hope, 148–149, 150, 154
    praise of memory, 92
    praise of silence, 20, 67–68, 69, 70
    seen and heard category, 73, 121
    self within culture, 150
    (*see also* Cree; Story/Stories, grandfather, High Cree)
names and naming (*see* Names and naming)
    (*see also* Grand/fathers/mothers/ parents'; Norman; Story/Stories, Jennifer's, Pesimwastchees', Rattler's, Swampy Cree, Tololwa's; Travers)
New Guinean, 116
    (*see also* Anonymous)
of pain and survival, 3–4, 7, 146–148, 150
Old woman truth, 169–170
Painted eyebrow (Chinese), 85–87, 104
    (*see also* Carpenter)
Pesimwastches',

background, 28
Beaver leg, 194–195
dream reality of childhood, 61
empathetic projection, 41–42
The exchange of powers between the wolf and the dog, 36
Groundhog for Grandma, 193–194
hope, 149–150, 154
metaphor of book, 94, 96
metaphor of campfire, 96
mission/residential school days, 28, 41, 97
The mourning of a hunter's spirit, 36
naming and birth, 40
Platonic, 20
pointed with his lips/gesture, 76
quietude as nongesture, 77
redundancy/repetition, 36, 41
The spirit moans, 33, 77
spiritual lives of the young, 96
Wesakychak and the creation of the earth, 36
Western world, 19
woodland tea fires, 61–62
writing Cree, 92–93
(*see also* Cree; Story/Stories, English, grandfather; Trickster/trickstering/tricksterish, elders)
plurality of other stories, 270
principle of three, 272
Rattler's,
  adventure, accident, and ceremony, 44
  Alberta box heater, 61
  artful hesitancy, 78
  artful redundancy/repetition, 34–35
  background, 18, 28
  Big Mike and the ghost camp, 166–169
  body gestures, 76
  The carbon ghost, 182–183
  as connective, 18
  death lodges (Blackfoot), 57–58, 143–144
  dreaming place, 124
  elder freedom, 90
  empathetic projection, 43–44
  Grandma's copper kettle, 205–206
  first days of teaching, 56–57, 74–75
  forgetting his name, 39, 56
  holy land, 122–127, 129, 130, 132
  hope, 139–144, 146, 147, 154
  ideal principal, 57, 90
  key words, 38, 39
  metaphor of book, 87–92
  Old Mexico ranch, 206–207
  One room knife, 43
  open circle theme, 58
  oral additives, 31, 32
  passion, 123
  quest for truth, 167–170
  reincarnation, 253–254
  shape of silence, 74–75
  The social credit cabinet minister, 219
  spiralling literacy, 91
  Spirit River peyote, 183–184
  Willow flight, 181–182
  (*see also* Cree; Story/Stories, English, grandfather; Narrative pluralities; Trickster/trickstering/tricksterish, elders)
relationship of self to (*see* Self/Selves)
repetition, 272
Sabochees', 16, 19, 33, 58–61
  body engagement, 77, 127
  death of an elder, 93–94
  holy land, 127–130, 132
  ideal teacher, 93
  lost metaphoric power, 94
  metaphor of book, 93–94
  metaphor of night, 59–60
  Misisikak, 202–204

nephew Nitotem, 20, 60–61
praise of memory, 92
silence is a sacred place, 69
town time, 228
upturned hands gesture, 76
Woodland Cree Masquematuay (spiritual bag of meat), 16, 135
woodland tea fires, 61
(*see also* Cree; Story/Stories, grandfather, High Cree)
Sakastenohk
 round dance, 211–212
shifting place, 42
(*see also* Place/s; Transformation/Transubstantiation)
silence after/in (see Silence/d/s)
South Korean bridegroom and the spirits of, 14–15
(*see also* Zong)
Spanish, 47
(*see also* Anaya; Y Maestas)
Sparrow's
 adventure (imagined), 43, 73
 air guitar concert, 185
 angels, 251–252
 background, 28 (*see also* Story/Stories, English, French, Ukrainian)
 cattle, 185
 childhood and silence, 73
 Cinderella, 159–161
 closet, 62
 culture clash, 72
 David and Goliath, 138–139
 dress in the future, 185
 empathetic projection, 42–43
 eyes and fingers gesture, 76
 Fern Gully, 187
 ghosts, 252
 holy land, 18, 117–119, 123

hope and continuity, 122, 137–139, 141, 142, 145, 154
 name, 73
 narrative joy/spontaneity, 31, 35–36, 42–43
 metaphor of book, 98–104
 one liners, 212–213
 oral triad, 35
 passion, 35
 transformation/transubstantiation, 99–104, 119
 West Edmonton mall and Fantasyland, 161–162
Swahili, 28
Swampy Cree, 9, 62
Tololwa's, 20, 28, 29, 33, 39, 40
 grandmother's hearth/stones, 48, 52, 61
 holy land, 131–132
 honey gathers, 196
 trickster rabbit, 195
 (*see also* Grand/father/mother/parents; Names and Naming; Story/Stories, Arusha Masai, Swahili)
 As truth, 164
Ukrainian, 28
White crane, 157–159
Woodland Cree, 58
Yiddish, 28
Story-teachers, 1–2, 3, 7
Storyteller/s
 and children/child's sense of story, 3, 7, 138
 choosing, 21
 and circles (*see* Circle/d/s)
 first sound of first, 122
 as gods, 17
 and holy land (*see* Holy land/place/s)
 as inhabitants of oral culture/s, 28, 41
 and literary expression, 37, 85–112

my littlest/youngest, 18, 31, 35, 73, 98, 116, 139 (*see also* Story/Stories, Sparrow's holy land called childhood)
live as, 121
most elderly, 20 (*see also* Story/Stories, Mosum's)
as multiliterate, 28, 89
and originality, 35, 38 (*see also* Goody)
and primary reality, 47
as shapeshifters, 201–220
shape/use of silence, 74, 75
and spiralling literacy, 91
spiritual powers of, 129
as teacher(s), 3, 92, 126, 127
who live and tell of gryphons, 3
Storytelling
as becoming situated, 4, 19, 37–41 (*see also* Key words; Names and naming)
hoopedness of, 23
impulse, 16
and literary expression, 37, 85–112
overview of, 15 (*see also* Pellowski)
possession and person in, 21
and sense of the self (*see* Self/Selves)
theatrical, 15, 18, 72, 89, 102
(*see also* Pellowski)
Story webs, 4
Student(s)
as colleague, 8
as little elders-in-waiting, 7
youngest, 18
"Sunrise on Narrative Hill" (Sewall), viii
Swarthout, G., 85
Synchronicity, 51, 118

Tan, A., 17
Tannen, D., 69, 70, 72
Tay John (O'Hagan), 21
Teaching moments

first day/s, 38–39, 43, 55–56, 74–75 (*see also* One room knife)
first year (Sewall's), 44
great teaching of all the greatest teachers, 92 (*see also* Campbell)
as spiritual guide, 115–132
suspended between contraries, 24
Technology
education and, 57 (see also Literacy)
muffled, 123
and oral culture, 5, 14, 54–55 (*see also* Literacy)
and pollution, 137
silence not visible in, 76
voice and, 16
Therapeutic/medicine stories, 4, 7, 10, 15, 94, 115–174
(*see also* Pellowski; Storytelling, overview of)
Todorov, T., 131
Toelken, B.
traditional moments, 24
Townsend, J. R., 121, 131
Transformation/Transubstantiation, 53, 54, 68, 71, 85–112, 119
(*see also* Story/Stories, Dafna's, passion/ate; Sparrow's; Interplay in stories/storytelling, literate silence and oral silence, strangers into family)
Translator's presence, 23
Travers, P. L., 38, 39, 80, 132
Trickster/trickstering/tricksterish, 1, 171
elders, 9, 18–20, 28, 36, 40, 42, 90–91, 94–96, 97, 125, 126, 141–143, (*see also* Cree; Story/Stories, English, High Cree, Pesimwastches', Rattler's)
imitation and incongruity, 206
and laughter, 7, 9, 18–19, 32, 33, 44, 90–91, 94–96, 122, 123, 126, 141–143 (*see also* Cree; Gesture/s;

Nanooch; Oral additives; Story/
Stories, English, High Cree,
Pesimwastches', Rattler's)
and silence, 78
Wesakychak Cree Trickster, 9, 36, 78
Triumph of good,
over proved and privileged, 18
(*see also* Wrightson)
Truth, 157–174
where intellect overlaps emotion, 164
(*see also* Fidelity)

Voice
folkloral, 13, 24
and technology, 16
Van der Post, L., 66–67, 80, 228
(*see also* Story/Stories, African, about silence; Travers)

Wesakychak, 216
Wesakychak and the creation of the earth, 36
(*see also* Story/Stories, Pesimwastches'; Rattler's)
Western,
culture and celebration, 5, 94, 96
lands, 2
society and fire, 55
world, 19
Widdows, P. F.
Wilder, T., 157, 161
Woodward, K., 260, 261, 262
Wrightson, P., 18, 19
(*see also* Triumph of good)
Writing as a chosen/holy undertaking, 71, 86, 92–93, 108–112
(*see also* Story/Stories, Dafna's; *Painted eyebrow*)

Y Maestas, J., 14, 47
Yanagita, K., 112

Zong, I. -S., 14–15
(*see also* story/stories)